GS 1083

Conversations between
The British and Irish Anglican Churches
and
The Nordic and Baltic Lutheran Churches

TOGETHER IN MISSION AND MINISTRY

The Porvoo Common Statement
with
Essays on Church and Ministry in Northern Europe

CHURCH HOUSE PUBLISHING
Church House, Great Smith Street, London SW1P 3NZ

COPYRIGHT

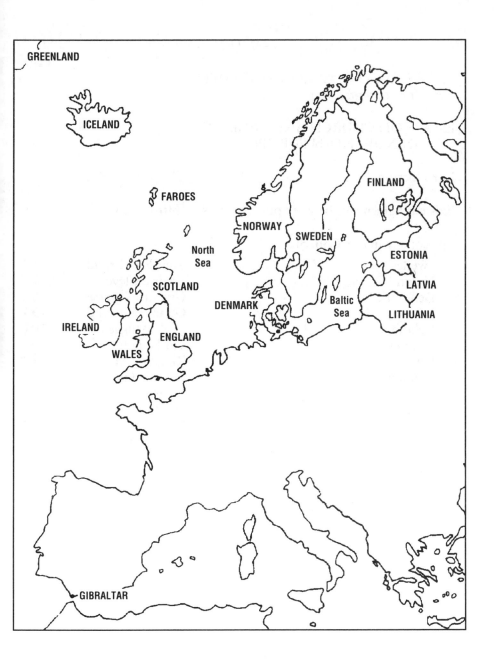

GREENLAND

ICELAND

FAROES

FINLAND

NORWAY

SWEDEN

ESTONIA

North
Sea

LATVIA

SCOTLAND

DENMARK

Baltic
Sea

LITHUANIA

IRELAND

ENGLAND

WALES

GIBRALTAR

CONTENTS

Conversations between
The British and Irish Anglican Churches
and
The Nordic and Baltic Lutheran Churches

THE PORVOO COMMON STATEMENT

Text agreed at the fourth plenary meeting,
held at Järvenpää, Finland, 9-13 October 1992

CONTENTS

Biblical quotations are from the *Revised Standard Version* except where otherwise shown. *REB* denotes the *Revised English Bible*.

The English text is definitive.

FOREWORD
by the Co-Chairmen

1. Dramatic changes have swept across Northern Europe in recent years. Many new links of commerce, education, tourism and consultation on environmental matters are now being actively developed across the Nordic/Baltic and British/Irish region. In this fast-changing scene the Anglican and Lutheran churches have a key rôle to play, and the present report offers the vision of twelve such churches – with a total membership of some 50 million Christians – entering into closer communion and joining in various forms of practical co-operation as they carry out their contemporary mission.[1] It is a cause of great joy that the Anglican and Lutheran strands of Western Christendom, which have so many common roots and display remarkably similar characteristics, have rediscovered one another in the present century and begun growing closer together.

2. *The Porvoo Common Statement* is the result of several major influences. The first was the series of Theological Conversations which took place between Anglicans and Lutherans in the Nordic and Baltic region during 1909-1951, and the agreements to which these talks gave rise.[2] Secondly, acquaintance between these churches was greatly strengthened by other joint events not directly concerned with church unity negotiations, notably the series of Anglo-Scandinavian theological conferences (begun in 1929) and pastoral conferences (begun in 1978) which still continue. Thirdly, a new climate of theological debate was created at world level by the bilateral and multilateral ecumenical dialogues of the 1970s and '80s, as evidenced by the following reports in particular: Pullach 1973, Lima (*BEM*) 1982, Helsinki 1982, Cold Ash 1983 and Niagara 1988.[3] This last report in particular has thrown new light on old questions of faith and order.

---

[1] For details of the churches represented in the Conversations, see pp. 38-42 below.

[2] See C. Hill, 'Existing Agreements between our Churches' in the *Essays on Church and Ministry in Northern Europe* appended to the Common Statement in the full edition of the report, entitled *Together in Mission and Ministry. The Porvoo Common Statement with Essays on Church and Ministry in Northern Europe* (London, 1993).

[3] See para. 30 below.

1

3. The immediate stimulus to move beyond the earlier agreements came from the personal initiative of Archbishop Robert Runcie (Canterbury) and Archbishop Bertil Werkström (Uppsala), coupled with the efforts of those officers who set preliminary arrangements in hand: Canon Christopher Hill and Canon Martin Reardon (England), together with Dean Lars Österlin (Sweden) and Prof. Ola Tjørhom (Norway). We owe them a debt of gratitude for their vision and determination, which evoked a positive response in each participating country.

4. A further impulse was added by the Lutheran-Episcopal Agreement of 1982 in the USA and by *The Meissen Common Statement* of 1988 between the Church of England and the Evangelical churches in East and West Germany. Each of these agreements led to mutual eucharistic hospitality, a limited degree of sharing ordained ministry, occasional joint celebrations of the eucharist and a commitment to common life and mission. Representatives who had been involved in both these ventures told us about them at first hand.

5. Four plenary sessions of official Theological Conversations were held during 1989-92, interspersed by meetings of a small Drafting Group.[4] We take this opportunity of thanking members of the Drafting Group, especially Bishop Stephen Sykes (Ely), Bishop Tord Harlin (Uppsala) and Dr Lorenz Grönvik (Finland), who gave their time unstintingly in carrying this extra burden. We also wish to record our appreciation and warm thanks to other particular persons: those who generously provided accommodation and hospitality during our meetings; our consultants and ecumenical observers for their sensitive encouragement and constructive advice; Director Gunnel Borgegård for her work in co-ordinating the Nordic translations; all those involved in making this report available in other languages; and those staff members who contributed their theological and administrative skills: Dr Mary Tanner, the Reverend Geoffrey Brown, Mr Colin Podmore and the Reverend Kaj Engström.

6. The aim of these Conversations was to move forward from our existing piecemeal agreements towards the goal of visible unity. By harvest-

---

[4] See p.34 below.

2

ing the fruits of previous ecumenical dialogues we hoped to express a greater measure of common understanding, and to resolve the long-standing difficulties between us about episcopacy and succession. We found that we had similar histories and faced similar challenges in contemporary society, and that there were no essential differences between us in the fields of faith, sacramental life or ministry (each church already being episcopal in structure). We became convinced that the way was now open to regard one another's churches, each with its own distinctive character, as sister churches. The time was ripe to move close together and to implement a practical agreement which would be relevant to laity and clergy alike in carrying out our common mission.

7. This purpose proved so attractive to Anglicans and Lutherans in neighbouring countries that our membership was extended. The original participants came from the five Nordic countries (Denmark, Finland, Iceland, Norway and Sweden) together with Latvia, Estonia and England. From the outset and at every stage of the Conversations full information was shared with church representatives in Lithuania as well as Ireland, Scotland and Wales. Their attendance and full membership was encouraged by Archbishop George Carey who, before his translation to Canterbury, had been one of the original English delegates, and was warmly welcomed when it came about. A full list of those who took part is shown on pages 34-36.

8. The final text was agreed unanimously on Tuesday, 13th October 1992 at Järvenpää, and entitled *The Porvoo Common Statement* after the name of the Finnish city in whose cathedral we had celebrated the eucharist together on the previous Sunday. Indeed, the context of worship in which Anglicans and Lutherans shared the eucharist and daily morning and evening prayer throughout these meetings played an important rôle in bringing us, under God, to a common mind.

9. As regards the structure and content of this report we offer the following brief commentary:

Chapter I sets the scene, both historically and today, and anchors the ensuing doctrinal discussions firmly in the context of the Church's mission. In this respect it follows the perspective of the Niagara Report.

3

Chapter II spells out our agreement on the nature of the Church and the goal of visible unity. Especially crucial to the later argument are paras 20 and 28.

Chapter III records in brief compass the substantial areas of belief and practice which Anglicans and Lutherans have in common. The twelve sections of para. 32 draw on the doctrinal agreements reached in earlier dialogues.

Chapter IV begins by identifying in para. 34 the major problem to be resolved: namely, episcopal ministry and its relation to succession. The report then breaks new ground, signposted in para. 35. The sections which follow deserve close attention. In seeking to unlock our churches from limited and negative perceptions, this chapter spells out a deeper understanding of apostolicity, of the episcopal office, and of historic succession as 'sign'. This theological argument is again linked in para. 54 to a mission context, and its conclusions are summarized in paras 56-57.

Since this part of the report arises from the empirical reality of church life in twelve different countries, we refer the reader to the series of twelve historical essays on Episcopacy in our Churches and Canon Christopher Hill's Introduction to the *Essays on Church and Ministry in Northern Europe*.[5] Regarding the Lutheran understanding of ordination in the Nordic and Baltic churches, Anglican readers will be helped by Canon John Halliburton's analysis of the ordinals in current use. Local similarities and differences over the ministry of deacons and initiation and confirmation are described and evaluated in further essays. In mentioning these materials we add our grateful thanks to all the writers, and especially to Canon Hill for his work as editor of the Essays.

Chapter V contains in para. 58 the Porvoo Declaration which will be laid before the appropriate decision-making bodies of each church for approval. Clause b(v) makes clear that the interchange of ordained ministers must be 'in accordance with any regulations which may from time to time be in force'. This implies a realistic acceptance of certain restrictions which already apply within our communions, e.g. regarding the ministry of women bishops (and those ordained by them) or women priests in particular places, the requirements of reasonable fluency in the local language, appropriate professional qualifications, State employment regulations, taking of customary oaths, etc.

---

[5] Cf. footnote 2 above.

10. We now offer this report to the participating churches for their scrutiny. The text is being translated into each of the languages concerned, but the English text remains definitive. As paras 60 and 61 make clear, these proposals do not conflict with existing ecumenical relationships. Yet we are clear that this report does have implications for other churches too, and we would urge that advisory responses be sought from our ecumenical partners during the process of response. The method adopted by this report is, in principle, one which could be applied between other ecumenical partners. To them, as well as to our own church authorities, we submit these proposals with humility.

11. We have a keen hope that all the participating churches will approve the Porvoo Declaration. If so, this will be a very significant contribution towards restoring the visible unity of Christ's Church. As soon as one of the Anglican churches and one of the Lutheran churches has approved the Declaration, its provisions can begin operating between them, subject to any necessary changes being made by each church to its own laws or regulations. Only in the course of time will the full consequences of the Declaration be able to be gauged. It is envisaged that public celebrations to mark our new relations will not take place until all the participating churches have made their response.

12. During the eucharist in Porvoo Cathedral on the final Sunday of our Conversations we were reminded by the preacher that to rejoice in our Anglican and Lutheran traditions is not enough. If the gospel is to be allowed to define and shape the life of our communities, this requires us not only to be faithful to the tradition which we have inherited, but also to be responsive to new issues. A special challenge faces those who belong to national churches: to exercise a critical and prophetic rôle within the life of their own nation, and also to witness to a unity in Christ which transcends national loyalties and boundaries. We believe that the insights and proposals contained in this report offer a way to bring us closer together in answering that challenge, and in enabling our churches to bear effective Christian witness and service not only within their particular nations and cultures but also within a broader European setting.

+ DAVID GRIMSBY   TORE FURBERG
The Right Reverend David Tustin,   The Right Reverend Dr Tore Furberg,
Bishop of Grimsby   Former Bishop of Visby

Johannesburg, February 1993

I SETTING THE SCENE

A A New Opportunity

1. Through the gracious leading of God, Anglicans and Lutherans all over the world are sharing together in mission and service, and discovering how much they have in common. In Europe our churches have lived side by side in separate nations for centuries. For a considerable time our churches have maintained in each other's countries chaplaincies, which are of growing significance with the increased mobility of population between the churches. Where both church traditions are present in the same place, as in North America and Southern and East Africa, new relationships have developed and new local agreements have been made. At the same time there is a growing closeness between European Anglicans and Lutherans, which convinces us that the time has come for us to review and revise the existing agreements.

2. These agreements,[1] which make possible differing degrees of communion, have been only partially implemented. For example, the political situation of the Baltic states hindered effective implementation for fifty years from 1939 to 1989. The agreements differ widely because in the past Anglicans have distinguished between the different Lutheran churches, principally on the criterion of the historic episcopate. However, the Nordic and Baltic churches have always enjoyed eucharistic communion. Moreover, the Nordic countries are increasingly regarded as one region and the churches now co-operate closely with one another and within the Nordic Bishops' Conference and the Nordic Ecumenical Council. Political change in Eastern Europe has given new hope to the churches of the Baltic countries. They are now developing their own life and are increasingly making their contribution to the wider fellowship. Co-operation with them becomes more important in a rapidly changing situation offering new possibilities for the churches.

---

[1] See C. Hill, 'Existing Agreements between our Churches' in the *Essays on Church and Ministry in Northern Europe* appended to the Common Statement in the full edition of the report, entitled *Together in Mission and Ministry. The Porvoo Common Statement with Essays on Church and Ministry in Northern Europe* (London, 1993).

3. The Nordic and Baltic churches wish to relate to the Anglican churches in Britain and Ireland not only as separate national churches, but also as groups of churches. The Commission is glad of new links with the Lutheran Church in Lithuania. It believes that the possibility of a new agreement, which will not differentiate between our churches, is opening up before us.

4. We are encouraged in this belief by an evident theological convergence in several Anglican-Lutheran conversations.[2] Furthermore, the official acceptance of *The Meissen Common Statement* by the Church of England and the Evangelical Church in Germany indicates a growing common understanding of the Church.

5. Anglicans and Lutherans are also helped by the broader ecumenical convergence, to which Orthodox, Roman Catholic and Protestant churches have contributed, on the doctrines of the Church, the ministry and the sacraments. This convergence has enabled us to move beyond both ways of thought and misunderstandings which have hindered the quest for unity between Anglicans and Lutherans. Of particular importance is the understanding of the mystery of the Church as the body of Christ, as the pilgrim people of God, as fellowship *(koinonia)*, and also as participation through witness and service in God's mission to the world. This provides a proper setting for a new approach to the question of the ordained ministry and of oversight *(episcope)*.

6. Above all, we face a common challenge to engage in God's mission to the people of our nations and continent at a time of unparalleled opportunity, which may properly be called a *kairos*.

B Our Common Ground as Churches

7. The faith, worship and spirituality of all our churches are rooted in the tradition of the apostolic Church. We stand in continuity with the Church of the patristic and medieval periods both directly and through the insights of the Reformation period. We each understand our own church to be part of the One, Holy, Catholic Church of Jesus Christ and truly participating in the one apostolic mission of the whole people of

---

[2] A bibliography of the most significant Anglican-Lutheran ecumenical texts is appended to the full edition of the report.

God. We share in the liturgical heritage of Western Christianity and also in the Reformation emphases upon justification by faith and upon word and sacrament as means of grace. All this is embodied in our confessional and liturgical documents and is increasingly recognized both as an essential bond between our churches and as a contribution to the wider ecumenical movement.

8. Despite geographical separation and a wide diversity of language, culture and historical development, the Anglican and Lutheran churches in Britain and Ireland and in the Nordic and Baltic countries have much in common, including much common history. Anglo-Saxon and Celtic missionaries played a significant part in the evangelization of Northern Europe and founded some of the historic sees in the Nordic lands. The unbroken witness of successive bishops in the dioceses and the maintenance of pastoral and liturgical life in the cathedrals and churches of all our nations are an important manifestation of the continuity of Christian life across the ages, and of the unity between the churches in Britain and Ireland and in Northern Europe.

9. Each of our churches has played a significant rôle in the social and spiritual development of the nation in which it has been set. We have been conscious of our mission and ministry to all the people in our nations. Most of our churches have had a pastoral and sometimes a legal responsibility for the majority of the population of our countries. This task is today increasingly being carried out in co-operation with other churches.

C Our Common Mission Today

10. Our churches and their nations are today facing new tasks and opportunities, in the context of many ideological, social and political changes in Europe. These include:

(a) a growing awareness by the European nations of their interdependence and mutual responsibility, and the need to rectify injustices resulting from the European wars of many centuries, but especially the twentieth century, which have affected the whole world;

(b) new opportunities – which are especially dramatic in the Baltic context – for evangelism, re-evangelism and pastoral work in all our countries, and the challenge to restate the Christian faith in response to both a prevalent practical materialism and a yearning among many people for spiritual values;

(c) a need to react to the vacuum arising from the collapse of a monolithic political system in Eastern Europe and to the increasingly pluriform character of society in Britain and Ireland and in the Nordic countries;

(d) opportunities to work for peace, justice and human rights, to diminish the imbalance between the prosperous nations and those impoverished and suffering from undue economic dependency, and to protect the rights and dignity of the poor and desolate – in particular, migrants, refugees and ethnic minorities;

(e) an ecological debate within and between the countries of Northern Europe, to which the churches have begun to bring a positive theology of creation and incarnation according permanent value to the earth and life in all its forms;

(f) a need for dialogue and understanding with people of other races, cultures and religious traditions as partners and fellow-citizens of a new Europe.

11. All the major European churches are now consulting together about these issues, especially in the follow-up to the European Ecumenical Assembly (Basel, 1989), co-sponsored by the Conference of European Churches (CEC) and the Council of Catholic Bishops' Conferences in Europe (CCEE). We are committed to encouraging this process of consultation and to playing an active part in the initiatives arising from it. Through such joint efforts in witness and service we shall build upon the unity we already enjoy, and contribute to a deeper unity which lies ahead of us.

12. Within the wider relationship of the Lutheran World Federation and the Anglican Communion our churches have become aware of the necessity of facing problems and undertaking tasks in a global perspective.

13. In the face of all the questions arising from our common mission today, our churches are called together to proclaim a duty of service to the wider world and to the societies in which they are set. Equally, they are called together to proclaim the Christian hope, arising from faith, which gives meaning in societies characterized by ambiguity. Again they are called together to proclaim the healing love of God and reconciliation in communities wounded by persecution, oppression and injustice. This common proclamation in word and sacrament manifests the mystery of God's love, God's presence and God's Kingdom.

II THE NATURE AND UNITY OF THE CHURCH

A   God's Kingdom and the Mystery and Purpose of the Church

14.   Our times demand something new of us as churches. Our agreement, as set out in this text, about the nature of the Church and its unity has implications for the ways in which we respond to the challenge of our age. We have come to see more clearly that we are not strangers to one another, but 'fellow-citizens with God's people, members of God's household... built on the foundation of the apostles and prophets, with Christ Jesus himself as the cornerstone' (Eph. 2. 19-20 *REB*). By the gift of God's grace we have been drawn into the sphere of God's will to reconcile to himself all that he has made and sustains (2 Cor. 5. 17-19), to liberate the creation from every bondage (Rom. 8. 19-22) and to draw all things into unity with himself (Eph. 1. 9f). God's ultimate purpose and mission in Christ is the restoration and renewal of all that he has made, the coming of the Kingdom in its fullness.

15.   To bring us to unity with himself, the Father sent his Son Jesus Christ into the world. Through Christ's life, death and resurrection, God's love is revealed and we are saved from the powers of sin and death (John 3. 16-18). By grace received through faith we are put into a right relationship with God. We are brought from death to new life (Rom. 6. 1-11), born again, made sons and daughters by adoption and set free for life in the Spirit (Gal. 4. 5, Rom. 8. 14-17). This is the heart of the gospel proclamation of the Church and through this proclamation God gathers his people together. In every age from apostolic times it has been the purpose of the Church to proclaim this gospel in word and deed: 'It is this which we have seen and heard that we declare to you also, in order that you may share with us in a common life *(koinonia)*, that life which we share *(koinonia)* with the Father and his Son Jesus Christ' (1 John 1. 3 *REB*).

16.   Faith is the God-given recognition that the light has come into the world, that the Word was made flesh and dwelt among us and has given us the right to become children of God (John 1. 1-13). Faith, as life in communion with the triune God, brings us into, and sustains and nourishes us in, the common life of the Church, Christ's body. It is the

gift of forgiveness which delivers us from the bondage of sin and from the anxiety of trying to justify ourselves, liberating us for a life of gratitude, love and hope. By grace we have been saved, through faith (Eph. 2. 8).

17. Into this life of communion with God and with one another *(koinonia)*, we are summoned by the gospel. In baptism the Holy Spirit unites us with Christ in his death and resurrection (Rom. 6. 1-11; 1 Cor. 12. 13); in the eucharist we are nourished and sustained as members of the one body by participation in the body and blood of Christ (1 Cor. 10. 16f). The Church and the gospel are thus necessarily related to each other. Faith in Jesus, the Christ, as the foundation of the reign of God arises out of the visible and audible proclamation of the gospel in word and sacraments. And there is no proclamation of the word and sacraments without a community and its ministry.[3] Thus, the communion of the Church is constituted by the proclamation of the word and the celebration of the sacraments, served by the ordained ministry. Through these gifts God creates and maintains the Church and gives birth daily to faith, love and new life.

18. The Church, as communion, must be seen as instrumental to God's ultimate purpose. It exists for the glory of God to serve, in obedience to the mission of Christ, the reconciliation of humankind and of all creation (Eph. 1. 10). Therefore the Church is sent into the world as a sign, instrument and foretaste of a reality which comes from beyond history – the Kingdom of God. The Church embodies the mystery of salvation, of a new humanity reconciled to God and to one another through Jesus Christ (Eph. 2. 14, Col. 1. 19-27). Through its ministry of service and proclamation it points to the reality of the Kingdom; and in the power of the Holy Spirit it participates in the divine mission by which the Father sent the Son to be the saviour of the world (1 John 4. 14, cf. John 3. 17).

19. The Holy Spirit bestows on the community diverse and complementary gifts. These are for the common good of the whole people and are manifested in acts of service within the community and to the world.

---

[3] See W.A. Norgren and W.G. Rusch (eds), *Implications of the Gospel. Lutheran-Episcopal Dialogue, Series III* (Minneapolis and Cincinnati, 1988) *(LED III)*, ch. III, paras 33-7, 51-7. (The full text of paragraphs cited in the footnotes is appended to the full edition of the report.)

All members are called to discover, with the help of the community, the gifts they have received and to use them for the building up of the Church and for the service of the world to which the Church is sent.[4]

20. The Church is a divine reality, holy and transcending present finite reality; at the same time, as a human institution, it shares the brokenness of human community in its ambiguity and frailty. The Church is always called to repentance, reform and renewal, and has constantly to depend on God's mercy and forgiveness. The Scriptures offer a portrait of a Church living in the light of the Gospel:

— it is a Church rooted and grounded in the love and grace of the Lord Christ;

— it is a Church always joyful, praying continually and giving thanks even in the midst of suffering;

— it is a pilgrim Church, a people of God with a new heavenly citizenship, a holy nation and a royal priesthood;

— it is a Church which makes common confession of the apostolic faith in word and in life, the faith common to the whole Church everywhere and at all times;

— it is a Church with a mission to all in every race and nation, preaching the gospel, proclaiming the forgiveness of sins, baptizing and celebrating the eucharist;

— it is a Church which is served by an ordained apostolic ministry, sent by God to gather and nourish the people of God in each place, uniting and linking them with the Church universal within the whole communion of saints;

— it is a Church which manifests through its visible communion the healing and uniting power of God amidst the divisions of humankind;

— it is a Church in which the bonds of communion are strong enough to enable it to bear effective witness in the world, to guard and interpret the apostolic faith, to take decisions, to teach authoritatively, and to share its goods with those in need;

---

[4] *Baptism, Eucharist and Ministry* (WCC Faith and Order Paper No. 111, 1982) *(BEM), Ministry*, para. 5.

— it is a Church alive and responsive to the hope which God has set before it, to the wealth and glory of the share God has offered it in the heritage of his people, and to the vastness of the resources of God's power open to those who trust in him.

This portrait of the Church is by no means complete; nevertheless, it confronts our churches with challenges to the fidelity of our lives and with a constant need for repentance and renewal.

B   The Nature of Communion and the Goal of Unity

21.   The Scriptures portray the unity of the Church as a joyful communion with the Father and with his Son Jesus Christ (cf. 1 John 1. 1-10), as well as communion among its members. Jesus prays that the disciples may be one as the Father is in him and he is in the Father, so that the world may believe (John 17. 21). Because the unity of the Church is grounded in the mysterious relationship of the persons of the Trinity, this unity belongs by necessity to its nature. The unity of the Body of Christ is spoken of in relation to the 'one Spirit..., one hope ..., one Lord, one faith, one baptism, one God and Father of us all' (Eph. 4. 4-6). Communion between Christians and churches should not be regarded as a product of human achievement. It is already given in Christ as a gift to be received, and 'like every good gift, unity also comes from the Father through the Son in the Holy Spirit'.[5]

22.   Viewed in this light, disunity must be regarded as an anomalous situation. Despite our sins and schisms, the unity to which we are summoned has already begun to be manifested in the Church. It demands fuller visible embodiment in structured form, so that the Church may be seen to be, through the Holy Spirit, the one body of Christ and the sign, instrument and foretaste of the Kingdom. In this perspective, all existing denominational traditions are provisional.

23.   Visible unity, however, should not be confused with uniformity. 'Unity in Christ does not exist despite and in opposition to diversity, but is given with and in diversity'.[6] Because this diversity corresponds with

---

[5] Roman Catholic / Lutheran Joint Commission, *Ways to Community* (Geneva, 1981), para. 9.

[6] *Ibid.,* para. 34.

13

the many gifts of the Holy Spirit to the Church, it is a concept of fundamental ecclesial importance, with relevance to all aspects of the life of the Church, and is not a mere concession to theological pluralism. Both the unity and the diversity of the Church are ultimately grounded in the communion of God the Holy Trinity.

24. The maintenance of unity and the sustaining of diversity are served by bonds of communion. Communion with God and with fellow believers is manifested in one baptism in response to the apostolic preaching; in the common confession of the apostolic faith; in the united celebration of the eucharist which builds up the one body of Christ; and in a single ministry set apart by prayer and the laying on of hands. This unity is also manifested as a communion in love, implying that Christians are bound to one another in a committed relationship with mutual responsibilities, common spiritual goods and the obligation to share temporal resources. Already in the Acts of the Apostles we can discern these bonds: 'Those who received [Peter's] word were baptized... And they devoted themselves to the apostles' teaching and fellowship, to the breaking of bread and the prayers... And all who believed were together and had all things in common' (Acts 2. 41ff).

25. In the narrative of the Acts of the Apostles this sharing in a common life is served by the apostolic ministry. We are given a picture of how this ministry fosters the richness of diversity while also maintaining unity. Through the mission of the apostles Peter and Paul, the Gentiles also are baptized. In the face of the threat of division, this radical decision is ratified by the coming together of the Church in council (Acts 15). Here is illustrated the role of apostolic leaders and their place within councils of the Church.

26. Such an understanding of communion has been described in the following terms:

> The unity of the Church given in Christ and rooted in the Triune God is realized in our unity in the proclaimed word, the sacraments and the ministry instituted by God and conferred through ordination. It is lived both in the unity of faith to which we jointly witness, and which together we confess and teach, and in the unity of hope and love which leads us to unite in fully committed fellowship. Unity needs a visible outward form which is able to encompass the element of inner differentiation and spiritual diversity as well

14

as the element of historical change and development. This is the unity of a fellowship which covers all times and places and is summoned to witness and serve the world.[7]

27. Already in the New Testament there is the scandal of division among Christians (1 Cor. 1. 11-13, 1 John 2. 18-19). Churches not outwardly united, for reasons of history or through deliberate separations, are obliged by their faith to work and to pray for the recovery of their visible unity and the deepening of their spiritual fellowship. Set before the Church is the vision of unity as the goal of all creation (Eph. 1) when the whole world will be reconciled to God (2 Cor. 5). Communion is thus the fruit of redemption and necessarily an eschatological reality. Christians can never tolerate disunity. They are obliged not merely to guard and maintain, but also to promote and nurture the highest possible realization of communion between and within the churches.

28. Such a level of communion has a variety of interrelated aspects. It entails agreement in faith together with the common celebration of the sacraments, supported by a united ministry and forms of collegial and conciliar consultation in matters of faith, life and witness. These expressions of communion may need to be embodied in the law and regulations of the Church. For the fullness of communion all these visible aspects of the life of the Church require to be permeated by a profound spiritual communion, a growing together in a common mind, mutual concern and a care for unity (Phil. 2. 2).

---

[7] Roman Catholic / Lutheran Joint Commission, *Facing Unity. Models, Forms and Phases of Catholic-Lutheran Church Fellowship* (n.pl., 1985), para. 3.

III WHAT WE AGREE IN FAITH

29.   Anglicans of Britain and Ireland and Lutherans of the Nordic and Baltic lands have at no time condemned one another as churches and have never formally separated. But a deeper realization of communion is certainly desirable, and now seems possible, without denying that proper and fruitful diversity which has developed, in course of time, into a distinctive way of confessing and expressing our faith. Anglicans have tended to stress the importance of liturgy as expressing the faith of the Church. Lutherans, whilst not denying this, have tended to lay more emphasis on doctrinal confession. Both, however, see *lex orandi* and *lex credendi* as closely related. The Augsburg Confession and the Thirty-Nine Articles of Religion were produced in different circumstances to meet different needs, and they do not play an identical rôle in the life of the churches. They contain much common formulation and bear common witness to the faith of the Church through the ages. Building on this foundation, modern ecumenical contact and exchange have substantially helped to clarify certain residual questions, bringing out with greater precision the degree to which we retain a common understanding of the nature and purpose of the Church and a fundamental agreement in faith. We are now called to a deepening of fellowship, to new steps on the way to visible unity and a new coherence in our common witness in word and deed to one Lord, one faith and one baptism.

30.   To this end, we set out the substantial agreement in faith that exists between us. Here we draw upon *Baptism, Eucharist and Ministry* (the Lima text) and the official responses of our churches to that text. We also draw upon previous attempts to specify the range and nature of Anglican-Lutheran agreement. These include the Pullach Report of 1973,[8] the Helsinki Report of 1983,[9] the Cold Ash Report of 1983,[10]

---

[8] *Anglican-Lutheran International Conversations. The Report of the Conversations 1970-1972 authorized by the Lambeth Conference and the Lutheran World Federation* (London, 1973) (*Pullach*), paras 17-82.

[9] *Anglican-Lutheran Dialogue. The Report of the European Commission.* Helsinki, August-September 1982 (London, 1983) (*Helsinki*), paras 17-51.

[10] *Anglican-Lutheran Relations. Report of the Anglican-Lutheran Joint Working Group.* Cold Ash, Berkshire, England, 28 November-3 December 1983 (London and Geneva, 1983).

Implications of the Gospel of 1988,[11] *The Meissen Common Statement* of 1988[12] and the Niagara Report of 1988.[13] These texts all testify to a substantial unity in faith between Anglicans and Lutherans. We have benefited from the insights from these texts as a contribution to our agreement in faith. Furthermore, we have made considerable use of the results of the respective Anglican – Roman Catholic and Roman Catholic – Lutheran dialogues.

31. The agreement in faith reached in the Anglican-Lutheran texts was affirmed in a resolution of the Lambeth Conference of 1988, where it is stated that the Conference

> recognises, on the basis of the high degree of consensus reached in international, regional and national dialogues between Anglicans and Lutherans and in the light of the communion centred around Word and Sacrament that has been experienced in each other's traditions, the presence of the Church of Jesus Christ in the Lutheran Communion as in our own.[14]

There is a parallel affirmation in a resolution of the Eighth Assembly of the Lutheran World Federation in Curitiba in February 1990:

> This Assembly resolves that the LWF renew its commitment to the goal of full communion with the churches of the Anglican Communion, and that it urge LWF member churches to take appropriate steps towards its realization... that the LWF note with thanksgiving the steps towards church fellowship with national/regional Anglican counterparts which LWF member churches have been able to take already and that it encourage them to proceed.[15]

32. Here we declare in summary form the principal beliefs and practices that we have in common:

---

[11] *(LED III).*

[12] *The Meissen Common Statement. On the Way to Visible Unity.* Meissen, 18 March 1988 (in *The Meissen Agreement: Texts* – CCU Occasional Paper No. 2, 1992) *(Meissen)*, paras 14-16.

[13] Anglican-Lutheran International Continuation Committee, *The Niagara Report. Report of the Anglican-Lutheran Consultation on Episcope.* Niagara Falls, September 1987 (London, 1988), paras 60-80.

[14] *The Truth Shall Make You Free: The Lambeth Conference 1988* (London, 1988), p. 204: resolution 4, para. 4.

[15] *I Have Heard the Cry of My People: Proceedings of the 8th Assembly of the Lutheran World Federation, Curitiba, Brazil, 29 January - 8 February 1990,* p.107.

a. We accept the *canonical scriptures* of the Old and the New Testaments to be the sufficient, inspired and authoritative record and witness, prophetic and apostolic, to God's revelation in Jesus Christ.[16] We read the Scriptures as part of public worship in the language of the people, believing that in the Scriptures – as the Word of God and testifying to the gospel – eternal life is offered to all humanity, and that they contain everything necessary to salvation.

b. We believe that God's *will and commandment* are essential to Christian proclamation, faith and life. God's commandment commits us to love God and our neighbour, and to live and serve to his praise and glory. At the same time God's commandment reveals our sins and our constant need for his *mercy*.

c. We believe and proclaim *the gospel*, that in Jesus Christ God loves and redeems the world. We 'share a common understanding of God's justifying grace, i.e. that we are accounted righteous and are made righteous before God only by grace through faith because of the merits of our Lord and Saviour Jesus Christ, and not on account of our works or merits.... Both our traditions affirm that justification leads and must lead to "good works"; authentic faith issues in love'.[17] We receive the Holy Spirit who renews our hearts and equips us for and calls us to good works.[18] As justification and sanctification are aspects of the same divine act, so also living faith and love are inseparable in the believer.[19]

d. We accept the faith of the Church through the ages set forth in *the Niceno-Constantinopolitan and Apostles' Creeds* and confess the basic Trinitarian and Christological dogmas to which these creeds testify. That is, we believe that Jesus of Nazareth is true God and true Man, and that God is one God in three persons, Father, Son and Holy Spirit.[20] This faith is explicitly confirmed both in the Thirty-Nine Articles of Religion [21] and in the Augsburg Confession.[22]

---

[16] *Pullach*, para. 17.

[17] *Helsinki*, para. 20 and *Meissen*, para. 15 (vi).

[18] *All Under One Christ. Statement on the Augsburg Confession by the Roman Catholic / Lutheran Joint Commission*. Augsburg, 23 February 1980 (published with *Ways to Community* (Geneva, 1981)), para. 14.

[19] *Salvation and the Church. An agreed Statement by the Anglican - Roman Catholic International Commission* — ARCIC II (London, 1987), para. 19.

[20] *Meissen*, para. 15 (ii); cf. *Pullach*, paras 23-25.

[21] See Article VIII.

[22] See Articles I and III.

e. We confess and celebrate the apostolic faith in *liturgical worship*. We acknowledge in the liturgy both a celebration of salvation through Christ and a significant factor in forming the consensus fidelium. We rejoice at the extent of our 'common tradition of spirituality, liturgy and sacramental life' which has given us similar forms of worship and common texts, hymns, canticles and prayers. We are influenced by a common liturgical renewal and by the variety of expression shown in different cultural settings.[23]

f. We believe that *the Church* is constituted and sustained by the Triune God through God's saving action in word and sacraments. We believe that the Church is a sign, instrument and foretaste of the Kingdom of God. But we also recognize that it stands in constant need of reform and renewal.[24]

g. We believe that through baptism with water in the name of the Trinity God unites the one baptized with the death and resurrection of Jesus Christ, initiates into the One, Holy, Catholic and Apostolic Church, and confers the gracious gift of new life in the Spirit. Since we in our churches practise and value infant baptism, we also take seriously our catechetical task for the nurture of baptized children to mature commitment to Christ.[25] In all our traditions *baptism* is followed by a rite of *confirmation*. We recognize two practices in our churches, both of which have precedents in earlier centuries: in Anglican churches, confirmation administered by the bishop; in the Nordic and Baltic churches, confirmation usually administered by a local priest. In all our churches this includes invocation of the Triune God, renewal of the baptismal profession of faith and a prayer that through the renewal of the grace of baptism the candidate may be strengthened now and for ever.

h. We believe that the body and blood of Christ are truly present, distributed and received under the forms of bread and wine in *the Lord's Supper (Eucharist)*. In this way we receive the body and blood of Christ, crucified and risen, and in him the forgiveness of sins and all other benefits of his passion.[26] The eucharistic memorial is no mere calling to mind of a past event or of its significance, but the Church's

---

[23] Cf. *Meissen*, para. 15 (iii).

[24] *Meissen*, para. 15 (vii); cf. *Helsinki*, paras 44-51; see also paras 14-20 above.

[25] *Meissen*, para. 15 (iv); cf. *Helsinki*, paras 22-25.

[26] *Pullach*, para. 67.

effectual proclamation of God's mighty acts.[27] Although we are unable to offer to God a worthy sacrifice, Christ unites us with himself in his self-offering to the Father, the one, full, perfect and sufficient sacrifice which he has offered for us all. In the eucharist God himself acts, giving life to the body of Christ and renewing each member.[28] Celebrating the eucharist, the Church is reconstituted and nourished, strengthened in faith and hope, in witness and service in daily life. Here we already have a foretaste of the eternal joy of God's Kingdom.[29]

i. We believe that *all members of the Church* are called to participate in its apostolic mission. All the baptized are therefore given various gifts and ministries by the Holy Spirit. They are called to offer their being as 'a living sacrifice' and to intercede for the Church and the salvation of the world.[30] This is the corporate priesthood of the whole people of God and the calling to ministry and service (1 Peter 2. 5).

j. We believe that within the community of the Church *the ordained ministry* exists to serve the ministry of the whole people of God. We hold the ordained ministry of word and sacrament to be an office of divine institution and as such a gift of God to his Church.[31] Ordained ministers are related, as are all Christians, both to the priesthood of Christ and to the priesthood of the Church.[32] This basic oneness of the ordained ministry is expressed in the service of word and sacrament. In the life of the Church, this unity has taken a differentiated form. The threefold ministry of bishop, priest and deacon became the general pattern in the Church of the early centuries and is still retained by many churches, though often in partial form. 'The threefold ministry of bishop, presbyter and deacon may serve today as an expression of the unity we seek and also as a means for achieving it.'[33]

k. We believe that a ministry of *pastoral oversight (episcope)*, exercised in personal, collegial and communal ways, is necessary as

---

[27] *Anglican-Roman Catholic International Commission. The Final Report.* Windsor, September 1981 (London, 1982) (ARCIC 1), *Eucharistic Doctrine,* para. 5.

[28] *BEM, Eucharist,* para.2.

[29] Cf. *Helsinki,* para. 28.

[30] *BEM, Ministry,* para. 17.

[31] cf. *Niagara,* para. 68, *Meissen,* para. 15 (viii) and *Helsinki,* paras 32-42.

[32] *BEM, Ministry,* para. 17.

[33] *BEM, Ministry,* para. 22.

witness to and safeguard of the unity and apostolicity of the Church.[34] Further, we retain and employ the episcopal office as a sign of our intention, under God, to ensure the continuity of the Church in apostolic life and witness. For these reasons, all our churches have a personally exercised episcopal office.[35]

l. We share *a common hope* in the final consummation of the Kingdom of God, and believe that in this eschatological perspective we are called to work now for the furtherance of justice, to seek peace and to care for the created world. The obligations of the Kingdom are to govern our life in the Church and our concern for the world. 'The Christian faith is that God has made peace through Jesus "by the blood of his cross" (Col. 1. 20), so establishing the one valid centre for the unity of the whole human family.'[36]

33. This summary witnesses to a high degree of unity in faith and doctrine. Whilst this does not require each tradition to accept every doctrinal formulation characteristic of our distinctive traditions, it does require us to face and overcome the remaining obstacles to still closer communion.

---

[34] Cf. *Niagara*, para. 69 and *Meissen*, para. 15 (ix).

[35] See *Niagara*, paras 23-30, 41-59 and 81-110 and *Pullach*, paras 79-82.

[36] *God's Reign and Our Unity. The Report of the Anglican-Reformed International Commission 1981-1984.* Woking, England, January 1984 (London, 1984), para. 18; *Niagara*, para. 70 and *Meissen*, para. 15 (x).

IV EPISCOPACY IN THE SERVICE OF THE APOSTOLICITY OF THE CHURCH

34. There is a long-standing problem about episcopal ministry and its relation to succession. At the time of the Reformation all our churches ordained bishops (sometimes the term superintendent was used as a synonym for bishop) to the existing sees of the Catholic Church, indicating their intention to continue the life and ministry of the One, Holy, Catholic and Apostolic Church. In some of the territories the historic succession of bishops was maintained by episcopal ordination, whereas elsewhere on a few occasions bishops or superintendents were consecrated by priests following what was believed to be the precedent of the early Church.[37] One consequence of this was a lack of unity between the ministries of our churches and thus a hindrance to our common witness, service and mission. The interruption of the episcopal succession has, nevertheless, in these particular churches always been accompanied by the intention and by measures to secure the apostolic continuity of the Church as a Church of the gospel served by an episcopal ministry. The subsequent tradition of these churches demonstrates their faithfulness to the apostolicity of the Church. In the last one hundred years all our churches have felt a growing need to overcome this difficulty and to give common expression to their continuous participation in the life of the One, Holy, Catholic and Apostolic Church.

35. Because of this difficulty we now set out at greater length an understanding of the apostolicity of the whole Church and within that the apostolic ministry, succession in the episcopal office and the historic succession as a sign. All of these are interrelated.

A The Apostolicity of the Whole Church
36. 'In the Creed, the Church confesses itself to be apostolic. The Church lives in continuity with the apostles and their proclamation. The same Lord who sent the apostles continues to be present in the Church. The Spirit keeps the Church in the apostolic tradition until the fulfilment

---

[37] For this see the Introduction, the historical essays on Episcopacy in our Churches and J. Halliburton, 'Orders and Ordination' in the *Essays on Church and Ministry in Northern Europe* appended to this Common Statement in the full edition of the report (cf. footnote 1 above).

of history in the Kingdom of God. Apostolic tradition in the Church means continuity in the permanent characteristics of the Church of the apostles: witness to the apostolic faith, proclamation and fresh interpretation of the Gospel, celebration of baptism and the eucharist, the transmission of ministerial responsibilities, communion in prayer, love, joy and suffering, service to the sick and needy, unity among the local churches and sharing the gifts which the Lord has given to each.'[38]

37. The Church today is charged, as were the apostles, to proclaim the gospel to all nations, because the good news about Jesus Christ is the disclosure of God's eternal plan for the reconciliation of all things in his Son. The Church is called to faithfulness to the normative apostolic witness to the life, death, resurrection and exaltation of its Lord. The Church receives its mission and the power to fulfil this mission as a gift of the risen Christ. The Church is thus apostolic as a whole. 'Apostolicity means that the Church is sent by Jesus to be for the world, to participate in his mission and therefore in the mission of the One who sent Jesus, to participate in the mission of the Father and the Son through the dynamic of the Holy Spirit.'[39]

38. God the Holy Spirit pours out his gifts upon the whole Church (Eph. 4. 11-13, 1 Cor. 12. 4-11), and raises up men and women, both lay and ordained, to contribute to the nurture of the community. Thus the whole Church, and every member, participates in and contributes to the communication of the gospel, by their faithful expression and embodiment of the permanent characteristics of the Church of the apostles in a given time and place. Essential to its testimony are not merely its words, but the love of its members for one another, the quality of its service of those in need, its use of financial and other resources, the justice and effectiveness of its life and its means of discipline, its distribution and exercise of power, and its assemblies for worship. All these are means of communication which must be focused upon Christ, the true Word of God, and spring from life in the Holy Spirit.

39. Thus the primary manifestation of apostolic succession is to be found in the apostolic tradition of the Church as a whole. The succession

---

[38] *BEM, Ministry*, para. 34.
[39] *Niagara*, para. 21.

is an expression of the permanence and, therefore, of the continuity of Christ's own mission in which the Church participates.[40]

40. Within the apostolicity of the whole Church is an apostolic succession of the ministry which serves and is a focus of the continuity of the Church in its life in Christ and its faithfulness to the words and acts of Jesus transmitted by the apostles.[41] The ordained ministry has a particular responsibility for witnessing to this tradition and for proclaiming it afresh with authority in every generation.[42]

B Apostolic Ministry

41. To nourish the Church, God has given the apostolic ministry, instituted by our Lord and transmitted through the apostles. The chief responsibility of the ordained ministry is to assemble and build up the body of Christ by proclaiming and teaching the Word of God, by celebrating the sacraments and by guiding the life of the community in its worship, its mission and its caring ministry.[43] The setting aside of a person to a lifelong ordained office by prayer, invocation of the Holy Spirit and the laying on of hands reminds the Church that it receives its mission from Christ himself and expresses the Church's firm intention to live in fidelity to and gratitude for that commission and gift. The different tasks of the one ministry find expression in its structuring. The threefold ministry of bishops, priests and deacons became the general pattern of ordained ministry in the early Church, though subsequently it underwent considerable change in its practical exercise and is still developing today.[44]

42. The diversity of God's gifts requires their co-ordination so that they enrich the whole Church and its unity. This diversity and the multiplicity of tasks involved in serving it calls for a ministry of co-ordination. This is the ministry of oversight, *episcope*, a caring for the life of a whole community, a pastoring of the pastors and a true feeding of Christ's

---

[40] *BEM, Ministry*, para. 35.
[41] Cf. *BEM, Ministry*, para. 34: commentary.
[42] *BEM, Ministry*, para. 35.
[43] *BEM, Ministry*, para. 13.
[44] Cf. *BEM, Ministry*, para. 22.

flock, in accordance with Christ's command across the ages and in unity with Christians in other places. *Episcope* (oversight) is a requirement of the whole Church and its faithful exercise in the light of the gospel is of fundamental importance to its life.

43. Oversight of the Church and its mission is the particular responsibility of the bishop. The bishop's office is one of service and communication within the community of believers and, together with the whole community, to the world. Bishops preach the word, preside at the sacraments, and administer discipline in such a way as to be representative pastoral ministers of oversight, continuity and unity in the Church. They have pastoral oversight of the area to which they are called. They serve the apostolicity, catholicity and unity of the Church's teaching, worship and sacramental life. They have responsibility for leadership in the Church's mission.[45] None of these tasks should be carried out in isolation from the whole Church.

44. The ministry of oversight is exercised personally, collegially and communally. It is personal because the presence of Christ among his people can most effectively be pointed to by the person ordained to proclaim the gospel and call the community to serve the Lord in unity of life and witness. It is collegial, first because the bishop gathers together those who are ordained to share in the tasks of ministry and to represent the concerns of the community; secondly, because through the collegiality of bishops the Christian community in local areas is related to the wider Church, and the universal Church to that community. It is communal, because the exercise of ordained ministry is rooted in the life of the community and requires the community's effective participation in the discovery of God's will and the guidance of the Spirit. In most of our churches today this takes synodical form. Bishops, together with other ministers and the whole community, are responsible for the orderly transfer of ministerial authority in the Church.[46]

45. The personal, collegial and communal dimensions of oversight find expression at the local, regional and universal levels of the Church's life.

---

[45] *BEM, Ministry,* para. 29.

[46] Cf. *BEM, Ministry,* paras 26, 29.

C The Episcopal Office in the Service of the Apostolic Succession

46. The ultimate ground of the fidelity of the Church, in continuity with the apostles, is the promise of the Lord and the presence of the Holy Spirit at work in the whole Church. The continuity of the ministry of oversight is to be understood within the continuity of the apostolic life and mission of the whole Church. Apostolic succession in the episcopal office is a visible and personal way of focusing the apostolicity of the whole Church.

47. Continuity in apostolic succession is signified in the ordination or consecration of a bishop. In this act the people of God gather to affirm the choice of and pray for the chosen candidate. At the laying on of hands by the ordaining bishop and other representatives with prayer, the whole Church calls upon God in confidence of his promise to pour out the Holy Spirit on his covenant people (Is. 11. 1-3, cf. *Veni Creator Spiritus*). The biblical act of laying on of hands is rich in significance. It may mean (among other things) identification, commissioning or welcome. It is used in a variety of contexts: confirmation, reconciliation, healing and ordination. On the one hand, by the laying on of hands with prayer a gift of grace already given by God is recognized and confirmed; on the other hand it is perfected for service. The precise significance or intention of the laying on of hands as a sign is determined by the prayer or declaration which accompanies it. In the case of the episcopate, to ordain by prayer and the laying on of hands is to do what the apostles did, and the Church through the ages.

48. In the consecration of a bishop the sign is effective in four ways: first it bears witness to the Church's trust in God's faithfulness to his people and in the promised presence of Christ with his Church, through the power of the Holy Spirit, to the end of time; secondly, it expresses the Church's intention to be faithful to God's initiative and gift, by living in the continuity of the apostolic faith and tradition; thirdly, the participation of a group of bishops in the laying on of hands signifies their and their churches' acceptance of the new bishop and so of the catholicity of the churches;[47] fourthly, it transmits ministerial office and its authority in accordance with God's will and institution. Thus in the act of consecration a bishop receives the sign of divine approval and a permanent

---

[47] Cf. *Niagara*, para. 91.

commission to lead his particular church in the common faith and apostolic life of all the churches.

49. The continuity signified in the consecration of a bishop to episcopal ministry cannot be divorced from the continuity of life and witness of the diocese to which he is called. In the particular circumstances of our churches, the continuity represented by the occupation of the historic sees is more than personal. The care to maintain a diocesan and parochial pattern of pastoral life and ministry reflects an intention of the churches to continue to exercise the apostolic ministry of word and sacrament of the universal Church.

D The Historic Episcopal Succession as Sign

50. The whole Church is a sign of the Kingdom of God;[48] the act of ordination is a sign of God's faithfulness to his Church, especially in relation to the oversight of its mission. To ordain a bishop in historic succession (that is, in intended continuity from the apostles themselves) is also a sign.[49] In so doing the Church communicates its care for continuity in the whole of its life and mission, and reinforces its determination to manifest the permanent characteristics of the Church of the apostles. To make the meaning of the sign fully intelligible it is necessary to include in the service of ordination a public declaration of the faith of the Church and an exposition of the ministry to which the new bishop is called. In this way the sign of historic episcopal succession is placed clearly in its full context of the continuity of proclamation of the gospel of Christ and the mission of his Church.

51. The use of the sign of the historic episcopal succession does not by itself guarantee the fidelity of a church to every aspect of the apostolic faith, life and mission. There have been schisms in the history of churches using the sign of historic succession. Nor does the sign guarantee the personal faithfulness of the bishop. Nonetheless, the retention of the sign remains a permanent challenge to fidelity and to unity, a summons to witness to, and a commission to realize more fully, the permanent characteristics of the Church of the apostles.[50]

---

[48] See paras 17-20 above.

[49] See paras 47-48 above.

[50] See para. 36 above.

52. Faithfulness to the apostolic calling of the whole Church is carried by more than one means of continuity. Therefore a church which has preserved the sign of historic episcopal succession is free to acknowledge an authentic episcopal ministry in a church which has preserved continuity in the episcopal office by an occasional priestly/presbyteral ordination at the time of the Reformation. Similarly, a church which has preserved continuity through such a succession is free to enter a relationship of mutual participation in episcopal ordinations with a church which has retained the historical episcopal succession, and to embrace this sign, without denying its past apostolic continuity.[51]

53. The mutual acknowledgement of our churches and ministries is theologically prior to the use of the sign of the laying on of hands in the historic succession. Resumption of the use of the sign does not imply an adverse judgement on the ministries of those churches which did not previously make use of the sign. It is rather a means of making more visible the unity and continuity of the Church at all times and in all places.

54. To the degree to which our ministries have been separated, all our churches have lacked something of that fullness which God desires for his people (Eph. 1. 23 and 3. 17-19). By moving together, and by being served by a reconciled and mutually recognized episcopal ministry, our churches will be both more faithful to their calling and also more conscious of their need for renewal. By the sharing of our life and ministries in closer visible unity, we shall be strengthened for the continuation of Christ's mission in the world.

E A New Stage

55. By the far-reaching character of our agreement recorded in the previous paragraphs it is apparent that we have reached a new stage in our journey together in faith. We have agreed on the nature and purpose of the Church (Chapter II), on its faith and doctrine (Chapter III), specifically on the apostolicity of the whole Church, on the apostolic ministry within it, and on the episcopal office in the service of the Church (Chapter IV).

---

[51] The historical background is set out in the *Essays on Church and Ministry in Northern Europe* (cf. footnote 1 above).

56. On the basis of this agreement we believe

— that our churches should confidently acknowledge one another as churches and enter into a new relationship;

— that each church as a whole has maintained an authentic apostolic succession of witness and service (IV A);

— that each church has had transmitted to it an apostolic ministry of word and sacrament by prayer and the laying on of hands (IV B);

— that each church has maintained an orderly succession of episcopal ministry within the continuity of its pastoral life, focused in the consecrations of bishops and in the experience and witness of the historic sees (IV C).

57. In the light of all this we find that the time has come when all our churches can affirm together the value and use of the sign of the historic episcopal succession (IV D). This means that those churches in which the sign has at some time not been used are free to recognize the value of the sign and should embrace it without denying their own apostolic continuity. This also means that those churches in which the sign has been used are free to recognize the reality of the episcopal office and should affirm the apostolic continuity of those churches in which the sign of episcopal succession has at some time not been used.

V TOWARDS CLOSER UNITY

A Joint Declaration
58. We recommend that our churches jointly make the following Declaration.

THE PORVOO DECLARATION

We, the Church of Denmark, the Church of England, the Estonian Evangelical-Lutheran Church, the Evangelical-Lutheran Church of Finland, the Evangelical-Lutheran Church of Iceland, the Church of Ireland, the Evangelical-Lutheran Church of Latvia, the Evangelical-Lutheran Church of Lithuania, the Church of Norway, the Scottish Episcopal Church, the Church of Sweden and the Church in Wales, on the basis of our common understanding of the nature and purpose of the Church, fundamental agreement in faith and our agreement on episcopacy in the service of the apostolicity of the Church, contained in Chapters II – IV of *The Porvoo Common Statement*, make the following acknowledgements and commitments:

a (i) we acknowledge one another's churches as churches belonging to the One, Holy, Catholic and Apostolic Church of Jesus Christ and truly participating in the apostolic mission of the whole people of God;

(ii) we acknowledge that in all our churches the Word of God is authentically preached, and the sacraments of baptism and the eucharist are duly administered;

(iii) we acknowledge that all our churches share in the common confession of the apostolic faith;

(iv) we acknowledge that one another's ordained ministries are given by God as instruments of his grace and as possessing not only the inward call of the Spirit, but also Christ's commission through his body, the Church;

(v) we acknowledge that personal, collegial and communal oversight (*episcope*) is embodied and exercised in all our churches in a variety of forms, in continuity of apostolic life, mission and ministry;

(vi) we acknowledge that the episcopal office is valued and maintained in all our churches as a visible sign expressing and serving the Church's unity and continuity in apostolic life, mission and ministry.

b We commit ourselves:

(i) to share a common life in mission and service, to pray for and with one another, and to share resources;

(ii) to welcome one another's members to receive sacramental and other pastoral ministrations;

(iii) to regard baptized members of all our churches as members of our own;

(iv) to welcome diaspora congregations into the life of the indigenous churches, to their mutual enrichment;

(v) to welcome persons episcopally ordained in any of our churches to the office of bishop, priest or deacon to serve, by invitation and in accordance with any regulations which may from time to time be in force, in that ministry in the receiving church without re-ordination;

(vi) to invite one another's bishops normally to participate in the laying on of hands at the ordination of bishops as a sign of the unity and continuity of the Church;

(vii) to work towards a common understanding of diaconal ministry;

(viii) to establish appropriate forms of collegial and conciliar consultation on significant matters of faith and order, life and work;

(ix) to encourage consultations of representatives of our churches, and to facilitate learning and exchange of ideas and information in theological and pastoral matters;

(x) to establish a contact group to nurture our growth in communion and to co-ordinate the implementation of this agreement.

B Liturgical Celebration

59. We recommend that this agreement and our new relationship be inaugurated and affirmed by three central celebrations of the eucharist at which all our churches would be represented. These celebrations would be a sign of:

— our joyful acceptance of one another;

— our joint commitment in the faith and sacramental life of the Church;

— our welcome of the ministers and members of the other churches as our own;

— our commitment to engage in mission together.

These celebrations would include:

— the reading and signing of the Porvoo Declaration;

— a central prayer of thanksgiving for the past and petition for the future, offered by Lutherans for Anglicans and Anglicans for Lutherans;

— the exchange of the Peace;

— a jointly celebrated eucharist;

— other verbal and ceremonial signs of our common life.

C Wider Ecumenical Commitment

60. We rejoice in our agreement and the form of visible unity it makes possible. We see in it a step towards the visible unity which all churches committed to the ecumenical movement seek to manifest. We do not regard our move to closer communion as an end in itself, but as part of the pursuit of a wider unity. This pursuit will involve the following:

— strengthening the links which each of our churches has with other churches at local, national and international level;

— deepening relationships within and between our two world communions and supporting efforts towards closer communion between Anglican and Lutheran churches in other regions, especially in relation to agreements being developed in Africa and North America;

— developing further existing links with other world communions, especially those with whom we have ecumenical dialogues and agreements;

— supporting together our local, national and regional ecumenical councils, the Conference of European Churches and the World Council of Churches.

61. The common inheritance and common calling of our churches, spelt out in this agreement, makes us conscious of our obligation to contribute jointly to the ecumenical efforts of others. At the same time we are aware of our own need to be enriched by the insights and experience of churches of other traditions and in other parts of the world. Together with them we are ready to be used by God as instruments of his saving and reconciling purpose for all humanity and creation.

MEETINGS OF THE CONVERSATIONS

I	Sigtunastiftelsen, Sigtuna, Sweden	2-7 August 1989
	Drafting Group: Swedish Church, London	9-12 January 1990
	Drafting Group: Tallinn, Estonia	5-12 May 1990

II	Emmaus House, West Wickham, England	18-24 September 1990
	Drafting Group: Swedish Church, London	14-16 January 1991
	Drafting Group: Swedish Church, London	2-4 May 1991

III Sankt Lukas Stiftelsens feriehjem, Smidstrup Strand, Gilleleje, Denmark
21-27 September 1991
Drafting Group: St Columba's House, Woking, England:
12 -15 February 1992

IV Seurakuntaopisto, Järvenpää, Finland   9-13 October 1992

PARTICIPANTS

Members

Church of England

The Rt Revd David Tustin (Bishop of Grimsby) — Co-Chairman
The Rt Revd Stephen Sykes (Bishop of Ely)
The Rt Revd John Hind (Bishop of Horsham)
The Very Revd John Arnold (Dean of Durham)
The Venerable David Silk (Archdeacon of Leicester)
Mrs Maryon Jägers

Church of Ireland

The Revd Paul Colton

Scottish Episcopal Church

The Rt Revd Robert Halliday (Bishop of Brechin)

Church in Wales

The Very Revd Huw Jones (Dean of Brecon)

Church of Denmark
The Rt Revd Henrik Christiansen (formerly Bishop of Aalborg)
The Revd Dr Gerhard Pedersen

Estonian Evangelical-Lutheran Church
The Revd Dr Toomas Paul
Mr Tiit Pädam

Evangelical-Lutheran Church of Finland
The Rt Revd Dr Erik Vikström (Bishop of Borgå)
The Revd Dr Lorenz Grönvik

Evangelical-Lutheran Church of Iceland
The Revd Dr Hjalti Hugason

Evangelical-Lutheran Church of Latvia
The Very Revd Ringolds Muziks

Evangelical-Lutheran Church of Lithuania
The Revd Aldonis Putce
The Revd Jonas Kalvanas

Church of Norway
The Rt Revd Dr Andreas Aarflot (Bishop of Oslo)
The Revd Associate Professor Ola Tjørhom

Church of Sweden
The Rt Revd Dr Tore Furberg (formerly Bishop of Visby) — Co-Chairman
The Rt Revd Dr Tord Harlin (Bishop of Uppsala)

Consultants
The Revd Dr Risto Cantell
The Revd Professor Fredric Cleve
The Revd Canon John Halliburton
The Revd Canon Christopher Hill
The Revd Canon Stephen Platten
The Revd Canon Martin Reardon

Observers
The Revd Dr Eugene Brand (Lutheran World Federation)
Director Gunnel Borgegård (Nordic Ecumenical Council)
The Revd Dr Günther Gassmann (World Council of Churches)
The Revd Henrik Roelvink, OFM (Roman Catholic Church:
  Nordic Catholic Bishops' Conference)
The Revd Lennart Sjöström (Lutheran Council of Great Britain)

Staff
Dr Mary Tanner
Mr Colin Podmore
The Revd Pirjo Työrinoja

Former Members
The Most Revd and Rt Hon Dr George Carey
  (as Bishop of Bath and Wells)
The Rt Revd Gunnar Lislerud (as Bishop of Borg)

Former Participants
The Revd Dr Walter Bouman
The Revd Canon Dr Robert Wright
The Revd Geoffrey Brown
The Revd Kaj Engström
Mr Anders Hess
The Revd Jón Baldvinsson

Observers appointed by the Anglican Consultative Council and the Evangelical Church in Germany were unable to attend any of the meetings, but received all papers. The Roman Catholic Church in England and Wales chose to receive all papers rather than send an observer. All papers were also circulated to the Conference of European Churches and to the Most Revd Antonius Glazemaker, Archbishop of Utrecht.

SELECTED PAPERS PRESENTED TO THE CONVERSATIONS

1989

David Tustin,	'The Meissen Document seen in Context'.
Ola Tjørhom,	'The Goal of Unity: Searching for a Common Ecumenical Vision', *One in Christ*, xxvi (1990), 80-93.
Martin Reardon,	'The Goal of Unity'.
John Halliburton,	'The Episcopal Office'.
Fredric Cleve,	'The Episcopal Office'.
Sven-Erik Brodd,	'Episcopacy in the Agreement on Intercommunion between the Anglican Communion and the Church of Sweden: the Church of Sweden Perspective'.

1990

Colin Podmore,	'Conciliar and Collegial Structures of the Church of England'.
David Tustin,	'Ecumenical Update'.
Gerhard Pedersen,	'Structure and Function of the Danish National Church'.
Hjalti Hugason,	'The National Church of Iceland', *Studia Theologica*, xliv (1990), 51-63.
John Halliburton,	'Sign and Place'.
Ola Tjørhom,	'The Dialogue Process between the Church of England and the Nordic and Baltic Lutheran Churches — An Introduction'.
Ola Tjørhom,	'Bilateral Dialogues involving the Churches of the Nordic Countries — A Provisional Survey'.

THE CHURCHES REPRESENTED IN THE CONVERSATIONS

Anglican Churches

Church of England

Population of England, the Isle of Man and the Channel Islands: 48 million

In a recent survey about 55% of respondents described themselves as members of the Church of England. If grossed up, this would represent some 21 million adult nominal members.

1990 Christmas communicants:	1,556,000 (4% of over 15s)
1990 electoral rolls:	1,396,000 (c.3% of over 15s)
1990 usual Sunday attendance:	1,143,000 (2.4%)

In 1989 it was estimated that on a given Sunday adult church attendances were divided roughly equally between the Church of England, the Roman Catholic Church and the Free Churches.

2 provinces, 44 dioceses, 13,060 parishes

Primate of All England:	The Archbishop of Canterbury
Primate of England:	The Archbishop of York

10,954 full-time stipendiary diocesan clergy
perhaps 1,500 non-diocesan clergy
   (prison, hospital, Forces, school, college and industrial chaplains; officials)
over 1,000 non-stipendiary clergy
some 6,000 retired clergy hold a licence to officiate

Church of Ireland

Population:	Republic of Ireland:	3.5 million
	Northern Ireland:	1.6 million
Membership:	Republic of Ireland:	95,000 (1981 census)
	Northern Ireland:	c.281,000

2 provinces, 12 dioceses, 420 parishes

Primate of All Ireland:	The Archbishop of Armagh
Primate of Ireland:	The Archbishop of Dublin

520 full-time stipendiary clergy (including bishops)
58 auxiliary clergy
265 retired clergy

Scottish Episcopal Church
Population of Scotland: 5.1 million
1990 membership: 58,000
1990 communicants: 35,000
1 province, 7 dioceses, 322 congregations
Primate: The Primus (currently the Bishop of Edinburgh)
352 active clergy

Church in Wales (Yr Eglwys yng Nghymru)
Population of Wales: 2.8 million
1992 Easter communicants: 106,000
1991 electoral rolls: 100,000
1991 usual Sunday attendance: 62,000
1 province, 6 dioceses, 1,142 parishes
Primate: The Archbishop of Wales
                                      (currently the Bishop of St Asaph)
680   full-time stipendiary diocesan clergy
?   non-diocesan clergy (number unknown)
75   non-stipendiary clergy
335   retired clergy

Nordic Churches
Church of Denmark (Den danske Folkekirke)
Population of Denmark, Greenland and the Faeroe Islands: 5.2 million
1992 membership: 4,554,000 (88.2%)
1991 communicants: 2.3 million
11 dioceses (12 from 1994), 2,300 parishes. The eleventh diocese is that of the Faeroe Islands and the twelfth will be that of Greenland.
2,095 active clergy

Evangelical-Lutheran Church of Finland (Suomen evankelis-luterilainen kirkko)
Population of Finland: 5 million
1992 membership: 4,370,000 (86.5%)
1991 weekly attendance: 118,000 (3.7%)
8 dioceses, 598 parishes
1,800 diocesan clergy

300 hospital, family counselling, school and industrial chaplains
750 church musicians
1,100 diaconal workers
1,300 youth workers
2,800 children's work personnel

Primate: The Archbishop of Turku and Finland

Evangelical-Lutheran Church of Iceland (Thjódkirkja Islands)

Population of Iceland:	262,000
Membership:	242,000 (92.2%)
Confirmations:	97% of those eligible

Church attendance (once a month or more often) 10%

1 diocese, 115 parishes, 288 congregations

130 full-time clergy

Bishop: The Bishop of Iceland

Church of Norway (Den norske kirke)

Population of Norway:	4.3 million
Estimated membership:	88.8%
1992 usual Sunday attendance:	136,900 (3.6% of the members)

1992 average attendance at Sunday services: 99 people

1992 baptisms: 49,000 (81.7% of live births)

11 dioceses, 625 parishes, 1,359 congregations, 1,700 churches and chapels

1,083 full-time parochial clergy

Praeses of the Bishops' Conference: The Bishop of Oslo (The *Praeses* or Chairman is elected annually. Hitherto, the Bishop of Oslo has always been elected.)

Church of Sweden (Svenska Kyrkan)

Population of Sweden:	8.6 million (of whom 8.2 million are Swedish citizens)
1991 membership:	7.6 million (88.8%) (92.3% of citizens)
church attendance (all services):	23.4 million attendances per year (5.9% of members each week)
church attendance (main Sunday services):	8.4 million attendances per year (2.1% of members each week)

communicants (all communion services): 2.3 million per year
communicants (main Sunday services): 1.6 million per year

baptisms:	72.7% of all infants
confirmations:	57.7% of those elegible
marriages:	63.2% of all marriages
funerals:	89.9% of all funerals

13 dioceses, 2,552 parishes

Primate of Sweden: The Archbishop of Uppsala

5,194 clergy (including 1,485 retired clergy)

In 1989 the Church of Sweden had about 28,000 employees, a large proportion of them engaged in the upkeep of cemeteries and in keeping population records. Following relinquishment of responsibility for population records, the number of employees is probably now somewhat lower.

Baltic Churches

Estonian Evangelical-Lutheran Church (Eesti Evangeelne Luterlik Kirik)

Population of Estonia: 1.6 million, of which 62% are Estonians

According to a recent survey, 60% of Estonians consider themselves Lutherans

Passive membership: 204,000
Active membership: c.75,000 (attendance at Holy Week services)

154 congregations
95 pastors and 24 deacons

The Church forms one diocese, headed by an Archbishop and a Bishop, and is divided into twelve deaneries.

Evangelical-Lutheran Church of Latvia (Latvijas evangeliski luteriska baznica)

Population of Latvia: 2.5 million
Latvians abroad: 200,000

Membership: 350,000 (Latvia); 50,000 (abroad)

300+ congregations in Latvia; 149 congregations abroad
105 clergy + 22 pastoral assistants in Latvia, 66 clergy (46 retired) abroad

The church in Latvia (one diocese) and the Latvian Lutheran Church abroad (one diocese) are about to be re-united. At present, the church in Latvia is headed by a bishop, while the diocese abroad is vacant.

41

Evangelical-Lutheran Church of Lithuania (Lietuvos Evangeliku Liuteronu Baznycia)

Population of Lithuania:	3.8 million
Confirmed members:	25-30,000
Active communicant members:	c.15,000

1 diocese, 41 parishes
12 clergy (including deacons)

Essays on Church and Ministry
in Northern Europe

CONTENTS

INTRODUCTION

The Essays on Church and Ministry in Northern Europe tell the fasci-
nating and sometimes heroic story of the British and Irish Anglican
churches and the Nordic and Baltic Lutheran churches, with particular
reference to the episcopate. They also include a summary of our earlier
agreements, a study of the episcopal ordination rites of our churches,
and material on the diaconate and on confirmation and initiation. The
earlier agreements between the Church of England and the Nordic and
Baltic churches differed from each other not only in their being nego-
tiated separately and at different times over a period of over forty years;
they also differed significantly in theological substance. The agreements
discriminated between those churches which possessed the episcopate
in a historic personal succession and those churches in which the
episcopate was transmitted initially at the Reformation by presbyteral
succession. Needless to say, the Lutheran churches themselves made no
such distinction. The unsatisfactory and partial nature of these agreements obviously requires resolution if all our churches are to come
together into the fuller communion *The Porvoo Common Statement*
now proposes. But this will require of Anglicans and Lutherans a better
understanding of the history of the episcopate in all our countries. It also
requires a renewed understanding of the nature of the Church and its
apostolic succession in faith and order. The extensive material in these
Essays will, it is hoped, provide all our churches with accurate information which, coupled with the rich ecumenical ecclesiology of *The Porvoo
Common Statement,* will enable them to perceive afresh a true apostolic
continuity in *all* our churches, effectively signalled in a commonly
recognized episcopate.

Bishops, Apostolic Succession and the Church

Anglicans and Lutherans will need to preface a fresh appraisal of the
significance of our histories by reminding themselves of the understanding of bishops, apostolic succession, and the Church offered in *The
Porvoo Common Statement.* The Common Statement is careful to avoid
a simplistic equation between personal episcopal succession and the
apostolic succession of the whole Church. The laying on of hands in the
context of prayer is seen as a sign of the apostolic succession of the

45

Church, though not an isolated guarantee of the continuity of the apostolic life of the Church. This is to understand the historic episcopate as sacramental rather than mechanical. It is not to depreciate the historic episcopate as Anglicans have received and understood it; it is rather to find an ecumenical way of understanding it and thus enabling those Lutheran churches which do not yet accept it to re-appropriate this sign of the apostolic succession without implying that their churches had ceased to be in authentic apostolic faith and continuity. Our agreement builds upon the understanding of apostolic succession in the *Baptism, Eucharist and Ministry* report of the Faith and Order Commission of the World Council of Churches, already widely received by the Lutheran churches and the churches of the Anglican Communion.

Agreement on the Church and on the Faith of the Church
There is another necessary preliminary to the reconsideration of our histories. Increasingly in all ecumenical conversations it has become recognized that agreement on the nature of the Church (ecclesiology) is the essential context for any agreement on the ordained ministry. Agreement on the Church as sign, instrument, and foretaste of God's Kingdom, that is that the Church is 'sacramental', is central to *The Porvoo Common Statement*. If the Church of Christ, professing apostolic faith and life, can be truly recognized in another Christian community, it follows that we can have confidence that that church has an authentic ministerial oversight (*episcope*), even if this has taken a different form from that with which we are familiar in our particular tradition. So our agreement on the nature of the Church and the summary forms of agreement in faith are integral and absolutely necessary parts of our total agreement and become the essential context in which we are able to move forward towards the fuller mutual recognition of our ministries and closer ecclesial communion. So too is our agreement on what fuller communion must imply by way of structures for joint decision making in the future.

Our Past Questions
Anglicans and Lutherans from our countries have often asked each other different kinds of questions. On the Anglican side the questions have varied over the centuries. When a new Danish church was built in London in 1692, visiting Anglicans were somewhat shocked by its

Roman-looking interior and because its priest wore eucharistic vestments. Yet from 1710 to 1725 the Society for Promoting Christian Knowledge (founded in 1698) gave financial support to the Danish-Halle Mission to India (in Tranquebar), and from 1728 onwards actually employed Lutheran pastors in the English Mission to India. Between 1728 and 1825 (when its Indian work was transferred to the Society for the Propagation of the Gospel) the SPCK employed or supported some sixty missionaries who had received Lutheran ordination. Distinguished seventeenth-century divines such as Bishop Lancelot Andrewes and Archbishop William Laud were clear that salvation was truly to be found in continental Lutheran and Reformed churches. Laud spoke explicitly of the Swedish and Danish Churches. Making the distinction between 'the thing and the name', he recognized the reality of episcopacy even where the name was not used.[1]

In the nineteenth century, however, the dominant Anglican opinion drew a sharp distinction between the Swedish episcopal succession and that in the Danish, Norwegian and Icelandic Churches. An influential article in the *Church Quarterly Review* of 1891 wistfully admired the continuing sacramental and liturgical tradition in the Danish Church, but bewailed 'the loss of the succession'.[2] That view was maintained in the official discussions between the Church of England and the Nordic and Baltic churches which led to the several 'intercommunion' agreements of this century.

Lutheran questions to Anglicans have perhaps been more consistent. When the English reformer Miles Coverdale, Bishop of Exeter, fled during the Marian persecution to Denmark he was generously offered a parish, which he sensibly declined because of his lack of Danish. But by the eighteenth century there were some Danish hesitations about Anglicans. When a Danish commission was considering whether Danish bishops could ordain priests for the Anglican Church in the USA (before the consecration of William Seabury for the Episcopal Church) reservations were expressed about Anglican leanings towards Calvinistic

---

[1]   W. Laud, *Works* (Library of Anglo-Catholic Theology), iii, 386.

[2]   A.J. Mason, 'The Loss of the Succession in Denmark', *Church Quarterly Review,* xxxii (1891), 149-187.

sacramental doctrine. In the present conversations Anglicans have sometimes been surprised to be asked to give assurance to their Nordic and Baltic colleagues that they are sound on the real presence of Jesus Christ in the eucharist. Questions of a quite different kind have arisen since the nineteenth century over an apparent Anglican emphasis on the absolute necessity for the historic episcopal succession and a distinction *de jure divino* between the three orders of ministry. *The Reply of the Bishops of the Church of Sweden* to the Lambeth Conference of 1920 constitutes a classical and irenical exposition of these questions.[3] Nor have the questions been absent from our present discussions.

Why we Ask the Questions we Do

Because we wanted to go beyond our traditional interrogation of the other ecclesial tradition, we decided to include in this report a considerable amount of historical material to show *why* we ask our questions.

When Anglicans read the dismal story of the late medieval abuse of episcopacy in Denmark, for example, they will begin to be more sympathetic to the urgency of the Danish reformers. Patient attention to this history will also show Anglicans a clear intention to *reform* the existing Church, and not to create a new one. Against this background Anglicans may begin to understand more sympathetically the Lutheran emphasis on the ordained ministry as both divinely instituted and yet nonetheless subservient to the word and sacraments. An awareness of the sharp historical dispute between Lutheran and Reformed over the eucharist will also alert Anglicans to the reasons Lutherans have for wanting a strong affirmation of the presence of Christ in the eucharist.

The story of the Church in Britain and Ireland will, it is hoped, show Lutherans why Anglicans have so emphasized the historic episcopate. In the reign of Elizabeth I it was only just possible to secure four bishops to consecrate Archbishop Parker on the death of Cardinal Pole in 1559. In Ireland there was an independent Anglican succession, but only where English rule was able to be imposed. In Scotland the abuse of episcopacy was in some ways similar to that in Denmark; episcopacy and the threefold ministry waxed and waned in a predominately Reformed

---

[3]   G.K.A. Bell (ed.), *Documents on Christian Unity 1920-4* (London, 1924), pp.184-195.

church, being finally excluded from the established Church of Scotland from 1689. Meanwhile, episcopacy had also been abolished in England in 1646, and had the Interregnum lasted even just ten years longer than it did, the Anglican episcopal succession might well have been extinguished completely. The oscillating history of episcopacy in the British Isles in the sixteenth and seventeenth centuries explains the heightened emphasis on the threefold ministry of bishops, priests and deacons at the Restoration of Church and monarchy embodied in the 1662 Act of Uniformity, Prayer Book and Ordinal. This was in reaction to Presbyterian, Congregationalist and Independent polity, rather than against the continental Lutheran churches.

Re-reading our Histories

As we read the others' history, and re-read our own, we may learn a new humility and discover surprising similarities. Anglicans may well be a little less emphatic about an unbroken episcopal succession when they see how precarious their succession was in the first 150 years after the Reformation. Or about the threefold ministry when they consider the spasmodic provision for deacons as a distinct order in the episcopally ordered Church of Scotland during parts of the seventeenth century. Surprising convergence can be discovered in considering episcopacy and the Tractarians. It is undoubtedly true that the Oxford Movement emphasized the importance of the continuity of the episcopal succession. But this was to emphasize the 'apostolical' origins of the Church over and against the state; bishops were not so much erastian officers of the state as successors to the Apostles. Here there are strong similarities with some of the Nordic and Baltic churches. Opposition to the historic and apostolic office of bishop in the Nordic and Baltic churches often occurred because other forms of ecclesiastical government were perceived to be more susceptible to manipulation by government or aristocracy, for example in Sweden and in Estonia.

We can also recognize a historical distortion of twentieth-century ecumenical discussion of the episcopate due to the dramatic condemnation of Anglican Orders by Leo XIII in 1896. This was at the time of the first official discussion between the Church of England and the Church of Sweden. In reaction to the Roman condemnation, Anglicans of all schools became over-anxious to establish their episcopal credentials.

Arguably, Anglican ecumenical conversations became preoccupied with episcopal succession in relation to Lutheran, Old Catholics and Orthodox.

The Baltic History

The agreement between the Church of England and the Churches of Latvia and Estonia in 1938 was eclipsed almost immediately by the Second World War and the occupation of these countries by the Nazis and the Soviets. But their subsequent story is one of individual heroism and corporate courage. Anglican and Nordic readers can only be inspired by the way episcopacy has come to be seen as a mark of the apostolicity of the churches of the Baltic region. Where the personal succession has been interrupted it has consciously been restored by prayer and the laying on of hands by a bishop within the succession, giving eloquent testimony to the intention of the Baltic churches to retain the office of bishop in its fullness. The story of the episcopate in Estonia in particularly moving. Political pressures from occupying powers or the conflicts of war have twice caused the interruption (with subsequent restoration) of a personal succession. Episcopacy is seen as witness to the gospel in the face of oppression and persecution.

Continuity of Apostolic Life

With such a fresh historical and theological perspective it is possible for Anglicans and Lutherans to look with new eyes at the complex history of the episcopate in all our countries and to discern an apostolic continuity. There were significant changes at the time of the Reformation. But there was also a real continuity in the pastoral life of word and sacrament, in administration and in episcopal oversight. Indeed, pastoral care and the proclamation of the gospel were enhanced. The pattern of parochial and diocesan life continued in the majority of the ancient Nordic and Baltic sees just as in Britain and Ireland. Moreover, in Denmark, even though the office of bishop was continued by one himself only in presbyteral orders (though exercising *episcope*), care has been taken ever since to maintain that episcopate through a personal succession, as is also the case in Norway and Iceland. The conscious care with which that succession has been maintained surely reflects a deep concern for the apostolic continuity of the ordained ministry.

The Intention to Continue the Office of Bishop

The evidence of the episcopal ordination rites of all our churches endorses such a view. It is to the text and liturgical context of such rites that the Christian must turn to learn what a church believes about its ordained ministry. It is here that the 'sacramental intention' or 'mind of the Church' can be discerned, not in the personal views of those ordaining or being ordained. The analysis of the various Anglican and Lutheran ordination rites demonstrates very clearly that those churches, including the Churches of Denmark, Norway and Iceland, intend by explicit prayer and the laying on of hands to ordain priests to a distinct episcopal ministry.

The Threefold Ministry

This clear ecclesial intention to continue the apostolic office of bishop is more significant than any particular Anglican theology of the threefold ministry of bishop, priest and deacon, or any Lutheran theology of the unity of ministerial order. The various forms of diaconal ministry in our churches point towards a revival of understanding of the diaconate as a distinctive ministry admitted to by prayer and the laying on of hands, whether it has traditionally been regarded as a lay or a clerical ministry. Moreover, as Anglicans have preserved the diaconate only by making it in effect a probationary step towards the priesthood, they may well have sympathy with the various forms diaconal ministry has taken in the Nordic and Baltic churches and their present tendency towards a distinctive diaconate.

Initiation and Confirmation

Similarly, neither Anglicans nor Nordic and Baltic Lutherans can claim a totally coherent theology or practice of initiation and confirmation. Anglicans, in particular, ought to be cautious about making presbyteral confirmation a bar to closer communion, since both the Roman Catholic and the Orthodox Churches generally confirm by the ministry of priests rather than bishops. Anglicans will admire the extensive and systematic training for confirmation in the Nordic and Baltic churches. They will also reflect upon the substantial variations in the practice of the rite of confirmation throughout Christian history — for example, by unction or the laying on of hands. As with different understandings of the diaconate, variations in the practice of confirmation are surely compatible with fuller communion.

Conclusion

On the basis of our agreement on the Church and its faith, on apostolic succession and the episcopate, the members of the Conversations believe that Anglicans will now be able to discern an authentic historic continuity of episcopal ministry in *all* the Nordic and Baltic Lutheran churches as well as the Anglican churches of Britain and Ireland. Equally, the way is opened for the restoration of the historic episcopal succession in those Lutheran churches where this has not yet been accepted because it would have been perceived as calling in question their past ministry. Our agreement therefore calls for changes of attitude and practice amongst both Anglicans and Lutherans. But we believe that these would be changes soundly based in both theology and history. We believe that these changes can be made with integrity. They are now demanded by the imperative for unity and the exigencies of the times in the Europe of today. At the end of the article already referred to bewailing 'the loss of succession', the readers of the *Church Quarterly Review* were asked to pray for the opening of the way by which our churches might share the fullness of their inheritance. One hundred years later we are close, I believe, to the fulfilment of that prayer.

CHRISTOPHER HILL

EXISTING AGREEMENTS BETWEEN OUR CHURCHES

Sweden

Prior to the first Lambeth Conference of 1867, the Revd Charles Kingsley had been in correspondence with Archbishop Longley of Canterbury, urging the desirability of inviting the Swedish bishops to attend. Thereafter there was occasional discussion about relations with the Church of Sweden in the Church of England Convocations and at the Lambeth Conferences of 1888 and 1897. This led to the establishment, at the Lambeth Conference of 1908, of an Anglican Communion commission, under the chairmanship of Bishop H.W.Ryle of Winchester, to confer with Swedish bishops and theologians. This had been prompted by the presence of the Bishop of Kalmar, Dr H.W.Tottie, at the Lambeth Conference — a presence encouraged by Professor (as he then was) Nathan Söderblom. The Swedish commission was led by Archbishop J.A.Ekman of Uppsala and included Söderblom.

The Anglican report was published in 1911 and was presented to the Lambeth Conference of 1920. It declared that the Swedish succession of bishops 'had been unbroken', that the Church of Sweden had 'a true conception of the episcopal office', 'rightly conceived the office of priest', and intended to hand them on. It recommended that members of the Church of Sweden should be permitted to receive Holy Communion in the Church of England, that Swedish clergy should be permitted to preach in the Church of England, and that occasionally there should be mutual participation in episcopal consecrations. The term 'intercommunion' was avoided. The Lambeth Conference of 1920 accepted these recommendations, but no action was taken by the Convocations of the Church of England. In 1922 the bishops of the Church of Sweden replied to the Lambeth acceptance of the Commission's recommendations, approving of Anglican reception of Holy Communion in the Church of Sweden and recommending that invitations to take part in Anglican episcopal consecrations should be accepted subject to the direction of the Archbishop of Uppsala. They nevertheless qualified their acceptance of the agreement to the effect that the Church of Sweden could not recognize 'any essential difference, *de jure divino*, between the two or three Orders into which the ministry of grace may have been divided'.[1]

By the Lambeth Conference of 1930 there had been consecrations at Uppsala (1920) and Canterbury (1927) in which one or more bishops of the other church had participated. On both sides the ultimate responsibility for the invitation to participate in episcopal consecrations has rested with the Archbishops of Canterbury and Uppsala respectively.[2] Mutual consecrations continued on an occasional basis until they were informally suspended by Archbishop Geoffrey Fisher of Canterbury in 1959 over the prospect of the ordination of women in the Church of Sweden. They were resumed in 1976 by Archbishop Donald Coggan after the General Synod declared that there were 'no fundamental objections' to the ordination of women.

A synodical consideration of Anglo-Swedish relations by the Church of England came in 1954.[3] After debating the report of a committee under the chairmanship of Bishop G.K.A.Bell, the Convocations recognized the due succession of the Swedish episcopate. They recommended that duly qualified members of the Church of Sweden should be able to receive Holy Communion and that Swedish clergy should be permitted to preach in the Church of England. The report did not treat of a participation in episcopal consecrations.

In May 1960 the Lower House of the Canterbury Convocation requested a review of relations between the Church of England and the Swedish Church. This was in the light of the situation created by the

---

[1] The Church of Sweden Conference of Bishops: 'To the Conference of Bishops in the Anglican Communion', *Kyrkohistorisk Årsskrift* 23 (1923), 374-381. Reprinted in: Vilmos Vajta (ed.), *Church in Fellowship: Pulpit and Altar Fellowship Among Lutherans* (Minneapolis, 1963), pp.181-188; G.K.A.Bell (ed.), *Documents on Christian Unity 1920-4* (London, 1924), pp. 185-195.

[2] Outside Europe interconsecration between Anglican and Swedish bishops met with setbacks in South Africa (1958) and in Uganda (1962) due to Lutheran caution. But in 1962 a Swedish bishop took part in the consecration of the Anglican Assistant bishop of Central Tanganyika (now Tanzania) and mutual participation in consecrations has continued. There are many current examples of mutual participation in consecrations in Africa, Malaysia, the Near East and Europe.

[3] H. Riley and R.J. Graham (eds), *Acts of the Convocations of Canterbury and York: 1921-1970* (London, 1971), pp.194-195.

ordination of women in Sweden in April of that year. A committee under the chairmanship of the Dean of Worcester (the Very Reverend R.L.P.Milburn) reported to the Lower House of Canterbury in October 1961.[4] The report was received and its resolutions were adopted. It re-affirmed that Swedish clergy should be permitted to preach and recommended that they should be given permission to celebrate Holy Communion *according to their own rite* or assist at the Anglican rite when in Anglican churches. Women priests were excluded from these provisions.

Finland

The Lambeth Conference of 1930 asked Archbishop Lang to appoint a Church of England commission to examine relations with the Church of Finland. It met with a similar Finnish commission at Lambeth Palace, London in 1933 and in Helsinki in 1934. The respective chairmen were the Bishop of Gloucester, Dr A.C.Headlam, and the Bishop of Tampere, Dr A.Lehtonen. The joint body was of the 'opinion that both Churches hold the most fundamental doctrines of the Christian faith'.[5] In 1935 its recommendations relating to admission to communion and participation in episcopal consecrations were accepted by the Convocations of Canterbury and York,[6] though not without some difficulties in the Convocation of Canterbury over an admitted break in the historic succession at the end of the nineteenth century (gradually to be restored through the Swedish succession). The term 'intercommunion' was avoided by the Anglican co-chairman, who spoke of 'economic communion'. In 1936 Archbishop Kaila of Turku wrote to Archbishop Lang of Canterbury in official reply to the resolutions of the Church of England Convocations. He acknowledged that, in spite of differences of emphasis, there was 'a fundamental agreement in Christian doctrine'. But the Church of Finland could not look upon the historic episcopate 'as a *conditio sine qua non* for a valid ministry'. He also endorsed the qualifications spoken of by the Swedish bishops in 1922 regarding the threefold ministry. Nevertheless he warmly welcomed the agreement and its

---

[4] *Ibid.*, pp.195-196.

[5] *Lambeth Occasional Reports 1931-8* (London, 1948), pp.115-187.

[6] *Acts of the Convocations*, pp.176-178.

pastoral recommendations on behalf of the Church of Finland.[7] The first consecration with Anglican participation in Finland took place in 1951.

Latvia and Estonia

In 1937 the Archbishop of Latvia and the Bishop of Estonia wrote a joint letter to the Archbishop of Canterbury requesting an arrangement similar to that made with the Church of Finland. Accordingly, delegates were appointed from the three churches under the chairmanship of the Bishop of Gloucester (Dr A.C.Headlam), the Archbishop of Latvia (Dr T.Grünbergs) and the Bishop of Estonia (Dr H.B.Rahamägi). They met at Lambeth Palace, London in 1936 and in Riga and Tallinn in June 1938. Their short report agreed that their churches held 'the most fundamental doctrines of the Christian faith' in common. They recommended mutual participation in episcopal consecrations, the mutual admission of communicants to their respective altars, the invitation of the Baltic bishops to a future Lambeth Conference and the celebration of baptism and marriage by Anglican clergy for the Latvian and Estonian diaspora and vice-versa.[8] The last provision was to be of unforeseen pastoral benefit for the Latvian and Estonian refugee communities in Great Britain during and after the Second World War. The Church of England Convocations accepted the recommendations of the commission in January and May 1939.[9] By reason of the date of the agreement and subsequent European history, the first participation in an episcopal consecration took place only in 1989 when the Bishop of Gibraltar in Europe took part in the consecration of the Archbishop of Latvia.

Norway, Denmark and Iceland

In 1948 the Lambeth Conference invited the Archbishop of Canterbury to appoint a committee to confer with similar committees of the Churches

---

[7] Correspondence between Archbishop of Turku, Finland (Kaila) and Archbishop of Canterbury (Lang), March-April, 1936. In Vilmos Vajta (ed.), *op.cit.*, pp.202-205. Also in G.K.A.Bell (ed.), *Documents on Christian Unity: Third Series 1930-1948* (London, 1948), pp.149-153.

[8] *Lambeth Occasional Reports 1931-8*, pp. 207-261; G.K.A.Bell (ed.), *Documents on Christian Unity: Third Series 1930-1948* (London, 1948), pp.154-158.

[9] *Acts of the Convocations*, pp.179-181.

of Norway, Denmark and Iceland. This followed an informal conference between the three churches held in Chichester in 1947. The joint committee met in Oslo in 1951. Professor A.M.Ramsey (as he then was) was the Anglican chairman in place of the Bishop of Chichester, who was ill. The Bishop of Oslo, Dr E.Berggrave, led the Norwegian delegation and the Bishop of Aarhus, Dr S. Hoffmeyer, the Danish, and the Revd J.Jonsson represented the Church of Iceland. It was agreed that the four churches were in agreement with each other in the fundamental doctrines of the Christian faith. Similarities in pastoral and sacramental practice were noted, together with differences in regard to confirmation. The Lutheran churches spoke of themselves as unwilling to think of succession by episcopal consecration as 'an essential element in the continuity of the ministry and the Church'. The breach of succession by consecration was said by them to be necessary as the only way of recovering the office of bishop from its corruption. It was agreed that interconsecration between churches which did not yet mutually recognize their respective ministries was inappropriate. Each side recommended that communicants of good standing of the other tradition should be able to receive Holy Communion in their own. These recommendations came before the Convocations in 1953 and 1954.[10] There was debate as to whether communicants from Norway, Denmark and Iceland were to be 'admitted' or 'welcomed' to receive Holy Communion. The resolution finally read 'may be welcomed'.

The problem of intercommunion between the National Church of Denmark and the Church of England on the one side and the (Presbyterian) Church of Scotland on the other was discussed several times after the Second World War in the meetings of the Danish bishops. In January 1955 the bishops discussed a letter received from the Archbishop of Canterbury offering the hospitality of the Church of England to members of the Danish Church who were prevented from taking part in the eucharist of their own church. The bishops decided to ask the Ministry of Ecclesiastical Affairs to ensure a canonically suitable confirmation of the willingness on the part of the Danish Church to provide similar hospitality to members of the Church of England as well as the Church of Scotland to take part in the Lutheran eucharist.

---

[10] *Ibid.*, p.194.

At first the Ministry responded reluctantly, but on 5 April 1956 the hospitality was confirmed by a royal ordinance which stated: 'that there is given general admission for members of the Church of Scotland and the Church of England to take part in the Eucharist in the congregations of the Danish National Church, provided that the priest concerned is willing to administer to them'. This ordinance was communicated to the bishops by a departmental circular letter from the Ministry of Ecclesiastical Affairs dated 17 April 1956.[11]

This first step towards a closer fellowship should be understood against the background of the formerly very restricted practice of the Danish Church expressed in *The Book of Order of the Church of Denmark and Norway* of 1685, where it is stated in Chapter 5 ('The Sacrament of the Lord's Supper'): 'no person of foreign religion (confession) should be taken to the sacrament of the Altar before he is fully instructed in our faith and disclaims all connection with his former religion in face of the priest'. Exchanges of letters between Lambeth and Denmark in 1957 described the agreement as 'limited intercommunion'.

Acceptance by other Anglican Churches

In the earlier part of this century such negotiations were often conducted by the Church of England in the name of all Anglicans. The piecemeal agreements of the '20s, '30s and '50s were therefore generally accepted by the other Anglican churches in Britain and Ireland, as well as elsewhere within the Anglican Communion, especially where the initiative originally came from the Lambeth Conference. In the Scottish Episcopal Church the above agreements with Sweden, with Finland, and with Latvia and Estonia were explicitly endorsed by the Episcopal Synod after their approval by the Lambeth Conference of 1948. Relations with the Church of Sweden were further endorsed as identical with those of the Church of England in 1952.

More Recent Developments

Since the acceptance of the above agreements, the Church of England has authorized a wider eucharistic hospitality to all baptized persons who are communicant members in good standing of other Trinitarian churches (Canon B 15A, 1972). Similar provision has been made in the other Anglican churches.

CHRISTOPHER HILL

---

[11] Vilmos Vajta (ed.), *op.cit.*, pp.212-213.

EPISCOPACY IN OUR CHURCHES

SWEDEN

In his ecumenical theory on the unity of the Church, Nathan Söderblom (1866-1931), the Swedish archbishop and pioneer in the ecumenical movement, uses the Anglican 'branch theory' and divides the Christian Church into three parts: one Greek-Catholic Church, one Roman-Catholic Church, and one Evangelical-Catholic Church. In an exemplary way, he attributed evangelical catholicity to the Church of Sweden. He saw the catholicity of the Church being realized in a particular church. What made the Church of Sweden an evangelical-catholic church was to Archbishop Söderblom the fact that the Reformation in Sweden was a 'church improvement' and a 'process of purification' which did *not* create a new church. As a national church, the Church of Sweden succeeded in bringing together medieval Swedish tradition with the rediscovery of the gospel which the Reformation brought with it. Archbishop Söderblom included the historic episcopate in the tradition-transmitting elements. The Church of Sweden was, according to Söderblom, in an even higher degree than the Anglican Church a *via media*.

By way of introduction, I wish to comment on Nathan Söderblom's opinions on these matters, as they have, to such a high degree, come to characterize the Church of Sweden's attitude to the episcopate, not least in ecumenical contexts. Ever since the Reformation in the sixteenth century, the Church of Sweden has lived its life apart from other churches. So, when the Church of Sweden for the first time, at the beginning of the twentieth century, was to establish inter-communion with another Church, namely the Church of England, it was forced to reconsider theologically what the episcopate, as a heritage from the early days of the Church, really meant. Söderblom exerted a great influence on the answer to this question. I shall come back to all this.

The Episcopate in Sweden in the Middle Ages

Christian belief started to spread in Sweden during the latter half of the ninth century. In the oldest Swedish law material, one can see that the bishops were appointed by the election of the people. The first indication of a Swedish division into dioceses is to be found in the so-called Florence document of around 1120. The appointment of bishops then became attached to the cathedral chapters when they were established in the dioceses by a special decision in 1248. The problem with the episcopal appointments is a particular illustration of the wider conflict between Germanic law and canon law, which continued for a long time in Sweden. During the latter part of the Middle Ages, it was brought to the fore by the role the Swedish kings played in the elections and appointments of bishops.

The original Swedish dioceses date from the eleventh and twelfth centuries and remain more or less the same today. New dioceses have been added and others have been lost through changes in Sweden's political borders. Two new dioceses have come into being in modern times. Uppsala has been the archiepiscopal see since 1164.

The problem of the Church's relations to the state has, to a great extent, had to do with the question of the episcopal office. The bishops used to take an active part in Swedish politics and they belonged to the governing council surrounding the kings. At the same time, the Swedish kings often intervened in the running of the Church. The kings' interference in the internal affairs of the Church and the politicization of the episcopate are features of Swedish medieval history which prepare for the Reformation in the sixteenth century.

The Episcopate in the Era of the Swedish Reformation
The political and religious transition period, usually termed the Reformation, was actually the period during which Sweden became a nation-state with an hereditary monarchy. When the Reformation began, most of the episcopal sees, including the archiepiscopal see, were unoccupied.

When King Gustavus Vasa took office, he wanted, in a way not unusual for sovereigns in late medieval times, to restrict the bishop's political powers and confiscate the economic assets of the Church. Initially, King Gustavus Vasa had no intention of breaking with Rome. As five out of ten sees were unoccupied, there arose a critical situation for the Church. In 1524, Petrus Magni, the director of the Brigittine Community in Rome, was elected and consecrated Bishop of Västerås. He also received papal confirmation. At the coronation of the king in 1528, Petrus Magni was forced to consecrate another two bishops. But on this occasion there was no papal confirmation. A new archbishop was elected for the Uppsala archdiocese, and there was a request from Sweden for papal confirmation of the election. However, it failed to arrive. Faced with this fact and influenced by Lutheran theologians, King Gustavus announced that he would take over the pope's right of confirmation. A Lutheran theologian, Laurentius Petri, was then elected archbishop and consecrated in 1531. He remained archbishop until his death in 1573.

During the archiepiscopate of Laurentius Petri, the king made an attempt, in the 1540s, to abolish the episcopate, but he failed. When the successor of Laurentius Petri was consecrated in 1575 by Bishop Paul Juusten in Åbo, now in Finland but then a Swedish province, the succession (*successio manuum* and *successio sedis*) from the medieval episcopate was established in the Church of Sweden.

This brief survey of the ecclesiastical development during the Reformation covers a complicated process. Broadly, it involves a settlement between a German-influenced Lutheranism and a more conservative Swedish Reformation, which itself contains elements of the Lutheran humanism which appears in the Augsburg Confession and of medieval Swedish tradition. It is the latter which, in the end, emerges victorious from the struggle. At a provincial convocation in 1593, the Church of Sweden confirmed a decision made by an earlier (1571) convocation that the Augsburg Confession together with the Swedish Church Ordinance (also of 1571) would make up the *Confessio Suecana*. The 1571 Swedish Church Ordinance was written by Archbishop Laurentius Petri, and unlike other Lutheran church ordinances, it is also a theological document. It prescribes at length the status of the episcopate in the Church of Sweden.

According to the Church Ordinance of 1571, the episcopal office is warranted by its being found as far back as the Early Church. Moreover, it has been given to the Church by the Holy Spirit, it has been approved by all Christendom everywhere and at all times, and therefore it must remain for as long as the world will last. One episcopal duty is to ordain the clergy (and also, naturally, to consecrate other bishops). The bishop is obliged to visit his diocese, he has jurisdiction over his clergy, he is responsible for the teaching of the true faith and the sacraments being rightly administered in his diocese, but above all he is, together with all the

61

clergy of his diocese, the servant of the gospel — *verbi divini minister* — through the administration of the sacraments and the preaching of the Word of God.

The Powerful Bishops during Sweden's Period as a Great Power

During the seventeenth century (c.1617-1719), Sweden pursued an expansionist foreign policy which at times, especially through the many wars, made the country into one of the leading powers of Europe. For the episcopate, this development meant that its position in society was strengthened. During long periods, this fact caused strained relations with the Swedish royal power and the nobility. The office was, in the light of the Church Ordinance (1571), considered as *jure divino*. The bishops exercised a critical and prophetic function in relation to the king and nobility, and they secured the freedom of the Church by consolidating their power in the dioceses. However, the king still appointed the bishops, as had become the custom after the pope's refusal to confirm bishops for the Church of Sweden as far back as 1528.

With the help of royal power, the noblemen now tried to circumscribe the bishops' and the clergy's power by proposing a Church Board which would also include laymen. This proposal was presented in the Swedish *Riksdag* (parliament), however, which was at the time composed of the four estates — namely nobility, clergy, burghers, and freehold farmers— and where bishops with their clergy thus formed an independent part. Not until 1864 was the four-estate *Riksdag* replaced by a more democratic form of government.

There is another interesting phenomenon which occurred at the same time, the beginning of the seventeenth century. The areas which had in various ways been conquered by the Swedes were, with few exceptions, not placed under the care of bishops. Instead, they were placed under superintendents (who had the right of ordination). These superintendents came into existence at a time when the influence of German Lutheranism was again on the increase. It is worth mentioning, however, that if a superintendent was elected bishop of one of the old Swedish dioceses, he had then to be consecrated before he took office as bishop.

New Discussions about the Episcopate during the Eighteenth and Early Nineteenth Centuries

During the eighteenth and nineteenth centuries, new issues came to the fore. Gustavus III (1746-1792), the Swedish king, was strongly influenced by French culture and wanted to influence Sweden in accordance with continental thought. He visited the pope and had conversations with Roman Catholic theologians. The influence of German Lutheranism was weakened, the superintendencies were turned into dioceses, and the superintendents were consecrated bishops. The last of these consecrations took place in 1772 in the diocese of Visby, the capital of the island of Gotland, recently captured from the Danes.

In the consecration liturgy of 1811 (which replaced the liturgy in the Church Ordinance of 1571), it is laid down for the first time since the Reformation that the bishop to be ordained shall be given crosier and mitre at the consecration. The crosier had actually disappeared through Gustavus Vasa's confiscations of the church treasures. His son, King Johan III, did indeed purchase new crosiers, but it seems that the use of the crosier was rare. The same can be said of the mitre. But looking at the sepulchral monument of Bishop Therserus in Linköping Cathedral (c. 1680), one can see that he had been attired in his episcopal cope, mitre and stole (worn directly over the cassock). After the Reformation, the cope had become the episcopal sign of office, while the ordinary clergyman wore a chasuble (*casula*). Since 1811 the custom of Swedish bishops using crosier and mitre has endured.

Apart from the diocesan bishops, there was (during the years 1783-1883, and officially it has not yet been abolished) a special episcopal office attached to the royal Order of the Seraphim. The bishop was the Prelate of the Order, responsible for the chaplains who officiated at its 'charitable institutions'. 'Absolute consecrations', i.e. bishops being consecrated without receiving an actual diocese, have thus taken place in the Church of Sweden. Finally, it can be stated that during this period interest was expressed in the succession in the Church of Sweden, for example in a book written by Professor Erik Fant in 1790, *De Successione Canonica et Consecratione Episcoporum Sveciae*. Behind the interest in this matter, one can among other things detect increased contacts with the Anglican Church.

At the same time it should be mentioned that during the first half of the nineteenth century there was a certain body of opinion which wished to abolish the episcopate. One reason for this was that the bishops were obliged to be members of the *Riksdag*. They were often members of the government or had other prominent functions in the state. One result of this was that the pastoral care for the dioceses was weakened. Sometimes the bishops were looked upon less as spiritual leaders and more as representatives of state authority. Since 1868 the status of the episcopate has not been questioned.

The Episcopate at Present in the Church of Sweden

One way of describing the present Swedish episcopacy is to proceed from the liturgy for episcopal ordination which was authorized in 1986. The episcopal ordination takes place in Uppsala Cathedral before the other bishops and with the archbishop as the main consecrator. Bishops from other Lutheran churches and from the Anglican churches are invited.

The Episcopal Ordination consists of the following parts:

1. The reading of the bishop's Letter of Appointment;
2. The archbishop's address and the vows of the bishop-elect;
3. The Creed;
4. The Prayer for the Church;
5. The Ordination Prayer with a laying on of hands. The new bishop is attired in cope, mitre, episcopal cross, and crosier. He first wears the stole crossed, but during the ordination it is changed so that it finally hangs down straight.

In his speech on the bishop's mission, the archbishop says:

> A bishop shall have oversight over the diocese and its congregations and he is responsible for God's word being preached in purity and clarity, for the sacraments being rightly administered, and for the works of charity being practised according to God's will.
>
> A bishop shall ordain and inspect, visit, take and give counsel, listen, make decisions...
>
> Holding the office of bishop, he shall live as a servant of Christ and shall be a shepherd for God's flock.
>
> With vigilance and wisdom he shall serve the unity of the Church in Christ...

That which stands out as the core of the episcopal office is the pastoral task (superintendence of the diocese with *potestas iurisdictionis*, responsibility for the teachings with *potestas magisterii*, and the responsibililty for ordaining with *potestas ordinis*). The bishop is also the sign of unity. This is the office to which the bishop-elect is ordained. The apostolicity of ordination is expressed in the readings from the Bible, but also in the final words from the archbishop (the consecrator) where he says:

> In apostolic manner, by prayer and the laying on of hands in God's name, X has been ordained a bishop. Receive him as an ambassador for Christ.

An episcopal ordination in Uppsala Cathedral is a national event, concerning the whole Church of Sweden. When the newly ordained bishop comes to his diocese, he will be received there at a special service in the cathedral of that diocese. In essence, the reception liturgy consists of representatives of the priests and deacons, the parishes of the diocese, and diocesan bodies and church institutions recognizing the newly ordained bishop. This part of the liturgy is led by the dean, who begins the service by saying to the bishop, who stands forward in the sanctuary:

> You have received the crosier of this diocese,
> the sign of your pastoral mission.
> We receive you as the ambassador of Christ
> and as our colleague in the service of Christ.

The bishop becomes a member of the Bishops' Conference, which consists of all the bishops in the Church of Sweden. Collegiality and loyalty are also expressed by the presence of all the bishops at the ordination, and several of them are also co-consecrators, normally three, the archbishop being chief consecrator. The Bishops' Conference is not a canonical institution, but it plays an important part in the life of the Church. Among other things, the bishops jointly give opinion on ecclesiastical and theological questions in corporate pastoral letters.

A particular problem at present under discussion in the Church of Sweden is the threefold ministry. There is the question of how to regulate the diaconate canonically. It was confirmed in the Church of Sweden Service Book in 1987 that there is a threefold ministry in the Church of Sweden. This later received a theological interpretation in a pastoral letter from the Swedish Bishops' Conference in 1990. The interpretation has also been worked out by a committee which is elaborating a proposal for a new Church Ordinance to replace that of 1571.

The status of the bishops has changed considerably in the twentieth century. From chiefly having been the representative of the authorities and *pastor pastorum*, the bishop's role has now been broadened so that he has become the spiritual leader of the whole diocese.

In 1990, the Church of Sweden consecrated its first auxiliary bishop since the Reformation. This was, among other things, necessitated by the scope of the diocesan bishop's duties, and, in this particular case, also the archbishop's increased responsibilities in the Swedish Church as a whole.

The Swedish Episcopate in an Ecumenical Context

When, for the first time, the Church of Sweden formally came into a closer relation with another church, it was, strangely enough, not a Lutheran church but the Church of England.

It can be said that not until it developed ecumenical contacts with other churches was the Church of Sweden forced to reflect on its theological and ecclesial identity. Right into the twentieth century, the Church of Sweden was able to lead a comparatively isolated life. As late as the middle of the nineteenth century, it was a national church enclosing the whole society. Even though individual theologians and churchpeople have obviously had contacts with other churches, it was through Archbishop Nathan Söderblom that the Church of Sweden as such began its first relations with other national churches in Europe. The episcopate became an important part of this conscious ecumenical reorientation.

The fruits of the dialogue with the Church of England have significantly influenced the Church of Sweden's views on the episcopate. On the one hand, the Church of Sweden is itself — in accordance with its tradition and by its conviction that the episcopate is founded by the Holy Spirit —bound to keep and to honour the episcopal office. On the other hand, the Church of Sweden does not believe that it can require other churches to embrace the same teachings on episcopacy as it does itself, even though the function of *episcope* is presupposed. This has led to a certain tension, which has been resolved by the Church of Sweden acknowledging the ministries of other churches provided that they have a teaching on the ordained ministry and sacraments which can be accepted by the Church of Sweden, even though they do not formally have the same ministerial structure. There still remains, however, some tension between the Church of Sweden and Lutheran churches which do not have the historic episcopate. The Church of Sweden has tried to overcome these differences by encouraging Swedish bishops to consecrate bishops in these churches. This is the case, for example, in the Baltic states, in Tanzania, Malaysia, Zimbabwe, South Africa, and in the Tamil Church in India (which resulted in conflict with the German Lutheran mission).

In a speech given at the first World Conference on Faith and Order in Lausanne (1927), Nathan Söderblom interprets the Church of Sweden's views on the episcopate as follows:

> Now a few words about our peculiar Swedish position. We have the so-called constitutional episcopacy, and the episcopal and presbyteral continuity without break is proved beyond any doubt — which, of course, in no wise makes our priestly office perfect.

The archbishop continues by referring to the Church Ordinance, saying that 'the value of episcopacy was acccentuated by Laurentius Petri, Archbishop of Uppsala, in his Church Ordinance of 1571', and he adds that the Church Ordinance has 'authority in our Church as a kind of particular symbolic book'. He quotes the passage where it is stated about the order of episcopacy that 'this law was most useful, and without doubt proceeded from God the Holy Spirit, the Giver of all goodness; it was also univerally accepted and approved over the whole of Christendom, and has ever since been and ever must be so long the world endureth'.

Söderblom interprets the standpoint of the Church of Sweden by quoting the Swedish Church Commission which stated that

> The doctrine of freedom in no wise makes our church indifferent to the organization and the forms of ministry which the cravings and experiences of the Christian community have produced under the guidance of the Spirit in the course of history. We not only regard the peculiar forms and traditions of our church with the reverence due to a venerable legacy from the past, we realize in them a blessing from the God of history accorded to us.

When Söderblom thereafter deals with 'the doctrine of freedom', he does this on the basis not of what is necessary for the Church of Sweden but of what is necessary for Christian unity. Episcopacy is not a *sine qua non* for church fellowship: 'The only way for us to decide what part of formulated doctrine and church organization is necessary for unity, is to consider its ability to bring the supernatural divine content to man, society and mankind (Phil. 3. 4-8)'. The Commission continues:

> No particular organization of the Church and of its ministry is instituted *jure divino*, not even the order and discipline and state of things recorded in the New Testament, the great principle of Christian freedom, unweariedly asserted by St Paul against every form of legal religion, and instituted already by our Saviour Himself, as for instance when, in taking farewell of His disciples, he did not regulate their future work by *a priori* rules and institutions but directed them by the guidance of the Paraclete, the Holy Ghost.

To Söderblom, 'the guidance of the Holy Paraclete' is the main norm for church order, not, for example, the New Testament. And church order cannot be a condition for unity, because that would reshape Christianity to 'a form of legal religion'. Church order, including episcopacy, are in principle inclusive and uniting, never exclusive.

Not until the 1980s were there talks about episcopacy between the Church of Sweden and the Roman Catholic Church. A report on the episcopal office appeared in 1988. It was written by the official dialogue group of the Church of Sweden and the Roman Catholic diocese of Stockholm, which had been working on the issue since 1982.

A National Episcopate

In his 1927 Lausanne speech, Nathan Söderblom describes the Swedish episcopate as constitutional. The Church of Sweden was separated from the Roman Catholic Church in the sixteenth century and the king took charge of a number of canonical matters which had previously been administered in Rome. Then began both the close relationship between the episcopate and the government and also the power struggle between the king, and government, and the bishops. As time went on this was settled when democracy was achieved in Sweden. The last remnant of this is the fact that episcopal candidates are elected by the Church, then the government chooses one out of the three who gained the highest number of votes. This candidate is ordained bishop. In 1963 lay people, too, received the right to take part in episcopal elections. The reasons for this development include the fact that this practice already existed in medieval times; that the bishop is no longer considered mainly as the head of the clergy but as the shepherd of the whole diocese; and that the bishop's spiritual authority is strengthened by God's people as a whole taking part in the election.

The bishop is the chairman of the most important bodies and institutions in his diocese. The archbishop works, correspondingly, not only in his diocese but also in the decision-making bodies for the whole church. But the constitutional aspect lies in the fact that he can, in principle, be outvoted. A constitutional episcopate, like the historic tension between bishop and government, does expose a special problem for an episcopal national church, namely the lack of an international instrument with the capacity to correct national aberration. The problem can be seen in autocratic bishops, well-known from the history of the Church of Sweden and also in churches today, for example in Africa. The current situation in the Church of Sweden poses the opposite problem, namely the fact that the spiritual and religious status of the episcopate makes it canonically almost powerless. The question is whether this problem can be resolved when national episcopal churches form part of a greater international communion.

SVEN-ERIK BRODD

FINLAND

Finland was part of Sweden from the middle of the thirteenth century until 1809. The Finnish Church belonged to the ecclesiastical province of Uppsala. In Finland the bishop's office covered much the same duties as in Sweden. But historic events which concerned Finland in particular often affected the position of the Finnish bishops.

The Missionary Period: 1155-1248

The first bishop in the Finnish Church was an Englishman, Bishop Henrik. According to tradition he came to Finland together with the Swedish king, Erik Jedvardsson, Saint Eric, who made a crusade to south-western Finland, probably in the summer of 1155. The Finnish Church therefore regards the year 1155 as the year of its foundation. Bishop Henrik remained in Finland in order to organize the Church there. He took up his residence in Nousiainen (Nousis) about 40 km north of Turku. His activity in Finland did not last for long. He was murdered on 19 January 1156 by a Finnish peasant, Lalli. Bishop Henrik has later been regarded as Finland's patron saint.

During the latter part of the twelfth century the status of the Church and the Christians in Finland was still very unsettled. Missionary work was carried out both from the east and the west. The eastern missionaries came from Novgorod, the western ones from Sweden and Denmark. At the beginning of the thirteenth century the Western Church gained the upper hand. The Finnish Church was led by the energetic Bishop Thomas, an Englishman. He moved the episcopal see from Nousiainen to Räntämäki (St Mary) near Turku. He acquired a regular income for the Church and laid the foundations of Turku Cathedral in 1229. He carried out an active missionary work. In order to diminish the influence of the Eastern Church he urged Western Christians to undertake a crusade against Novgorod, but the crusaders were defeated in 1240 at the River Neva by the Novgorodian Duke Alexander, who after his victory was called Alexander Nevski.

The Medieval Church: 1248-1523

In 1248 Finland and Sweden become more firmly united. At the same time the Finnish Church developed closer relations with Rome. During the middle ages the whole of Finland belonged to the diocese of Turku. At the end of the fifteenth century the diocese had about 70 parishes. Most of them lay on the coast in the south and the west. A large part of the Finnish mainland was still uninhabited. Many of the bishops of Turku were outstanding men. The most prominent was Bishop Hemming (1338-1366). He was a close friend of Saint Bridget, who asked him to carry out many important commissions for her.

Between 1397 and 1523 all the Nordic countries formed a union. The bishops of Turku supported the union for a long time, but at the end of the fifteenth century they began to work for an independent state, consisting of Finland and Sweden. The Danes tried to keep the union together by force. The Danish king, Christian II, conquered Stockholm in 1520 and was enthroned there. After his coronation eighty leading Swedes, among them two bishops and the father of the future Swedish king, were sentenced to death and beheaded. The formal reason was that they had deposed the Archbishop of Uppsala, Gustav Trolle. The Finnish bishop, Arvid Kurck, escaped, because he did not take part in the coronation, but he perished in a storm two years later, when he fled from the Danes to Sweden.

The Reformation Period: 1523-1617
The Nordic union was dissolved when Gustavus Vasa was elected King of Sweden and Finland in 1523. Gustavus Vasa supported the Lutheran Reformation and used it to weaken the political power of the Church. At a diet in Västerås in 1527 it was decided that the word of God should be preached purely and clearly everywhere in the country. At an assembly in Uppsala in 1593 Sweden accepted the Augsburg Confession.

The see of Turku remained vacant for a long time. In 1527 Gustav Vasa appointed the Dominican prior, Martin Skytte, Bishop of Turku, and he was consecrated by the Bishop of Västerås, Petrus Magni, who had himself been canonically consecrated. The historic episcopate was thus preserved. The pope did not, however, confirm the election, and relations between Sweden and Rome were severed in 1529. Then the bishops lost the support of the international Church and became dependent on the king. The new Bishop of Turku found himself in a difficult position as the king confiscated most of his revenue and destroyed his castle, Kuusisto (Kustö).

After Skytte's death in 1550 the king again kept the see vacant. He tried to introduce a state church system, but it met with resistance within the Church. In 1554 he asked the Finnish reformer, Mikael Agricola, and his fellow worker Paul Juusten, to come and see him. He told them that he had founded a new diocese in Viipuri (Viborg), and that he had appointed Agricola Bishop of Turku and Juusten Bishop of Viipuri. The king emphasized that the new bishops did not need a papal confirmation, because the right to appoint bishops had passed from the pope to the king. Finland thus received its first Lutheran bishops. They were ordained by the Bishop of Strängnäs.

Sweden as a Leading European Power: 1617-1721

After 1617 Sweden was the leading nation of the Baltic region. The Swedish kingdom comprised peoples of different languages and cultures, the only common factor being their Lutheran confession. Religious unity was the determinative factor for the unity of the state, and it was promoted especially through the church law of 1686. The entire *Book of Concord* was accepted as the confession of the Church in 1664. The state and the Church shared a common interest in strengthening the Lutheran faith, and the bishops had a special responsibility for promoting it. They were obliged to confirm their loyalty both to the Lutheran confession and to the state by oath.

On the other hand, the bishops once again gained political influence. They were *ex officio* members of the Swedish Parliament, which had four houses: the nobility, the clergy, the burgesses and the freehold farmers. During the sessions of Parliament the bishops could also discuss common church matters.

The Church was closely connected with school and university. Turku gained a university, Abo Academy, in 1640. The professors of the theological faculty were members of the chapter. In Viipuri the lecturers of the cathedral school had the same position. The teachers in higher schools were pastors. Many pastors and bishops, though not theologians, held other academic posts.

The Eighteenth Century: 1721-1809

Sweden lost its position as a great power in the Great Nordic War (1700-1721). For Finland the war was disastrous. The Russians invaded the country between 1710 and 1714 and occupied it to the end of the war. The two bishops and many pastors fled to Sweden, while other pastors were deported to Russia. A dean, Jakob Ritz of Somero, assumed responsibility for the life of the Church in 1717, and ordained a number of students as pastors.

In the peace treaty of Uusikaupunki (Nystad) in 1721, Karelia was ceded to Russia, and Finland then received the same borders with Russia as it has today. Viipuri stayed on the Russian side. The see was therefore moved to Porvoo (Borgå) in 1723. After a second war between 1741 and 1743, yet another part of eastern Finland was taken by Russia. The Russian regions of the country did not have a bishop. The Church was governed by consistories in Viipuri and Hamina (Fredrikshamn).

The Autonomous Period: 1809-1917

The whole of Finland was united with Russia in 1809. At a diet in Porvoo that year, the Russian emperor, Alexander I, promised that Finland would become an autonomous nation, connected with the Russian Empire. The Russian tsar would be Grand Duke of Finland, as the Swedish king had been. The Swedish laws and instititutions, including the constitution of 1772 and the church law of 1686, were to remain in force. Finland was granted a parliament and a government of its own. The eastern parts of Finland, which had been ceded to Russia in the eighteenth century, were reunited with Finland in 1812. Ecclesiastically they were incorporated in the Porvoo diocese. In connection with the anniversary of the Reformation in 1817, the Bishop of Turku was entitled Archbishop. It was, in fact, an honorary title, but it symbolized that the Finnish Church had become an independent church.

The Finnish Parliament did not convene until 1863. One of its foremost tasks was to make a new church law. The law was passed in 1869. Whereas the former church law had covered all citizens, the new law only applied to members of the Finnish Evangelical-Lutheran Church. The Church was thus regarded as a separate entity in relation to the state. The Synod was established as a governing body for the Church. The Synod was given the right to make decisions on internal church matters and the right to propose new church laws. New bills had to be passed by the legislative authorities in order to become law, but the authorities did not have the right to alter the Church's proposals. The union between the Church and educational institutions was dissolved through the new church law. Since 1870 the diocesan chapters have consisted of the bishop, the dean of the cathedral, two elected pastors and a lawyer.

A new diocese was founded in Kuopio in 1850, and it was moved to Oulu (Uleåborg) in 1896. At the same time a diocese was founded in Savonlinna (Nyslott).

The bishops were *ex officio* members of the House of Clergy in the Finnish Parliament. The grand duke usually appointed the archbishops to be the speaker of the House of Clergy. The bishops thus had a political influence, which they lost when Finland established its one-chamber parliament in 1906. In church matters the co-operation between the bishops was continued by the Bishops' Conference, which was established in 1908.

The Independent Finland: 1917 onwards

Finland declared its independence on 6 December 1917 and had its constitution confirmed on 17 July 1919. According to the constitution, Finland as a state is neutral in religious matters. But the Evangelical-Lutheran Church is mentioned in the constitution and has an official status in the country. A law on religious freedom came into force in 1923.

There was a strong nationalistic movement among the Swedish population in Finland during the early years of the nation's independence. One result of this movement was that all parishes with a majority of Swedish-speaking members were united into one diocese, Borgå (Porvoo) diocese. The old Porvoo diocese was transferred to Tampere (Tammerfors). The Savonlinna diocese was moved to Viipuri in 1925.

In the independent Finland, the Church strove to establish good relations with other churches, especially with the Lutheran churches in the Nordic and Baltic states. In 1933 and 1934 conversations were held between the Finnish Church and the Church of England. The conversations resulted in an agreement that members from both churches would be allowed to take part in Holy Communion in the other church. Bishops from both churches would participate in episcopal consecrations in the other church. During the conversations, and even afterwards, the Finnish interpretation of episcopacy was discussed. In a letter to the Archbishop of Canterbury, Erkki Kaila, the Finnish archbishop, declared that the Finnish Church appreciated the historic episcopate as an extremely valuable form of ecclesiastical supervision and as an external sign of the unity of the Church throughout the ages. The Finnish Church did not, however, regard the historic episcopate as necessary for a valid ministry.

In 1939, just before the Second World War, a new diocese was founded in Kuopio. After the Winter War of 1939-40 Karelia was ceded to the Soviet Union. The whole population was moved to other parts of Finland. During the Continuation War (1941-44), some Karelians moved back to their original birthplaces, but they had to leave Karelia again after the cease-fire in 1944. The see of Viipuri was moved to Mikkeli (St Michael). In order to help the Karelian parishes, a central fund for the Church was founded in 1942. Rich parishes pay fees to the fund, which in turn uses them to support poorer parishes. The means of the fund can also be used for common church activities and for diocesan work.

Since the war the Church has been ecumenically active, especially within the framework of the Lutheran World Federation, the World Council of Churches and the Conference of European Churches.

New dioceses were founded in Lapua (Lappo) in 1956, and in Helsinki (Helsingfors) in 1959.

During the last twenty years a large reform of the church legislation has been in preparation. Its aim is to extend the independence of the Church in relation to the state. The church law has been divided into two sections, the church law proper and the church order. Only the church law, which contains matters affecting society as well, will henceforth have to be approved by the legislative authorities, while the Synod has the sole right to approve the church order. The reform was passed by the Synod in 1991, but has not yet been passed by the legislative authorities of the state. In the new church law and church order the position of the bishops will remain almost unchanged.

Episcopacy Today

(i)   The Appointment of a Bishop
The bishop is elected by pastors and laypeople. All pastors in the diocese have the right to vote. Non-ordained female theologians ('lectors') who

work in parishes also have the right to vote. At least one layperson from each parish takes part in the election. Large parishes get an additional elector for each 5,000 members. Among the clergy the electors nominate three pastors each, and list them in order of preference. The counting of the votes reduces the nominees to a total of three by means of a special set way of counting the votes cast. The President of the Republic appoints one of the three nominees as bishop. The president has thus retained the papal power which Gustavus Vasa assumed in 1528. Usually the president appoints the nominee who is placed first on the list. Only on two occasions since the Second World War has the president appointed the nominee who was second on the list. The president and the government have avoided using episcopal appointments as a means for church politics.

The bishops are paid by the state. They are, in a sense, representatives of the state in relation to the Church. During the period when religious unity was fundamental for the state this aspect was important. The state needed the bishops in order to effect (Lutheran) religious uniformity. Some bishops also saw themselves as state supervisors within the Church, even though they tried to preserve a certain independence for the Church at the same time. In a pluralistic society the bishops see themselves primarily as representatives of the Church in relation to the state.

(ii)   The Ordination of a Bishop
Each new bishop is ordained. The ordination usually takes places in the cathedral of the diocese. It is generally performed by the archbishop, who is assisted by other bishops and pastors. Usually Scandinavian bishops are present and sometimes an English bishop.

The Church law provides for the possibility of the Church losing all its bishops. In such an emergency a pastor can be commissioned to perform the ordination. In 1884 it actually happened that the Finnish Church lost four bishops within ten months. All three dioceses were without bishops. Before the ordination of the new archbishop different opinions were put forward as to how to handle this situation. There were some who suggested that a Swedish bishop should be asked to ordain the archbishop. Others were in favour of the stipulation in the church law. They argued that the main thing was that the archbishop was ordained and that whoever had been ordained to the one ministry of preaching the gospel and administering the sacraments could ordain another. In an emergency situation the emergency itself was looked upon as a special vocation from God to perform a bishop's duties. The new archbishop accepted the latter opinion, and was ordained by Axel Fredrik Granfelt, a professor emeritus of systematic theology at Helsinki University.

This event was discussed during the conversations between the Finnish Church and the Church of England in 1933-34. The Finnish delegates emphasized that the presence of Swedish and Estonian bishops at Finnish episcopal consecrations had not been an attempt to re-introduce the succession, but had been a witness to the unity of the Church of Christ. The same position was upheld by Archbishop Kaila in his letter to the Archbishop of Canterbury in 1936. The Finnish Church thus regards its episcopal office as valid regardless of what happened in 1884.

The ordinal had its place in the church law for a long time, but did not become part of the Finnish church manual until 1886. Then its title was 'On installing a bishop in his office'. Since 1963 it has had the title 'Ordination of a bishop'. The explanatory notes to the manual state: 'The ordination of a bishop is an installation', but the preamble to the ordination of a bishop in the present manual of 1984 states: 'The relevant parts of this formula can be used when a bishop, after having been translated from one diocese to another, is installed in his office'. This formulation indicates that the Church distinguishes between ordination and installation. The new church order does not settle this point, but the ordination rite includes the following.

The ordination begins with a procession and a hymn. The archbishop delivers a charge followed by the collect:

> Almighty God, beloved heavenly Father ... We beseech thee. Give thy Holy Spirit to this thy servant who now will be ordained bishop. Lord, make thy Church comply with thy will. May thy word bear fruit, thy name be hallowed and thy kingdom spread among us.

The clerk reads the letter of appointment given by the president of the Republic and gives it to the archbishop. The assistants read lessons from the Holy Scriptures. The following lessons are recommended: Matt. 28. 18-20, John 21. 15-17, Heb. 4. 14-15, Acts 20. 28, 1 Cor. 4. 1-4 and 2 Tim. 3. 14-15.

The bishop confesses his faith in the words of the Nicene Creed. He then gives three promises. He promises that he will administer the bishop's office in his diocese rightly and faithfully according to God's holy Word and the confession of the Church. He promises that he will ensure that the gospel is purely preached, that the sacraments are administered according to Christ's institution and that the congregations are cared for according to the order of the Finnish Church. He promises that he will promote everything that edifies the Church of Christ and that he himself will be an example for Christ's congregation.

The promises are confirmed by an oath. Already at the end of the sixteenth century an oath was demanded from new bishops. The present oath received its main content at the end of the eighteenth century. The oath does not differ very much from the promises, but it has some interesting details. It mentions explicitly the confession of the Evangelical-Lutheran Church and it also stresses loyalty to the secular authorities. The bishop gives an assurance that he will always promote peace in the country and obedience to the authorities and in all matters follow the law and order of the Church, and that he will seriously admonish and exhort the pastors to do the same. The oath is a survival from the time when state and Church were closely united. But it may be of interest also for a secular state that a large national Church with great privileges preserves its identity and remains loyal to the state. In the new church order the oath has been replaced by a solemn assurance, but the content is the same.

When the bishop has made his confession, given his promises and sworn his oath, the archbishop gives him his office. The archbishop says:

> With the authority which has been given me in the Church of Christ I entrust you with the bishop's office in the diocese of ... in the name of the Father, and of the Son, and of the Holy Spirit. Amen.

The archbishop gives the letter of appointment to the bishop. The assistants invest him with his episcopal vestments, and the archbishop gives him his crosier and his bishop's cross. The congregation sings *Veni Creator Spiritus*.

The bishop kneels. The archbishop and the assistants put their hands on his head, and the archbishop says:

> May the triune God bless thee and sanctify thee to serve Christ's Church always and everywhere.

Then an intercession for the bishop follows. The archbishop says:

> Almighty God, merciful Father ... We thank thee, that thou hast founded thy Church and given it shepherds. We beseech thee: give thy Holy Spirit to N.N. who now has been ordained bishop. Increase the gifts of grace which thou hast given him. Give him thy help that he may preach the Gospel purely and in every respect edify thy Church. Preserve him in thy word, that he in his teaching and his life may serve thee sincerely. Give him the ability to rightly govern this diocese. Help him to support his fellow-workers and those who carry responsibility for the diocese. Give him wisdom, patience, kindness and humility ...

The ordination ends with the Lord's Prayer, a commission and a blessing.

The ordination emphasizes that the bishop, even if he is appointed by the President of the Republic, is a minister of the Church. The office is given by the archbishop. The bishop is introduced into the succession of bishops who have been responsible for the diocese. The bishop is sent to his office through lessons from the Scriptures, through prayer and laying on of hands. The intercession, beseeching the Holy Spirit to increase the spiritual gifts given to the bishop, has a central place and is, in the first place, a prayer that the Holy Spirit may help the bishop to fulfil his duties rightly. The promises and the oath remind the bishop of the essentials of his office and assure the diocese and society that the bishop will preserve the identity of the Church and be loyal to the community.

The bishop stays in office until he retires. He must retire when he reaches the age of 70 (according to the new church law, 67). A retired bishop keeps the title Bishop, but has no episcopal rights.

(iii) The Ministry of the Bishop

The most important regulation concerning bishops in the church law reads: 'The bishop exercises, each in his diocese, the highest superintendence of the congregations and the clergy'. Since the Reformation the fundamental interpretation of episcopacy has been that the bishop supervises the pastors and the parishes. The biblical foundation for this interpretation is Acts 20. 28: 'Take heed therefore unto yourselves and to all the flock, over which the Holy Ghost has made you overseers, to feed the Church of God, which he hath purchased with his own blood'. At the same time the stipulation in the church law emphasizes that the ministry of the bishop is limited to his diocese, and that all bishops are equal as bishops. The archbishop is first among equals, *primus inter pares*. He is the bishop of the archdiocese of Turku. His special duties as archbishop concern the direction of the Church as a whole but do not interefere with the other bishops' governing of their dioceses.

The duties of a bishop cover six areas.

The bishop is to take care that the Word of God is preached pure and unfalsified in accordance with the confession of the Church, that the sacraments are rightly administered in accordance with the institution of Christ, that the services are held in accordance with valid regulations, that the teaching of Christian doctrine is carried out faithfully, in the parishes as well as in the educational institutions, that good order and morals are observed in the parishes and that missionary and diaconal work is carried out. The bishop fulfils these obligations through his visitations of the parishes. He is required to visit the parishes every fifth year, but the dioceses have so many parishes that the intervals tend to be longer. The bishop together with the chapter is also responsible for meeting the parishes' need for pastors. In the Finnish Church pastors cannot obtain permanent positions immediately after their ordination. They must be at the bishop's disposal for at least two years. He can send them anywhere where they are needed, and they can in a sense be regarded as deacons.

The bishop is also obliged to see to it that the finances of the parishes are duly administered, and that the administration of the parishes is attended to in accordance with the law and the regulations of the Church. These duties, too, are mainly fulfilled through the visitations.

The bishop has to ensure that the clergy and other parish workers impeccably observe the doctrine of the Church and lead a worthy Christian life. The bishop is *pastor pastorum*. He is to give pastoral care to the pastors in his diocese. But he has also judicial powers. The chapter functions as a court and can impose sentences on pastors and some other parish workers. According to the new church law the chapter will lose its function as a court, and in the future it will only have the right to impose disciplinary measures.

The bishop is obliged to ensure that everything is rightly attended to in matters of pastoral care and Christian order. This responsibility is mainly carried out during the visitations.

The bishop ordains pastors, installs rectors and chaplains and consecrates churches and cemeteries. In some cases he can delegate these duties to a dean. Even the ordination of pastors can be performed by the dean of a cathedral when the see is vacant or when the bishop is seriously ill. The father of the church law of 1869, Bishop Schauman, argued for this practice in the following way:

> According to the principles of the Roman Church, only the bishop is entitled to ordain priests. This principle is not acknowledged by the Protestant Church, but she has expressly stated in the Schmalkaldic Articles, that, contrary to this principle, an ordination performed by a pastor in his parish is valid according to divine law, as the ministry of the bishop on the one hand and that of the pastor on the other are not different in degree according to divine law.

It very seldom happens that the dean of a cathedral ordains a pastor, but the church law still permits this possibility.

Ordination by a dean was a theme for discussion during the conversations between the Finnish Church and the Church of England in 1933-34. The Finnish delegates suggested that in the case of a vacancy in a see, a pastor should be ordained in another diocese and then transferred to his own diocese. Archbishop Kaila supported this suggestion in his letter to the Archbishop of Canterbury. Nowadays this is the usual practice.

The bishop is, finally, regarded as the foremost theological teacher of the diocese. Together with the chapter he examines the candidates for ordination and the pastors who seek the right to apply for permanent incumbencies and chaplaincies in the parishes. During visitations the bishop often gives a lecture on doctrinal matters. Every fourth year he chairs a theological assembly of all pastors and lectors in the diocese. The regulations on episcopacy contained in the church law reflect the traditional Lutheran view that the bishop is the supervisor and theological teacher of his diocese.

The Lutheran churches, and the Finnish Church among them, give great responsibility to the individual pastor. The pastors are pledged by an oath at the ordination to observe the confession of the Church, and so they are made responsible for the faith as it is proclaimed by the Church, and they are also expected to be able to defend it.

The church law also stipulates that the rector of a parish 'is to be held responsible for the worthy and proper conduct of divine service, the holy sacraments and other church rituals, for the Christian education and teaching of young people, for faithful attendance to pastoral care, for maintaining church discipline and for the diaconal work'. Moreover, he is also responsible for all measures necessary to further the activities of the parish, and for strengthening the religious and moral life of the population within the bounds of his parish. The rector must 'also see to it that both the fixed and the movable property of his parish is properly attended to and used in accordance with the law and with the decisions taken by the parish'. The responsibility and the authority here conferred upon the rector indicate that he genuinely shares in oversight (*episcope*). This view, is, moreover, emphasized by the fact that the rector is entitled to confirm young people. The rector is elected by the parish and is representative of the parish rather than of the bishop. The parish is the basic unit in the Finnish Church. Each parish, within its territory, ought to represent the Church of Christ in all its functions. The parish is fully responsible for its spiritual as for its financial life. But the bishop has the highest oversight over both the rector and the parish.

Until the Second World War almost all spiritual life in the Church took place in the parishes. In missionary and diaconal work the parishes were supported by voluntary Christian societies. The dioceses had financial resources only for their internal administration. After the foundation of the central fund of the Church, the Church and the dioceses now have means for special activities, for example, in the field of liturgy, education, charity work and mission. In the dioceses these activities are led by the chapter, and this fact has strengthened the bishop's position as the spiritual leader of his diocese. The bishops are also often entrusted with the chairmanship of the centres for Christian education and spiritual development.

The Finnish archbishop is first and foremost bishop of the Turku archdiocese, a bishop among others. In addition to that the archbishop is chairman of the Synod, the Bishops' Conference and the Church Board. Together with the Council for Foreign Affairs he is responsible for the foreign relations of the Church. He is also *ex officio* chairman of the board for the Church's information centre and of the Finnish Missionary Society. The other bishops are *ex officio* members of the Synod and of the Bishops' Conference.

In the Finnish Church there are some tensions in the interpretation of episcopacy. According to traditional Lutheran theology the Church has only one ministry, the ministry of preaching the gospel and administering the sacraments. Within this one ministry there are different commissions, and episcopacy is one of them. According to another view pastors and bishops have different ministries. Both interpretations are represented in the Finnish Church, and the latter view has gained more support in recent years. The tension between these two interpretations is reflected in the stipulations in the church law, in the ordinal and in the exercise of episcopacy. Regardless of these tensions the Finnish Evangelical-Lutheran Church has preserved episcopacy throughout the whole of its history, and there is a unanimous opinion in the Church that episcopacy is an extremely valuable form of church government.

FREDRIC CLEVE

DENMARK

Episcopacy and the Reformation

On the threshold of the Reformation, episcopacy in the Danish Church was in state of grave decay. After 1519, the Archbishop of Denmark, residing in Lund, was neither consecrated bishop nor formally approved by the Roman pope, and in 1532 three further bishops exercised episcopal jurisdiction without being consecrated. The leading Danish theologian at the time, Paul Helgesen, a Carmelite, described these bishops as 'show-bishops'. Consequently, the ordination of priests had to be performed either by the remaining consecrated bishops or by specially consecrated 'ordination-bishops', who took care of the sacramental functions of the episcopal office, while the nominal bishop looked after the more secular matters such as the management of the property of the diocese.

Under pressure from the nobility, the Danish bishops had accepted that the approval of elections of bishops should no longer be given by the pope, but by the Archbishop of Lund. Since the archbishop himself was neither canonically elected nor consecrated, the nobility hoped that this method of approval might increase their own influence on what was developing into a 'national church' (i.e. a church cut off from the jurisdiction of the pope and ruled by the national bishops).

In the late 1530s Lutheran preaching spread thoughout the country, and in several churches in the towns there were both Roman Catholic and Lutheran services held one after the other. It also happened that priests ordained laymen to the ministry. Thus one of the leading figures of the Reformation, Hans Tausen, who was a priest in Viborg, ordained his brother-in-law Jørgen Jensen Sadolin to the priesthood. They were both among the first 'superintendents', who a little later were to succeed the former Catholic bishops as heads of the dioceses.

One can understand that the Catholic bishops were most unpopular and were rightly regarded as responsible for the decay of the Church. When the Reformation was finally carried through in 1536, they were dismissed from their offices by the king (Christian III) and put in prison, and both the noblemen and the burghers demanded a new leadership in the Church. This leadership was installed when Johannes Bugenhagen (vicar in Wittenberg and collaborator of Martin Luther) consecrated on 2 July 1536 seven new 'superintendents' (a word translating the biblical term *episcopos*) in the Church of Our Lady in Copenhagen. These 'superintendents' were given the oversight over the seven medieval dioceses of the Danish Church. By this consecration the episcopal succession according to canon law was broken, as Bugenhagen was an ordained priest but had not been consecrated bishop. This break, however, came about as a result of the contempt of the bishops for their own office, which I have tried to describe, and it is important to note that the medieval structure of dioceses led by bishops was kept intact.

In 1537 the *Ordinatio Ecclesiastica Regnorum Daniae et Norwegiae et Ducatuum Sleswicensis Holtsatiae etc.* was published, followed in 1539 by a Danish translation, *Den danske Kirkeordinans*. This very important source contains an order for the consecration of a bishop, which is supposed to be almost identical with the order used by Bugenhagen when he consecrated the first seven superintendents. According to this order, the consecration shall take place in the cathedral of the diocese in which the new bishop is to serve. (The first consecration probably took place not in the Cathedral of Roskilde but in Copenhagen, because this was the city where the king had his residence.) The consecration shall take place during a high mass and shall be presided over by the neighbouring bishop, assisted by priests of the diocese. The order contains the Pentecost anthem *Veni Sancte Spiritus*, psalms, readings from the Scriptures (Tit. 1. 5-9; Acts 20. 25-38 and 2 Tim. 4. 1-8), admonitions regarding the spiritual duties of the bishop, the Our Father and, finally, a prayer of consecration with the laying on of hands composed by Martin Luther.[1]

---

[1] This prayer has the following wording: 'O Almighty and everlasting God, who through thy only-begotten Son, our only Master, hast taught us: "The harvest is plenteous, but the labourers are few; pray ye therefore the Lord of the harvest, that he will send forth labourers into his harvest". These words remind us that we shall pray for good labourers, preachers and teachers in the churches by thy divine goodness with a serious and faithful prayer. Therefore we now pray thy ineffable goodness that thou graciously mayest accept this thy servant N.N. whom we elect in thy Name to the holy office of bishop in the Church, that he may be zealous in thy Word, to preach thy Son, Jesus Christ to be our only salvation, to teach and comfort the perplexed consciences, to give counsel, to admonish, and to punish with patience, so that others may learn and make progress thereby, that the most Holy Gospel permanently may remain with us, pure and right, without the admixture of human learning, that we may obtain eternal life as the blessed fruit thereof, through this thy Son, Jesus Christ our Lord.'

In this *Ordinance* (1537/39) there is a description of the tasks of a bishop which is still often quoted as relevant:

1. to study and teach Holy Scripture;
2. to preach the Word of God to the people in his diocese;
3. to keep the subjects obedient to the lawful authorities;
4. to see to it that the priests teach the Holy Gospel of Jesus Christ and lead a decent life;
5. to ordain priests and to send them to their congregation with a letter of recommendation;
6. to warn and eventually punish priests who bring their ministry into disrepute;
7. to give counsel in matters of conscience;
8. to visit the public schools;
9. to supervise help for the poor.

Lutheran Orthodoxy

In the years after the Reformation of 1536, the term Superintendent was still used in official documents, often as an apposition to 'the right bishops', but the term Bishop was still kept in use, and so when the next official book of order, *The Book of Order of Denmark and Norway (Danmarks og Norges Kirke-Ritual)* was published in 1685, the classical term Bishop was reintroduced.

At the same time a new formula for the handing over of the ministry was introduced in the order for the ordination of priests and in the eighteenth century (probably in 1771) even in the order for the consecration of bishops. This formula is reminiscent of the medieval formula for the handing over of a fief. A Danish church historian, P.G.Lindhardt, is of the opinion that the formula has its origin in the Anglican Ordinal of 1662, because the author of the Danish Ordinal, the Bishop of Sealand, Hans Bagger, studied in England in the 1660s. The text of 1685 runs as follows:

> Thus I hand over to you the holy ministry of priest and preacher according to the apostolic manner in the name of the Father, of the Son and of the Holy Ghost. I give you power and authority hereafter as true servants of

God and Jesus Christ to preach the Word of God privately and openly in the Church, to administer the Most Holy Sacraments according to Christ's institution, to bind the sin of the obstinate and loose the sin of the penitent and to do whatever belongs to this holy vocation of God, according to God's Word and our Christian custom.

This can be compared with the Ordering of Priests in the Anglican Ordinal (1662):

RECEIVE the Holy Ghost for the Office and Work of a Priest in the Church of God, now committed unto thee by the Imposition of our hands. Whose sins thou dost forgive, they are forgiven; and whose sins thou dost retain, they are retained. And be thou a faithful Dispenser of the Word of God, and of his holy Sacraments; In the Name of the Father, and of the Son, and of the Holy Ghost. Amen.

Then the Bishop shall deliver to every one of them kneeling, the Bible into his hand, saying,

TAKE thou Authority to preach the Word of God, and to minister the holy Sacraments in the Congregation, where thou shalt be lawfully appointed thereunto.

The Present Situation

The present order for the consecration of a bishop is almost the same as the order in the *Book of Order* of 1685. Alterations in a rationalistic direction dating from the first half of the nineteenth century were removed in the second half of that century, and the order of the ordination and consecration services was restored by the addition of a more 'catholic' ceremonial. This was done with conscious reference to the Anglican order for the consecration of bishops and to eventual negotiations on intercommunion. The Latin anthem *Veni Sancte Spiritus* was re-introduced, also for ecumenical reasons. This order was authorized in 1898 and was in use until the present ritual of 1987 was authorized.

As years passed, the formula of handing over thus became more important. However, this was not in harmony with the theology of the Reformers. Lutheran theology regards the calling of a person to the ministry by the congregation as the very calling of God himself. The ministry is given to the candidate by the call of the congregation. The ordination service with prayer and the laying on of hands is the confirmation of God's call by the bishop, who functions as a representative of the Church, sending the ordained person to serve in the congregation. As the bishop has already, through his vocation as a priest and through ordination, received the calling and sending to the ministry of the word and sacraments, he is not given a new ministry, but he is called into a wider responsibility in the Church, and is therefore commissioned by prayer with the laying on of hands. The ministry of the bishop is still the ministry of word and sacrament. The difference, in comparison with the priest, is that he has responsibility for a wider area and that he has the episcope, the oversight over his fellow pastors.

Our most recent liturgical commission, in publishing its proposal for ordination and consecration services in 1977, suggested moving the formula of handing over from its traditional position. The bishops followed this proposal, and the handing over is now located in the prayer with the laying on of hands.[2]

Furthermore, there has been a strong opposition to the introduction of the historic succession in the traditional sense of transfer by the mere laying on of hands. This was clearly illustrated when Swedish bishops were prevented from taking part in the laying on of hands in the consecration services according to the order of 1898. However, this practice has had no negative effect on the fellowship of the Scandinavian churches. In the present order of service the laying on of hands is done by the consecrating bishop together with the two neighbouring bishops and the priests from the diocese of the new bishop, so the laying on of hands by bishops from abroad is not provided for.

The conception of the office of a bishop has developed in the Danish National Church in recent years. Two examples may illustrate why this is so. In a society marked by religious pluralism, the need for guidance is obvious. Consequently, congregations and priests look to the bishop as the person who has the task of giving them guidance and seeing to it that those who have been entrusted with the ministry will preach in accordance with the Bible and the confession of the Church. The Danish National Church normally prides itself on being comprehensive. But in the last years several

---

[2] Cf. John Halliburton, 'Orders and Ordination' and the Rites of Ordination to the Episcopate, below.

bishops have made statements to the effect that in the modern pluralistic society comprehensiveness has its limits (e.g. belief in reincarnation) and the bishop is the person who is called to draw the borderline if necessary.

Another example: In the established Church there exists a fine balance between (i) the *episcope* of the Church, which is in the hands of the bishops and should remain there, and (ii) the legal structure, where the secular authority may function to the benefit of the Church. As the bishop is both a minister of word and sacrament and at the same time part of the official system of the state, it is part of his office to guard the subtle balance between the ecclesiastical and secular authorities which exist side by side in the one Church. This balance is a prerequisite for the order of the National Church. Bishops have a very important role to play as persons who guard the apostolic tradition in worship and the administration of sacraments, in preaching and teaching. And they have to fight against all tendencies to make the Church a confessionally neutral institution in the service of the state.

Many Danish theologians express the opinion that no person can speak on behalf of the Danish National Church. However, this is by no means an axiom. On some occasions the bishops have in fact been heard as speaking on behalf of the Church. This was the case during the German occupation when the bishops published a pastoral letter opposing the persecution of the Jews in Denmark. And in recent years the bishops have spoken out on several burning issues of our time. But there is no legal institution through which the bishops or others are able to speak or make decisions on behalf of the whole Church, except Parliament.

As a new feature in Danish church life one could mention that the meetings of all the bishops which take place several times a year have become more and more important for the daily life of the Church. Decision-making in Parliament and the daily administration by the Ministry of Ecclesiastical Affairs are influenced by these meetings. However, even so, the bishops never claim to speak as a *'collegium'* or make decisions binding for the whole Church. In this area there is a clear difference between the Danish and the Norwegian Church.

In current discussions on episcopacy some people express their longing for a stronger and more outspoken leadership in the Church. Others want to retain the state of affairs where Parliament makes decisions on behalf of the Church. And with the increasing importance of the bishops' meetings, some people express the need for a strengthening of the lay element in the administration of the dioceses and of the Church as a whole.

In comparison with the Norwegian Church two further differences could be noticed. First, Danish bishops regard themselves as representatives of their diocese — also in contact with sister churches. But most of them would not give their ecumenical task as high a priority as the Norwegian bishops. Secondly, Danish bishops no longer have any legal function in the state school system. Christianity is part of the curriculum, but the education is no longer under the oversight of the bishops.

In concluding this paper, I would like to stress that ecumenical relations have had both positive and negative effects on the developments of the episcopate in Danish theology and church life. In this century, many bishops have regarded themselves as administrators more than spiritual leaders. However, in recent years both the spiritual and the ecclesial aspect of *episcope* have been stressed. In my personal opinion this could open the way for a reappraisal of the office of the bishop, and I hope that future conversations with representatives of the Anglican tradition may have an inspiring effect on the debate.

GERHARD PEDERSEN

NORWAY

Historical Perspective

Christianity was brought to Norway by missionaries from the British Isles and from Central Europe around the year 1000. Supported by kings and noblemen who had taken the new faith, bishops and priests organized a church with strongholds mainly in the coastal areas. The earliest bishops were most often representatives of the English clergy of some monastic observance. After the final establishment of the Church following the death of Norway's patron saint, St Olav, in 1030, the first episcopal sees were established in Oslo, Bergen and Trondheim (Nidaros) shortly after 1050, followed by the see of Stavanger in 1125. A strong influence from English church traditions and spirituality is noticeable in this first century.

From the establishment of the archdiocese of Lund (then in Denmark) in 1103, the Norwegian dioceses were part of this province. In 1153, however, a separate Norwegian province was established, with Nidaros (Trondheim) as the archiepiscopal see. The papal legate who visited Scandinavia for that purpose, Cardinal Nicholas Breakspear, later became the first English-born pope as Hadrian IV. At the establishment of the province a fifth Norwegian episcopal see was added, and dioceses were organized in Iceland and the isles of the North Sea, as well as on the Isle of Man (six additional sees).

The introduction of Lutheranism in Denmark and Norway in 1537 severed relations with Rome and placed the Church of Norway under the authority of the Danish king (1537-1814).

During the years prior to the Reformation the churches in Denmark and Norway experienced a decline in church life and in church administration. The last Archbishop of Nidaros, Olav Engelbrektson, was a powerful church leader who at the same time became the spokesman for national independence. He fled the country in April 1537 and died later in the Netherlands. This flight marked the turning point in Norwegian church history and reinforced Norway's political dependence on Denmark.

As the Lutheran Reformation was introduced in Norway by royal edict, the Roman Catholic bishops were removed. The Bishop of Oslo, for instance, was forced to move to Denmark, but later he returned to Oslo in order to take up his responsibilities as leader of the Diocese of Oslo, now as a Lutheran superintendent/bishop.

In order to establish a new church structure, King Christian III, in consultation with Dr Martin Luther, called the parish minister of Wittenberg, Johannes Bugenhagen, to assist in the organization of the churches in Denmark and Norway. Bugenhagen ordained the new 'overseers', *episkopoi*, who took over the office of bishops. To start with, these *episkopoi* were called 'superintendents', but soon the old title of Bishop was used and consequently introduced into the church laws. In the Church Ordinance of 1685 only the title Bishop is used for the episcopal office. The Wittenberger Johannes Burgenhagen had not been consecrated bishop, therefore the Reformation superintendents in the Churches of Denmark and Norway were not consecrated into 'the order of apostolic succession', and this is the position even today.

The Lutheran reformers in Germany and in the Nordic countries had no special intention to remove the episcopal office from the evangelical churches, but hoped to free episcopacy from political 'malpractice' and the responsibility of exercising secular authority. The Lutheran bishop was furthermore expected to proclaim and uphold the gospel as confessed in the Lutheran confessions. As far as the kingdoms of Denmark and Norway were concerned, that meant the Ecumenical Creeds, the Unaltered Augsburg Confession (*Confessio Augustana*) and Luther's Small Catechism.[1]

Psychological Perspective

One could hardly use the term 'revolution' in connection with the introduction of the Lutheran Reformation in Norway in 1535/37. What happened was a renewal and restoration of the church structure. It opened up the way for a new understanding of the biblical message of justification by faith. The expressed policy of the king and his council was not to form a new church, but to renew and cleanse the same Church from unbiblical teachings and practices.

---

[1] Cf. *Confessio Augustana* (CA) XXVIII.

The 'new confession' was introduced in Denmark and Norway by a king who held it himself by conviction. In this way the Churches of Denmark and Norway became state churches as well as 'folk churches'. Thus there is a close relation between Church and state even up to this day.

The Evangelical-Lutheran faith was not totally strange to the peoples of Denmark and Norway. Students from the two kingdoms were enrolled at German universities. A few had even studied at Wittenberg, the centre of the Reformation. In the towns along the vast Norwegian coastline there was close contact in trade and shipping with the Continent, and the new evangelical teaching soon found its way to Norway. Further inland it took some time before evangelical priests could be called to proclaim the protestant understanding of justification by faith alone.

All the time the Church in Norway carried on her work as before, with divine services in the same churches, education programmes in the same schools and diaconal work often in the same institutions. After some time a new clergy was trained in Wittenberg, in Copenhagen and in theological schools linked to the bishop's sees. The Church continued to play an important part in the life of the people, and church work was carried on as before, with services, baptism, confirmation, weddings, funerals, etc. The Church had the confidence of the people and from generation to generation the Church transmitted Christian norms and value-systems to the people of Norway. During the Reformation period the Norwegian people therefore did not experience a new church, but the Church from the medieval era carried on her life as a renewed and restored church.

Theological Perspective

Throughout her history, the Church of Norway has maintained the episcopal office as the office for *episcope* — oversight.[2] As to the functions and responsibilities placed upon the bishop, there would hardly be any difference between the bishop in the Church of England and the bishop in the Church of Norway, except for the fact that in the Anglican churches confirmations are performed by the bishop, whereas in Norway this is one of the functions of the parish clergy.

---

[2] Cf. CA XXVIII.

When considering the different ministries in the Church, Lutheran theology would start with ecclesiology, i.e. concept of the Church, which according to CA VII is understood as the congregation of believers — *congregatio sanctorum*, 'in which the word is rightly preached (according to the gospel) and the sacraments rightly administered'. The gospel, and faith in the gospel, is therefore considered as the apostolic tradition in the Church. 'To obtain such faith, God instituted the office of ministry.'[3] The office of the ministry — *ministerium ecclesiasticum* — is accordingly the basic ministry in the Church, as the necessary instrument for communicating the gospel, which through the Holy Spirit works faith in those who hear the gospel. The minister is also charged with the responsibility of being the shepherd of the congregation.

According to this theology, the bishop is basically a pastor proclaiming the gospel and administering the sacraments. Through the rite of ordination the pastor/minister is given this authority *jure divino*, i.e. the ministry is instituted by God. No one can become a bishop without first being ordained priest. When a priest is called to the episcopal office, and consecrated as bishop, he is still a priest, but the Church, *jure humano*, places upon him additional responsibilities and duties.

The office of the bishop is defined and described in the Church Ordinances of 1537 and 1685,[4] and in the liturgies for the consecration of bishops, the latest being found in the Altarbook of 1990. The episcopal responsibilities are further described in different resolutions passed by Parliament and in various rules and regulations issued by the Department of Ecclesiastical Affairs, Church Assembly and Church Council — generally upon recommendation by the Bishops' Conference.

The Church of Norway is a 'folk church', comprising 90 per cent of the total population. The Church has the structure of a state church, but through the long process of different reforms the Church has her own Church Assembly, which meets once a year, and her own Church Council. Administration has gradually been transferred from the state Department of Ecclesiastical Affairs to the different church councils and their administration at parish, diocesan and national church levels. The

---

[3] CA IV.

[4] See Gerhard Pedersen, 'Episcopacy in our Churches: Denmark', above.

bishops are *ex officio* members of the Diocesan Council, and one of them must be a member of the 15-strong National Church Council. The eleven bishops are members of the Bishops' Conference, which meets twice a year and is defined as one of the central church organs. There is no archbishop, but the Bishop of Oslo is elected annually as *primus inter pares*.

In the present situation the episcopal office would include the following duties and responsibilities:

1. The ecumenical responsibility for the ministry of unity within the diocese, the national Church and the global ecumenical family.

2. The guardianship of faith: the bishop shall promote and defend the teachings of the Church among pastors and congregations, Church and society.

3. The ministry of oversight (*episcope*) over pastors and other church workers, congregations and councils. The bishop is *pastor pastorum*. The bishop gives pastoral care to clergy and other church workers.

4. The authority of ordination, i.e. examining and approving candidates for the ministry. The Church has entrusted the bishop alone with the right to ordain. The Diocesan Council may recommend candidates for ordination, but the final decision rests with the bishop.

5. The ministry of oversight (*episcope*) also includes the regular visitation of congregations and parishes, where the bishop is called upon as overseer, but increasingly also as '*inspirator*' and counsellor with the aim of renewal and spiritual growth.

6. In the areas of church planning and strategy there is a growing demand upon the bishop's counselling at the congregational, diocesan and national levels. The task is to build the body of Christ through the proclamation of the gospel and administration of the sacraments, to assist in the strengthening of congregational life with regard to fellowship (*koinonia*), liturgy, missionary outreach and diaconal work.

7. Collegial and synodical responsibilities. In the contemporary Church the bishop functions within the context of different councils both at diocesan and national levels. The bishop of today is not a sovereign ruler, but must exercise his responsi-

bilities in relation to collegial and synodical bodies, i.e. Bishops' Conference, Diocesan Council, Church Assembly and Church Council. In principle the Diocesan Council and the Church Council are given the responsibilities of administration in order to enable the bishop to concentrate more on the responsibilities related to spiritual oversight. However, councils and ministers share responsibility for spiritual life in the Church.

8. Counselling responsibility The bishop is expected to exercise a prophetic witness on social matters — for instance, in matters related to contemporary problems in social ethics, such as abortion, nuclear weapons, race-discrimination, war and peace, and the environment.

The Appointment of Bishops

Under the present church law, bishops are still appointed to their office by the government, as an expression of the constitutional clause that the king is the Supreme Head of the Church. However, there is an extended procedure of nomination and election, giving the voice of the Church a say in the process. Candidates for election are proposed by the Diocesan Council, and pastors and parishes in the diocese cast their vote for the three candidates they prefer in priority.

In addition, all rural deans in the other dioceses and the theological professors with full tenure also are entitled to give their vote. After the votes are counted, all the bishops are asked to state, with reasons, which candidate they find most suitable. Finally, the government is free to appoint, with due regard to the outcome of the election but with no requirement to choose from among the first three candidates.

Bishops are appointed for life, but are subject to the normal regulations for the retirement age of civil servants, which at present is between 65 and 70 years.

The deans of the cathedrals of the sees are *ex officio* proxies and take care of the episcopal office in vacancies. This may in practice include the ordination of pastors, but this opportunity is now rarely used, and may eventually become redundant.

In the Church of Norway the bishop has always been consecrated in a special act of ordination with one of the other bishops ordaining him, usually the Bishop of Oslo as *primus inter pares*. At the bishop's consecration through prayer and the laying on of hands, all the Nordic churches are represented by a bishop, who takes part in the consecration ceremony.

GUNNAR LISLERUD

ICELAND

Before commencing any discussion of the development of the episcopal office in Iceland, mention should be made of the fact that from 1262 Iceland was part of the Norwegian kingdom. After the dissolution of the Union of Kalmar, Iceland remained under Danish control and in 1662 it recognized the absolute rule of the Danish monarch. In 1918 the country obtained the status of a sovereign state in personal union with Denmark, and it finally became a republic in 1944.

The legal status of the country throughout the centuries was a major factor in shaping both secular and ecclesiastical legislation. Until 1662, however, the Icelandic national assembly, the *Althing*, shared legislative power with the monarch, a responsibility which it maintained in part right up to 1700. After that time the assembly functioned primarily as a court. A new constitution granted in 1874 restored to the *Althing* its legislative function in conjunction with the Danish monarchy. Norwegian and Danish laws were never directly applicable in Iceland. They had to be first translated into Icelandic and then presented to the *Althing*.

In 1106 the country was divided into two episcopal dioceses, the diocese of Skálholt, which extended over much of the eastern, southern, and western areas of the country, and the Hólar diocese, in the northern region. The two sees were eventually united in 1801, and since that time the see of the bishop of Iceland has been in Reykjavík.

During the period directly following christianization, Iceland was first under the jurisdiction of the archbishopric of Bremen, then (after their respective establishment) the archbishopric of Lund and finally the archbishopric of Trondheim. Following the Reformation the connections between the Church in Iceland and the Danish Church became successively stronger as the influence of the Danish Church increased throughout the Danish kingdom. The Bishop of Sealand thus informally became the superior bishop or *primus* of the Icelandic Church.

In early medieval times the country's bishops were chosen by representatives of both clergy and laity at the *Althing*. This was in fact a tradition inherited from the organization of the ancient Icelandic Church which had developed in the wake of christianization and was charac-

101

terized by the extensive influence which secular leaders exerted on the internal affairs of the Church.

In 1237 the custom of having the chapter in Trondheim elect the Icelandic bishops was adopted. The archbishop subsequently confirmed the choice and ordained the newly elected bishop. After 1277 the king of Norway was also called upon to approve the election. Around 1350 the pope began to select the Icelandic bishops, a situation which lasted for approximately a century. In 1450, however, the king forbade the Icelanders to recognize any bishop whose election he had not approved. Shortly after this it became customary for Icelandic bishops to be selected by a clerical synod in the diocese concerned, and this election was then confirmed by secular leaders, despite the fact that the right to elect the bishops remained formally in the hands of the chapter in Trondheim until the time of the Reformation.

The Reformation gained ascendancy in the two bishoprics in a rather different fashion and with an interval of ten years. In the diocese of Skálholt the Ecclesiastical Ordinance issued by King Christian III in 1537 was adopted in 1541. In the Hólar diocese the opposition was stronger, under the powerful leadership of the last pre-Reformation bishop. The Reformation was not effected until he had been executed in 1550, and the following year the new Ecclesiastical Ordinance was adopted in the diocese. It can hardly be said, however, that in either see an actual protestant movement had developed, as the majority of Icelanders were in reality far too isolated from contemporary developments abroad for this to have occurred. The Reformation was primarily a struggle conducted by a small number of educated individuals and representatives of the Danish monarchy.

The appointment of the first Lutheran bishop to the see of Skálholt took place without conflict. In 1539 the last pre-Reformation bishop sought to be relieved of his duties due to ill-health and blindness and suggested his former protegé and later assistant as a suitable successor to the bishopric. At the clerical synod and the *Althing* both the priests and secular leaders supported his appointment. The bishop-elect had studied abroad, had even travelled to Wittenberg, and had been influenced by Lutheran theology. As a result he had fallen into temporary disgrace with his predecessor, although he was later forgiven. It is not unlikely that the outgoing bishop felt that his former pupil had turned away from the theology of the protestant reformers, or else he had concluded that a religious and political compromise was necessary, one which could be effected by a successor who would support moderate reform of religious doctrine and practices in the diocese while himself satisfying the requirements laid down by the king for the necessary confirmation of his appointment.

The latter proved in fact quite willing to give his support to this candidate promptly in 1540, although his ordination as bishop had to wait until 1542, when it was performed by the Bishop of Sealand. It may be that the postponement of the ordination is an indication of a desire to introduce a moderate and gradual reformation, with more regard given to the circumstances existing within the episcopal see in question than to the ecclesiastical politics of the monarchy and developments within the Danish kingdom in general, where the Reformation had by this time gained considerably wider acceptance.

The appointment of the first bishop to the see of Hólar took place in a much more dramatic fashion, reflecting the general trend of the reformation developments within that diocese. After the last pre-Reformation bishop had been executed, the representatives of the clergy and laity chose his son to succeed him. The king refused to confirm his appointment and at his instigation a new candidate was chosen who had been strongly influenced by evangelical teachings. He was subsequently ordained by the Bishop of Sealand.

With the adoption of the Ecclesiastical Ordinance of Christian III, the same basic regulations were introduced governing religious practices in Iceland as had been enacted in Denmark several years earlier (1537/39). For a considerable period, however, uncertainty reigned with regard to a number of formal legal points concerning Christian practice and ecclesiastical law. When such questions arose, they were dealt with on the basis of the legal statutues of the medieval Catholic Church (i.e. Icelandic legislation regarding religious affairs and Christian practice), as well as both traditional and more recent Icelandic, Danish, or even Norwegian laws. The efforts of the monarchy were directed primarily towards harmonizing the religious practices in Iceland with Danish customs to the greatest possible extent.

To this there were substantial obstacles, as circumstances in Iceland were completely different, particularly as far as population distribution was concerned. The Icelandic Church always retained special status. The Ordinance on Church Ritual of 1685, for instance, never came into force in Iceland, although it is obvious that it had extensive influence on Christian practice. Icelandic bishops, for instance, were ordained on this basis just as their Danish or Norwegian colleagues were. In addition, Icelandic prayer books, compiled by the country's bishops, were used by the clergy. The Icelandic Church also received its own translation of the Bible at an early date, in 1584.

After the Reformation, Icelandic bishops were generally ordained by the Bishop of Sealand in Denmark according to the same rites as Danish bishops. A royal communication in 1789 authorized the ordination of bishops in Iceland, with the bishop of one diocese ordaining his counterpart in the other diocese. This actually only took place on one occasion, as the dioceses were united some ten years later. As there was only a single bishop serving the country, the Icelandic bishops once more received their ordination from the Bishop of Sealand. This continued until 1908, when the outgoing bishop ordained his successor.

From the foregoing account it becomes apparent that during the centuries following the Reformation Icelandic bishops had a similar status to their counterparts elsewhere in the Danish kingdom. They were usually ordained by the same bishop and according to the same rite (that of the diocese of Sealand). The same, or very similar, laws prescribed their powers and duties. Any special status of the Icelandic bishops, such as it was, arose primarily as a result of their isolation from the central power of the monarchy. The small size of the Icelandic nation, the relatively simple public administration in the country and the limited numbers of the educated and professional classes appear to have been the main reasons for the generally strong social and cultural position of the bishops in society. The post-Reformation bishops, in fact, appear to have been considered as influential as their pre-Reformation predecessors.

This is perhaps the explanation for the fact that the title 'superintendent' never became common practice, despite the original royal support for its usage. With the strengthening of absolutism, however, the power of the Icelandic bishops was gradually reduced and in the nineteenth century the Royal Governor (*stiftamtmadur*), the supreme representative of the Danish crown in Iceland, controlled most of the adminstrative affairs of the Church, including appointments. He shared with the bishop several additional responsibilities, and they were jointly titled 'diocesan authorities' (*stiftsyfirvöld*). The responsibilities of the bishop were mainly confined to ordaining ministers and to supervising and controlling the internal affairs of the Church. The position of bishop, however, appears to have been considered as essential within the Church and ministers were never ordained by anyone but the bishop. (Churches, on the other hand, were for centuries commonly consecrated by both ministers and deans. With improved transportation in more recent times the consecrating of churches has now become the exclusive responsibility of the bishops.)

In 1909 laws were passed creating the two so-called suffragan bishops, who functioned in areas corresponding to the country's traditional Hólar and Skálholt dioceses. They received a bishop's ordination, although their sole purpose was to ordain the country's bishops when circumstances prevented the outgoing bishop from so doing. They thus held no office as such.

At the same time the Icelandic Church adopted its own ritual for the ordination of bishops, based on the Danish example. New legislation passed in 1990 has changed the positions of the suffragan bishops, and the holders have been assigned more extensive duties, which they are to carry out as the representatives of the Bishop of Iceland. The country remains a single diocese, and the suffragan bishops have thus become a kind of assistant bishop.

The advent of the suffragan bishops at the beginning of this century, following the weakening of the political ties between the Iceland nation and the Danish government and the growing tension resulting from resurgent nationalism and the struggle for independence, clearly shows the high regard felt for the episcopate and the ordination of the bishops by the nation at the time. Even when the struggle for independence was at its peak and every effort was directed towards severing any and all connections between the two countries, there was never any question of doing away with the ordination of Icelandic bishops by their Danish counterparts, without provision being made for an alternative procedure which would ensure the historical continuity of the Lutheran episcopal office as it had developed up to that point within the Danish Lutheran Church. This was in fact the sole reason for the establishment of the positions of suffragan bishop.

This support was evident whenever the question came up for discussion as was the case more than once during the final decades of the nineteenth century. Proposals presented to the *Althing* at this time sought to simplify the country's central administration in both religious and secular spheres. They called for the office of bishop to be abolished and instead for special (regional) archdeacons to assume the bishop's duties. These proposals were never adopted.

The determination shown by Icelanders near the end of the nineteenth and the beginning of the twentieth century to preserve both the episcopate and the form of ordination which had developed within the Icelandic and Danish Churches since the time of the Reformation is even more remarkable in view of the fact that by this stage in the struggle for independence the country was under considerable cultural and religious influence from North America and the large numbers of Icelanders who had emigrated westward after 1870. One result of this influence was the movement towards independent congregations, a tendency which in many ways seemed to suit the contemporary striving for political independence. Lutheran doctrines and religious traditions, however, proved to be so dominant and firmly rooted in Iceland that the episcopate stood its ground.

From the survey presented here it should be apparent that developments in Iceland, with regard both to the legal position and responsibilities of the bishop and to the doctrinal influences which had a decisive role in shaping the ordination rite, were dictated to a large extent by the circumstances in Denmark from the time of the Reformation until the present century. The social and cultural position of the Icelandic bishops was probably considerably stronger than that enjoyed by their Danish counterparts.

In our own time, the position of the bishop within the Icelandic Church is a strong one. The legislation which prescribes the relationship between Church and state guarantees the former considerable independence as well as responsibility for its own affairs. From an administrative point of view the bishop enjoys considerable power, as he has neither chapter nor other form of diocesan administration to consider when taking decisions, only a Church Council which meets several times each year to discuss major issues and the Church Assembly, which convenes annually.

The bishops have generally employed only a small staff and have had no experts at their disposal in conducting the daily affairs of the Church. This has resulted in a concentration of power in the hands of the bishop himself and a relatively direct influence on his part on most areas of ecclesiastical affairs. In the eyes of the nation the bishop has an important role to play among the country's leaders.

With regard to the doctrinal conception of the episcopal office and ordination, one should recall the positive position adopted by the Icelandic National Church to the approach taken by the Lima Report *Baptism, Eucharist and Ministry*. It is also important to keep in mind the present form of the ordination of Icelandic bishops. It could be said that this reflects a development which can be witnessed in general in the Icelandic National Church as far as liturgy is concerned, i.e. a tendency to return to more classical liturgical forms.

The links between the Icelandic National Church and the Church of England have understandably been minimal right up to most recent times. During the nineteenth century a group within the Church of England advocated the development of closer ties with other Nordic churches, which would lead, for instance, to the revival of the historic succession where it had been broken. With this purpose in mind, it was suggested that Icelandic bishops receive their ordination in England instead of Denmark, as had previously been the case. The idea received a positive reception from the Icelandic side, but proved impossible to carry out because of the country's ties with Denmark. With the increased participation of the Icelandic National Church in ecumenical co-operation the contacts between the churches have increased.

To judge by the informal discussion which has taken place in Iceland, the position taken towards the historic episcopal succession would not appear to present any obstacle to the close co-operation between churches which have followed historically different courses of development and varying doctrines in this regard. Nor is there any barrier — on legislative, historical or doctrinal grounds — to prevent such co-operation from taking the visible and symbolic form of bishops in the historic episcopate participating in the laying on of hands in the ceremony of the bishop's ordination. Perhaps to reduce the tension even further, one could point to the fact that the chain of episcopal succession of Icelandic bishops was broken as a result of historical circumstances within the Danish and Norwegian Churches which sooner or later had to affect the Icelandic Church, and not as the result of any intentional disengagement with the Catholic Church in the country itself.

HJALTI HUGASON

ESTONIA

The Present Situation

The population of Estonian Republic is about 1.5 million. The greatest national minority are the Russians: 28 per cent. The Estonian Evangelical-Lutheran Church (EELC) with its episcopal-synodical structure is the largest church in Estonia. The second church by its membership is the Russian Orthodox Church, a quarter the size of the EELC. The Roman Catholic Church is one of the smallest in Estonia, having only two congregations and about 1,500 members.

In 1987 several denominations, under the leadership of the Lutheran Church, founded an alliance, the Council of Estonian Churches, which all the larger confessions have joined. Through this consultative council the Churches attempt to solve jointly problems in relation to the state and to co-ordinate co-operation in Christian service. It is also the task of the Council to resolve different opinions between the member churches. According to the constitution, the Church is disestablished, but dependent upon the political system; the Estonian state has a long tradition of intervention in the life of the Church. The EELC exists as one diocese, which consists of 153 congregations, forming 12 deaneries. At the head is the archbishop, who is elected by the Church Council, the highest ecclesiastical organ of power. It consists of the representatives of all the deaneries of the EELC, the Conference of Clergymen and the Theological Institute. According to the new Constitution of the Church, ratified by the Church Council on 27 June 1991, the archbishop convenes the Council at least once a year. In the interim the Church is led by the archbishop with the Consistory, which consists of six assessors who have been elected by the Church Council.

The candidates for spiritual office must study theology and pass an examination before the Consistory. Pastors and deacons are ordained by the bishop. Deacons are appointed as assistants by resolution of the Consistory. The pastors of congregations are always appointed by the Consistory on the nomination of the archbishop. Clergymen are responsible to the archbishop. Pastors have the casting vote on matters relating to the life of the congregation although the congregation is formally led by its board. During the period of Soviet rule, the EELC was the only church in the Soviet Union which refused to alter its constitution in order to remove pastors from the board of the congregation. Thus the pastor has the central role in the activity of the congregation, and this is maintained to the present day.

Membership of the EELC is counted by the number of adults who are baptized and confirmed and have given a nominal financial contribution to the congregation during the past year. Latent membership is probably four times greater.

Numerical Data:

Year	Members	Baptized	Confirmed	Marriages
1988	50,412	4,525	2,704	581
1989	59,376	12,962	8,837	1,426
1990	63,891	18,608	11,691	1,752

The Episcopate

Christianity began to extend to the area of Estonia at the end of the first millennium, but the official christianization was completed in 1227 by the archdiocese of Hamburg-Bremen. The first known bishop of the Estonians was a Benedictine monk, Fulco, who was consecrated Bishop of Estonia by Eskil, Archbishop of Lund, in 1165.

In the thirteenth century Estonia was conquered by Germans, Danes and Swedes. The people were baptized and the country was divided into three dioceses — each of them with its bishop and cathedral chapter. Riga, the capital of Livonia, became the archiepiscopal see. A peculiarity of Estonia was that the land was divided between the bishops and the Teutonic Order. These were at loggerheads, because in those districts that were under the secular jurisdiction of the bishops of the Order spiritual authority still belonged to the diocesan bishop. There was a constant power struggle between them. Cathedral chapters elected the bishops unless there was direct papal provision.

The Reformation movement arrived in Estonia in 1523-24, when the Archbishop of Riga (who was at the same time the Bishop of Tartu and Tallinn) was Johann IV Blankenfeld. He was a faithful apologist of the old doctrine and an opponent of the Reformation. The Bishop of Saare-Lääne was the famous Johannes IV Kyvel, who was a reforming bishop of the final period of Roman Catholicism.

After the Reformation there were hard and complicated days in Old Livonia. The Russian-Livonian War (1558-83) meant the end of the Teutonic Order. In the '90s of the same century the northern part of Estonia came under the power of Sweden and Russia gave up the southern part of Estonia to Poland. The southern region therefore came under the influence of the Counter-Reformation. This lasted up to 1621, when the whole region of Estonia came into Sweden's possession, except for Oesel (Saaremaa), which was under Danish rule from 1560 until 1645. Danish ecclesiastical laws were enforced in Saaremaa in 1562. In consequence there was no consistory, and bishops (or superintendents) were royal officials for the administration of the Church.

The King of Sweden recommended that in Swedish Estonia there should be bishops or visitors. They were ordained in Sweden and were inducted solemnly in Tallinn Cathedral. The first bishop in Estonia under Swedish rule was the previous Bishop of Turku, Peter Folling. He was followed by Christian Agricola (the son of the Finnish reformer and bishop, Mikael Agricola), David Dubberch, Johhannes Rudbecius, Joachim Thering and others. All these bishops did much good for the Church and intellectual life in general. The episcopate lasted up to the end of Swedish rule in Estonia, the last being Jakob Long (1701-1710). In 1686 the new Swedish church law was passed. It came into force in Estonia with some concessions.

The period of Russian rule (1710-1917), with the destructive Great Northern War beforehand, was a great setback for the Estonian achievements — even more than the time of annexation to Sweden. A number of elementary schools were closed and the Church (then a minority church compared with the Russian Orthodox) fell into greater dependence on the central government and the aristocracy. In spite of protests by the clergy, from then on the president of the Consistory was a layman — i.e. a representative of the aristocracy; the episcopate was abolished. It was easier to replace a superintendent than a bishop and thus to make the Church politically acceptable to the authorities. At the first opportunity Estonians restored the episcopate.

The Estonian Republic declared its independence on the 24 February 1918. Before that, on 31 May and 1 June, the first Church Congress had convened at Tartu and resolved to restore the episcopate in the Estonian Free People's Church. The second Church Congress on 10 and 11 September 1919 and the first Synod in 1920 elected Jakob Kukk as the first restored Estonian bishop. His consecration took place in Kaarli Church in Tallinn on 5 June 1921 by the Archbishop of Uppsala, Nathan Söderblom, and the Finnish bishop J.Gummerus, according to the same rite as had been used for the consecration of the Estonian bishops during the Swedish period. Bishop Jacob Kukk died on 25 July 1933 in Tallinn.

On 19 June 1934 the sixteenth Synod elected Hugo Bernhard Rahamägi, the pastor of the congregation of Tartu University, as the new bishop. He was consecrated on 16 September 1934 in Tallinn Cathedral by the Archbishop of Uppsala, Erling Eidem, assisted by Theodor Grünbergs, the Archbishop of Latvia and A.Lehtonen, the Bishop of Tampere. Under the leadership of Hugo Bernhard Rahamägi the contacts between English and Estonian Churches were established and the Agreement of Altar and Pulpit was signed in 1938. This had a very great importance for Estonians soon to be scattered in exile all over the world. In September 1939 the government interrupted the episcopate of Hugo Bernhard Rahamägi and appointed a trustee for the Church (Pastor Jaak Varik) until December of the same year when the EELC eventually received a new bishop. Hugo Bernhard Rahamägi died in 1942 in a prison camp in Siberia.

On 14 December 1939 the Electoral College elected Johan Kópp as the new Bishop of the EELC. According to the constitution of 1935 the bishop entered his office on election. The EELC requested the Archbishop of Uppsala, Erling Eidem, to consecrate him on 16 or 30 June 1940. This time was not suitable for Archbishop Eidem, and he suggested a new date in August 1940. The EELC also applied to the Archbishop of Canterbury, who did not find it possible to take part in the consecration because of the difficult situation in Europe and in Estonia itself. The Bishop of Gloucester suggested, in a letter of 1 January 1940, that a correct and canonical solution would be for Bishop Rahamägi to consecrate his successor. Because of the wartime situation Bishop Johan Kópp remained unconsecrated. He left Estonia in 1944 and was the first bishop and archbishop in exile until 1964. He died in Sweden in 1970.

On 2 June 1944, foreseeing the uncertain situation in Estonia, Bishop Johan Kópp had appointed substitutes from the senior clergy in case he or his deputy were removed. This was soon to happen: the assessor Anton Eilart began to perform the duties of the bishop until his own arrest on 25 November 1944. The pastor of Tallinn Cathedral, August Pähn, was elected chairman of the Provisional Arranging Committee in the place of the missing Anton Eilart on 17 January 1945. He was elected by the Episcopal Council as substitute of the bishop. August Pähn was considered to have vacated his office from 12 April 1948 because of his arrest and deportation. After his release from prison in 1956 and return to his homeland, he served the congregation of Vönnu until 1963. He died in Estonia on 4 June 1963.

The twenty-third Church Council of the EELC elected Jaan Kiivit, the pastor of the congregation of Jaani in Tallinn, Archbishop of the EELC. But once again because of the prevailing political situation, the churches of Scandinavia could not consecrate him. During his archiepiscopate the EELC joined the World Council of Churches (1952) and the Lutheran World Federation (1956). The archbishop, who was elected for life, retired to become emeritus archbishop on 12 October 1967 for health reasons. He died on 3 August 1971 in Tallinn.

On 12 October 1967 the Church Council elected Alfred Tooming as archbishop of the EELC. He was consecrated on 9 June 1968 in Tallinn Cathedral by the Archbishop of Finland, Martti Simojoki. Alfred Tooming died on 7 October 1977, and on 31 May 1978 the Church Council elected Edgar Hark as Archbishop of the EELC. He was consecrated on 31 October 1978 in Tallinn Cathedral by the Archbishop of Finland, Mikko Juva, assisted by the Archbishop of Uppsala, O.Sundby, and the Bishop of Hungary, Z.Kaldy. Edgar Hark died on 26 October 1986. In December 1992 the Bishop of Grimsby, David Tustin, Anglican Co-Chairman of the Anglican-Nordic-Baltic Conversations, represented the Archbishop of Canterbury at the consecration of E.Soone as Suffragan Bishop of Estonia in Tallinn Cathedral. This was the first time that the EELC had appointed a suffragan bishop, as well as the first occasion on which an Anglican bishop had taken part in an Estonian consecration.

On 11 June 1978 the pastor of Jaani Congregation in Tallinn, Kuno Pajula, was elected the new archbishop. He was consecrated on 15 November 1987 in Tallinn Cathedral by the Archbishop of Finland, John Vikström, assisted by Bishop G.Grappe from Sweden, Bishop Olob Lindegaard from Denmark, Bishop Fredrik Gronningsater from Norway, Bishop H.Gienke from Germany, Bishop Jan Michalko from Czechoslovakia and Bishop Dieter Knall from Austria.

The Estonian Evangelical-Lutheran Church is comparable to the Nordic churches in its structure and traditions in doctrine as in practice. Thanks to those churches the episcopate has once more been restored with the historic succession after interregnums caused by the politics of foreign domination.

Church Structure
The Estonian Evangelical-Lutheran Church bases its teaching upon the Old and New Testaments, the Apostles', Nicene and Athanasian Creeds, the Unaltered Augsburg Confession and the *Book of Concord*.

The EELC is an independent episcopal, synodically-structured church. The highest ruling body of the EELC is the General Synod, which is called together by the archbishop. It consists of the archbishop, members of the Consistory, the Revision Commission, the deans of each deanery, the pastor of the Toom-Niguliste Church and two representatives from each deanery, elected by the deanery synod. The General Synod makes changes in church laws, the calendar and other matters pertaining to the order of worship. It also elects the archbishop, and, for a three year-term, a six-member consistory and a three-member revision commission. The Consistory is the executive organ of the General Synod and implements the decisions made by the General Synod. In the event of the sudden death of the archbishop, the consistory appoints a successor. A new archbishop must be consecrated within a year of the vacancy.

The parish consists of confirmed members. It is led by its pastor and a three- to seven-member board, elected for three years. Every confirmed member of the congregation is allowed to vote, but to serve on the board, one must be a minimum of 25 years old and a member in good standing.

Each parish is part of a deanery, consisting of the churches in a given geographical area. Each dean calls together synods made up of the dean, parish pastors, and one representative from each congregation, congregations over 500 members having two representatives. It is at the deanery level that representatives are selected for the General Synod, one pastor and one lay person.

TIIT PÄDAM

LATVIA

The office of bishop in historic succession was introduced into the Lutheran Church of Latvia in 1920, which until then had been led by General Superintendents since the Reformation. Archbishop Nathan Söderblom (Uppsala) assisted by Bishop Jakob Kukk (Estonia) consecrated two Latvian bishops at separate ceremonies on the same day: Karlis Irbe for the Latvian-speaking congregations, and Harold Pelchau for the German-speaking congregations. Bishop Pelchau continued in office until 1938, when the bulk of the German-speaking population was drawn back into Nazi Germany.

Bishop Irbe resigned in 1932 over the plebiscite concerning the ownership of Riga Cathedral. Theodor Grünbergs was elected as his successor, and Archbishop Eidem of Uppsala was invited to consecrate him. However, Archbishop Eidem declined to do so unless Bishop Irbe also took part, and owing to the latter's conscientious refusal on the same grounds which had prompted his resignation, Archbishop Grünbergs was unable to obtain consecration. During official conversations with delegates of the Church of England in Tallinn in 1938 the Latvian delegation, led by Archbishop Grünbergs, submitted a statement which included the following:

> The representatives of the Evangelical Church of Latvia... hope that the Church of Latvia in its historical development in the future will adopt such forms of the episcopal office and will give it such validity as will promote the working out of the ecumenical unity of the Christian Church...'[1]

It was on the basis of this desire to regularize the position of their Bishop and establish a regular ministry that intercommunion with the Latvian Church was recommended to the Church of England and accepted by the Convocations.

During and after the Second World War the Latvian Church entered a period of great hardship and persecution. Many of its members were deported, and others fled into exile under threat of their lives. Archbishop Grünbergs went into exile in 1944, having left behind him an emergency leadership shared between several senior pastors; he died in

---

[1] *Lambeth Occasional Reports 1931-8* (London, 1948), p.243.

1962. Regular leadership was resumed by Archbishop Gustav Thurs (1955-1968), though he was unable to obtain consecration for political reasons. In 1968 both Peteris Kleperis and Albert Freijs were successively nominated to the office of Archbishop, but each died before taking office. The historic succession was restored in 1969 when Archbishop Janis Matulis was consecrated by Bishop Sven Dannell (Skara, Sweden).

The Situation in the Latvian Lutheran Church Today

(i) RELIGIOUS CONTEXT

After 50 years of atheism almost three generations have been brought up without any idea about religion. Other religions, as well as Christianity, were persecuted in the Soviet Union. Now people are thirsting for the spiritual side of life. Churches are being opened and many spiritual communities are established. People see how the old idols of Marxism-Leninism are dying, old systems are being destroyed. There is great poverty. Many people see that all previous values, including all stable and solid things, are going to be destroyed; what then of the things of the spirit? People mix different spiritual systems with salvation through Jesus Christ (e.g. because medical services are very bad, people are visiting nature healers).

(ii) POPULATION AND DENOMINATIONS

Latvia is a traditionally Lutheran country — Lutheran ideas came there directly from Germany and Martin Luther corresponded with Livonia. From Riga, the Reformation spread into other Baltic regions at that time. The eastern part of Latvia is Roman Catholic, because it was historically connected with Lithuania and Poland. Today in Latvia there are about 1 million Latvians (50 per cent of the population). Approximately 300,000 are Lutherans. Christians can be divided by denomination as follows: approximately 50 per cent Lutherans, 20 per cent Roman Catholics, 15 per cent Baptists (both Latvians and Russians), 10 per cent Russian Orthodox and 5 per cent other smaller Christian denominations. These are unofficial statistics. In Latvia there is also a Latvian Christian mission led by Jewish and Russian Christians. There are ecumenical groups which are active in Christian work, in orphanages, old people's homes, with the mentally ill people, and with prisoners.

(iii) CHURCHES AND CONGREGATIONS

In 1939 there were 300 Lutheran congregations with their own church buildings in Latvia. After Soviet occupation many of these buildings were bombed or burned down. The Communists started to use others as museums, amusement halls, store houses, etc. In 1960 under Kruschev persecution was especially hard. Only 100 congregations remained. Members of the congregations were old, because old people did not have anything to lose. Today Latvians have registered 264 Lutheran congregations. This means that (1) all who are involved in ministry must care for several congregations; (2) students of theology are involved in ministry as deacons; (3) there are problems between the generations in Latvian Lutheran clergy. There are two generations of pastors – old and young; there are very few in the middle. The old pastors were educated in the Faculty of Theology before the Second World War and they had to work under the Soviet regime. Now most of them are tired but still at work, and their congregations are passive (no confirmation classes, no charity work, no Bible studies, no *diaconia*). On the other hand, young pastors lack theological education, because they have graduated from ordinary Soviet schools without basic Christian teaching; sometimes they are narrow-minded.

Not all Lutheran congregations have their own church buildings; About 100 churches need repairing or are totally destroyed. In special cases (Christmas, Easter) some congregations celebrate their services in ruins. During the last years several churches were rebuilt by our own congregations and some with the help of the Swedish and North Elbian Churches.

(iv) EDUCATION

When Latvia was occupied by the Soviets in 1940 the Faculty of Theology was closed. After the Second World War the Latvian Lutheran Church developed academic theological courses, and later a seminary. The education was simple. Pastors studied for two years. In 1989 the Faculty of Theology was renewed in the University of Latvia. At the present time there are 130 students, 33 of them having been accepted in 1989. Studies are organized according to a four-year programme. There are seven professorial chairs in the Faculty. Important help has been received from the Latvian Lutheran Church outside of Latvia, which has sent theologians for longer periods of time to work with the Faculty. Some students are studying theology abroad, for example, in Germany and the USA. At the present time the Church is working on a new catechism for use both in Latvia and abroad.

(v) FOREIGN CONTACTS

The situation in the Latvian Lutheran Church has changed during the last years. First of all a very close co-operation between the Lutheran Church of Latvia and the Latvian Lutheran Church outside Latvia has been established. A committee of co-operation has been established and meets frequently.

Substantial help has been received from the Church outside Latvia from Finland and from the North Elbian Church. From the Church of Sweden we have received a printing press which is already in use.

In September 1989 the Bishop of Gibraltar in Europe, John Satter-thwaite, represented the Archbishop of Canterbury at the consecration of Archbishop Karlis Gailitis. This was the first time that an Anglican bishop had taken part in the consecration of a Latvian archbishop in fulfilment of the 1938 agreement. Archbishop Gailitis, who was a vice-president of the Lutheran World Federation, died in 1993.

RINGOLDS MUZIKS

LITHUANIA

It was many years before Lithuania became Christian. Only when King Mindaugas of Lithuania was crowned on the orders of Pope Innocent IV in 1253 was part of the court converted. The country at large remained pagan, mainly because there was no real zeal to christianize it but only to reign over it. However, in 1387 Grand Duke Jogaila began to address himself to the need, and with the help mainly of the Franciscan Order, Lithuania largely became Christian. An exception was the north-western part of Lithuania, known as Samogitia, which the Teutonic Knights wanted to capture and were in continual conflict with the Lithuanians over. Only after the battle of Tannenberg (1410) was won by the Lithuanian and Polish united forces could Lithuania proceed to be christianized by a more authentic Christianity, rather than purely for mercantile considerations. So by 1413 it could be said that Lithuania had officially became a Christian country. Yet mass baptisms performed by priests who did not speak Lithuanian could do little to instil real Christian spirit. The country was therefore ripe for something different from the old paganism and imposed, foreign forms of Christianity.

When the Reformation came to Lithuania in 1525, already preceded by Hussite teaching, the country was willing and ready to accept its ideas. Lithuania became a protestant country with Calvinists and Lutherans living their faith in a still semi-pagan but Roman Catholic ruled country. (At this time, talks were proceeding towards a union of Lithuania and Poland, creating a tense political atmosphere in a religiously uncertain country.) The bishop of Vilnius, V.Protasevicius, invited the Jesuit Order to counteract Reformation ideas. The rulers of the country remained Roman Catholics and strongly supported the Counter-Reformation. When King Zigmantas Vaza (1588-1632) became king there were only two Roman Catholics in the Senate. When he died only two protestants remained in the Senate. The Counter-Reformation was very thorough and strong. King Augustus II (1670-1733) had to become a Roman Catholic and to give a promise that no protestants would be permitted to serve in any high office. The untenable situation of the protestants was only alleviated after Pope Clement XIV suppressed the Jesuit Order in 1773.

Lithuania ceased to exist as a separate state in 1793, when Russia incorporated it. The Roman Catholic Church and the protestant churches remained, but had to live with the ever-increasing intervention of the Russian government, prompted by the Orthodox Church. The Latin alphabet was prohibited in Lithuania in 1864, and possession of literature in that alphabet meant immediate arrest and deportation or incarceration. This prohibition lasted until 1904 and claimed many lives. It obviously hindered the work of the Lithuanian churches, both protestant and Roman Catholic. In 1918 Lithuania again became independent and the indigenous churches began to flourish again. The largest denomination in Lithuania was the Roman Catholic Church. But the Evangelical-Lutheran Church in Lithuania began to grow in influence and numbers. By 1939 there were 70,000 members (30,000 Lithuanian, 26,000 German and 14,000 Latvian), with 55 parishes and congregations served by 51 pastors.

In the Evangelical-Lutheran Church in Lithuania at this time the highest authority was the Synod, which consisted of pastors and of laymen from each parish (one for 500). At the first Synod, held in Kaunas on 15 October 1919, it became clear that there was a need to call national synods for the three linguistic groups — Lithuanian, German and Latvian. Thus from 1920 there were three Synods. These Synods elected three clergy and three lay persons to form the Consistory, which was the highest executive organ of the Church as well as the highest registry office and matrimonial Court. The president and vice-president of the Consistory were elected by the Synods, but their nomination had to be approved by the president of the Republic. The Consistory executed synodical decrees and was responsible for the examination of candidates for the ministry, the acceptance of pastors selected by parishes for ministry, and the supervision of pastors, as well as the teaching of religion in schools, the liturgical order, religious and theological publishing, and overseas representation of the Evangelical-Lutheran Church in Lithuania.

The first Soviet occupation of Lithuania ended with the Second World War, but after the German occupation of the country the Soviets returned to power. Much of civil and religious activity was suppressed under both occupations.

The Lutheran Church was not, however, dormant. In January 1941 the Consistory elected Prof. Dr Stanaitis as its chairman. In 1946 a new Consistory elected as its chairman Pastor E.Leijeris, who was arrested in 1949 and died in Siberia. In 1968 the Evangelical-Lutheran Church in Lithuania was officially accepted as a member of the Lutheran World Federation. The first post-war Synod took place on 22 May 1955. At the second Synod, on 25 August 1970, Pastor Jonas Kalvanas was elected as chairman of the Consistory.

The Synod of 20 June 1976 re-elected Jonas Kalvanas to chair the Consistory and gave him the title Bishop. He was consecrated to the episcopate on the same day in the Martynas Mazvydas Church in Taurage, where he had been ordained as pastor on 28 July 1940 and where he still serves. During the consecration the Archbishop of the Estonian Evangelical-Lutheran Church, Alfred Tooming, said:

> In order to show that within the Church Militant throughout the centuries apostolic faith and gifts still live, I, Bishop of the Estonian Evangelical-Lutheran Church, myself having received the Apostolic Inheritance (*Successio Apostolica*) from the Archbishop of Finland, give to you the ministry of the Bishop of the Lithuanian Evangelical-Lutheran Church. You are ordained to an office of service, doing your duty with a loving heart. For all the tasks given you may Our Lord grant you from heaven his grace and his peace, his power and his blessing. Amen.

At present there are 41 active Lutheran parishes in Lithuania with a membership ranging from 20 to 3,000. Total Church membership is between 25,000 and 30,000. There are only 12 active ministers, not all of whom are ordained pastors. Theological education for ministers is conducted mainly in the Riga Seminary (Latvia), which is non-residential. Moreover, Lithuanian is not used. There is a church journal, *Kelias* ('The Way'). The name is taken from a former publication which ran between 1935 and 1939, published weekly in Klaipeda. The present *Kelias* appears as circumstances allow.

ALDONIS PUTCE

ENGLAND

The Edge of Empire

When Christians first landed in England is not known, but, as in other parts of the Roman Empire, it can be safely assumed that the faith was first carried by traders, administrators and soldiers. Tertullian speaks of Christians in Britain, inferring that Christ had reached areas the Imperial Army had been unable to penetrate (c.200). The first individual Christian we hear of is St Alban the martyr. Alban was a Roman soldier, a layman of the Roman city of Verulamium, now St Albans, who, according to the Venerable Bede, gave shelter to a Christian priest. Though the story is encrusted with legend, the date is now accepted by many scholars to have been c. 209 at the time of the persecution by Septimius Severus, rather than at the time of the Diocletian persecution a century later. By 314 there were at least three bishops in England, who attended the Council of Arles. They included bishops from London and York. St Athanasius tells us that the British Church accepted the decisions of the Council of Nicaea (325), though no bishops from England are recorded as being present. Some bishops did attend the Council of Rimini (359) — on imperial expenses! Christian symbols, such as the Chi-Rho sign, are found in Romano-British villas of this period in England, and there are remains of churches in Berkshire, Dorset, and Kent. Pelagius, the heretic, was a Romano-British monk, who taught on the Continent at this time. His teachings were countered in England and Wales by two bishops from Gaul, Germanus of Auxerre and Lupus of Troyes (from 429).

With the gradual abandonment of Britain by Imperial Rome in the fifth century, England was rapidly overrun by the Jutes, Angles and Saxons. The Romano-British inhabitants, of whom an unknown proportion were Christians, fled westwards to Cornwall and Wales or were absorbed by their pagan invaders. The Church was largely destroyed and for the time being the story of Christianity in Britain is to be found in Ireland, Scotland and Wales, where the 'Celtic' Church flourished. It was eventually to re-evangelize England from the north through the mission of St Columba of Iona at about the time St Gregory the Great sent St Augustine from Rome to re-convert England.

Missionary Episcopacy

St Augustine of Canterbury landed in Kent in 597. In King Ethelbert of Kent he met a civilized ruler, whose wife, Queen Bertha, was the Christian daughter of a Frankish king. She had already brought chaplains with her to Kent. Though Pope Gregory had originally intended Augustine to proceed to London, progress was slow and it was at Canterbury that St Augustine consolidated his ecclesiastical headquarters. St Mellitus came from Rome to London in 604 and St Paulinus journeyed from Canterbury to York in 625. Paulinus initiated a mission in the north which was revived by King Oswald of Northumbria (d.642), who had been reared in the Irish tradition on the island of Iona. Oswald sent for help from Iona, initiating the mission of the monk-bishop St Aidan (d.651). Aidan subsequently established his monastic headquarters on the island of Lindisfarne in Northumbria. The Iona mission in the north of England was also powerfully assisted by women's monastic communities, notably that led by St Hilda of Whitby (d.680).

The clash between 'Celtic' and 'Roman' customs has perhaps been over-emphasized. Nevertheless, with the King and Queen of Northumbria keeping Easter at different times there was need for harmonization. Hilda supervised a synod at Whitby (c.663), presided over by the king, who found in favour of the Roman calendrical arrangements. But the Synod of Whitby is best seen as a continuation of the debate about the dating of the Easter festival common throughout the Western Church at this time, rather than as a clash between so-called 'Celtic' and 'Roman' traditions, unhistorically perceived as monolithic.

Diocesan Consolidation and Reform

Uniformity of custom and consolidation of ecclesiastical organization was, however, achieved by a second Roman mission led by Theodore of Tarsus, St Paul's city in Asia Minor. Theodore reached Canterbury in 669. Finding few bishops left in either the north or south of England, he supplied bishops for all the politically separate kingdoms of England. He held a synod at Hertford in 672 which effectively created a united *Ecclesia Anglicana* for the first time; this made its own contribution to the later political unity of the country. Theodore was the first Archbishop of Canterbury whom the whole English Church obeyed. His diocesan boundaries are still recognizable today. He also prepared the way for the parochial system at the local level. The first regular synods owe their origins to Theodore, eventually to become the Convocations of Canterbury and York. During his primacy the English Church produced both scholars such as the Venerable Bede and missionaries such as St Boniface of Crediton, who evangelized in the Germanic speaking regions of the Continent.

The Norse invasions interrupted the development of the life of the English Church and standards fell. Archbishop Dunstan of Canterbury (d.988) reformed monastic communities and cathedrals, but the question remained open as to whether England would be drawn into the Scandinavian political orbit or the increasingly powerful Norman domain.

Duke William of Normandy's conquest of England in 1066 settled the matter decisively. Lanfranc, his Archbishop of Canterbury, together with other Norman bishops and abbots, led a religious revival. Old Saxon sees were moved to more important cities, and new dioceses were created (Ely and Carlisle). The great age of the building of the English cathedrals had begun. The supremacy of Canterbury over York was asserted, ecclesiastical organization was renewed at all levels, and most significantly the ecclesiastical and civil courts were separated, with the concomitant introduction of Roman canon law. This period saw the beginning of English evangelization in the Nordic countries.

Bishops, Church and State

During the twelfth century the struggle for spiritual independence dominated the Church in England, as elsewhere in Europe. The martyrdom of St Thomas Becket at Canterbury in 1170 reverberated all over Europe. He represented the reforming movement of the Hildebrandine papacy and indirectly the monastic reforms epitomized in the Cistercian movement. By the thirteenth century the theoretical freedom of the Church (and barons) over against an absolutist monarchy was established in *Magna Carta* (1215). As the century advanced the papacy exerted an increasing influence on episcopal appointments, especially to Canterbury. Roman canon law in England was further developed. The English episcopate at this time included fine scholars, pastors and administrators, the most distinguished of whom was Grosseteste of

Lincoln (d.1253). Under Edward I and Edward III parliamentary institutions were developed in England, but the lower clergy successfully established their right to meet in Convocation (synod) separately from the emerging lower house of Parliament. Bishops and abbots already met synodically and in the upper house of Parliament.

Church and Papacy

During the fourteenth century the financial exactions and appointments of the papacy, itself divided between Rome and Avignon, came increasingly under attack. So too were 'foreign' religious orders. A new nationalism strengthened the control of the monarchy over the Church. The fifteenth century saw the first beginnings of theological criticism of the papacy in England through the teachings of John Wycliffe. He emphasized the importance of Scripture as the sole authentic source of doctrine and authority in the Church and sought to free the eucharist of superstitious abuse.

Henry VIII's break with Rome in the sixteenth century, though immediately occasioned by his marital adventures and quest for a male heir, can also be seen as the final denouement of a long struggle for the control of the Church. In the first phase of the English Reformation few strictly theological changes were made. The vernacular was only partially accepted by the introduction of the (printed) Great Bible into parish churches. Luther's works were still banned. But the common lawyers had been decisively victorious over the canon lawyers. Henry VIII had subordinated the canon law to the Crown in place of the pope and became the fount of both civil and ecclesiastical jurisdictions. Meanwhile the monasteries were dissolved and their lucrative property appropriated.

Reformation and Episcopacy

The episcopate in England at the time of the Reformation was nevertheless more or less intact. Thomas Wolsey (d. 1530), it is true, was appointed to the diocese of Lincoln in 1514, only to be translated to the archdiocese of York the following year. In 1515 he was also created a cardinal and appointed Lord Chancellor of England. For various periods during the next 15 years he also nominally occupied the sees of Bath and Wells, Durham and Winchester. The diocese of Worcester was held by an Italian bishop who represented the King of England to the papal court. Nevertheless, most dioceses had resident bishops. Though the majority were far from sympathetic to radical Reformation theology, many acknowledged the need for the moderate reforms urged by Erasmus — for example, John Fisher of Rochester, who with Thomas More was eventually executed by Henry VIII for refusing to accept the king as 'Supreme Head' of the Church.

Nevertheless, Henry appointed the reforming Thomas Cranmer as his Archbishop of Canterbury. Under Edward VI, Cranmer was encouraged to produce the first two vernacular Prayer Books and Ordinals. The first Prayer Book (1549) was moderate in its theological changes, the second (1552) more unequivocally reformed. The Forty-Two Articles (a statement of doctrine) were published (1553), drafted by Cranmer, and formed the basis of the later Articles of Religion.

In the English Ordinal the ordination services in the Latin Pontifical were radically pruned, with considerable medieval material concerning a 'sacrificing priesthood' done away with. The word 'priest' was, however, consciously retained. The Ordinal, while abolishing the 'minor orders', provided for the continuation of the separate orders of deacon, priest and bishop. It unambiguously declared that these orders were found in the primitive Church and were now continued in the Church of England.

Under Mary Tudor communion with Rome, Papal Supremacy, and the Latin services were restored (1555), though the monastic communities were not re-founded. Many of the reforming party went into exile. Of those remaining a number were burned as heretics, including four bishops Thomas Cranmer, Hugh Latimer, Nicholas Ridley and John Hooper.

The Elizabethan Settlement

With the accession of Elizabeth I (1558) papal obedience was again repudiated and the Sovereign assumed the style of 'Supreme Governor'. A slightly more conservative English Prayer Book was re-introduced (1559). The Thirty-Nine Articles of Religion were published for assent, and Matthew Parker, Archbishop of Canterbury, attempted to achieve religious uniformity. But there remained Roman Catholic and Puritan minorities who refused to conform, or who conformed only nominally to Elizabeth's religious settlement. The Puritans remained *within* the

Church of England but strove for a 'purer' Reformed church. The Roman Catholic 'Recusants' refused to conform, especially after the papal excommunication of Elizabeth I in 1570. From then on, Roman Catholics were subject to sporadic but increasing persecution.

A scholarly apologetic for the Anglican position was developed during Elizabeth's reign, most notably by Bishop John Jewel of Salisbury and his even more famous protégé, Richard Hooker. The necessity for national reform was defended; appeal was made to the Scriptures, the Fathers and Reason (though not as equals); the notion of a *via media* between Rome and Geneva was propagated. Episcopacy was considered to be both scriptural and traditional, and therefore to be received and treasured from the past and handed on to the future for the good of the Church. But, significantly, no one theology of episcopacy was canonized; still less the absolute necessity for an unbroken historical chain of succession. The Lutheran and Reformed churches on the Continent were not unchurched. Nevertheless great care was taken to preserve the historic episcopal succession. At the consecration of Archbishop Matthew Parker (1559) in Lambeth Palace Chapel four bishops were duly found to take part in the laying on of hands, although all but one of Mary Tudor's bishops had gone into exile at her death and that of her Archbishop of Canterbury, Cardinal Reginald Pole.

Anglicanism, Episcopacy and Conflict

When James VI of Scotland ascended to the English throne as James I of England he united in the monarch's person two thrones and kingdoms. He personally emphasized the inter-connection between the 'Divine Right' of kings and the authority of the bishops in Church and state. A new code of canon law was published by the Convocations (synods) of Canterbury and York under royal licence (1604). Under James episcopacy was restored in Scotland (1610-12), three bishops being consecrated in England. Under Charles I the debate between the Anglican establishment and the Puritans was sharpened. William Laud, Charles' Archbishop of Canterbury, endeavoured to secure uniformity and high dignity in the conduct of the services of the Church. Laud was, however, as autocratic as his royal master. Episcopacy, dubbed 'prelacy' by the Puritans, and Anglicanism itself became a matter of conflict in the English Civil War. Scotland allied itself with the Parliamentarians after

Charles attempted to impose a Prayer Book (similar to the first, conservative, English book) on the Church of Scotland (1637), and to make the Scottish Church dependent upon Canterbury. The defeat of the king in the Civil War (1642-46) meant the disestablishment of the Anglican Church in favour of Presbyterianism. The bishops were deposed, some going into exile; loyalist clergy also went into hiding or maintained their Anglicanism secretly. Archbishop Laud was imprisoned in the Tower of London and eventually executed (1645). King Charles refused to barter his high Anglican principles to conciliate the Scots and the English Puritans on episcopacy. His execution in Whitehall (1649) was therefore regarded by royalist Anglicans as a martyrdom in defence of the Church.

From as early as 1651 concern grew amongst loyal churchmen that the Church of England's episcopal succession might die out, and indeed by the end of 1659 all but nine of the 27 sees were vacant. The exiled King Charles II repeatedly attempted to persuade the survivors to consecrate new bishops, but the were too fearful to act on his orders witin England, while age and infirmity held them back from travelling to the Continent. Had the Interregnum lasted even just ten years longer, the Anglican episcopal succession would probably have been extinguished.

In fact, at the Restoration episcopacy was re-established in England and Wales, Scotland and Ireland (1660). In England the Savoy Conference attempted to accommodate the Puritans, at first with some 'success'. But with the imposition of the revised Prayer Book and its enforcement by a new Act of Uniformity, 'dissenters' were ejected from parishes and their separation from the Church of England made complete (1662). From this time on the absolute invariability of episcopal ordination was required by law.

Charles II and James II attempted to introduce toleration for dissenters, Roman Catholic and protestant alike. But the Anglican establishment, both clerical and lay, felt the deprivations of the Civil War too strongly, and almost all attempts at toleration were successfully resisted. James II, a professed Roman Catholic, openly attacked the Church of England by incarcerating in the Tower of London seven bishops who opposed toleration, including the Archbishop of Canterbury. The 'Glorious Revolution' which ensued (1689), brought William of Orange from the

Netherlands and confirmed the protestant succession. Ironically, a number of bishops, including those who had been imprisoned by James, refused to accept William as king while James lived, because of the theory of the 'divine right' of kings. This included all the Scottish bishops; their deprivation finally eliminated episcopacy from the established Church of Scotland, which from then on remained Presbyterian in polity.

Comfortable Episcopal Establishment
The eighteenth century was considerably less dramatic. Both Church and state reacted against the fierce religious controversy of the previous century. In 1717 the Convocations of Canterbury and York were pro-rogued (dismissed) by King George I because they were about to condemn the notion that there is no scriptural authority for Church authority. They were not to meet again for the transaction of business until 1852 and 1861 respectively

The Methodist revival, from the 1740s onwards, was viewed with considerable suspicion by the bishops, although both John and Charles Wesley sustained their Anglican priesthood to the end. John Wesley's ordinations were a serious stumbling block. Also of importance was the degree of support for Methodism among the artisans of the Industrial Revolution. The bishops, hampered by their alliance with the political establishment, saw Methodism as a threat to the *status quo*. Their hostility to Methodism was one reason for its eventual secession from the Church of England, though by the end of the century Methodism had also assimilated important elements of continuing protestant non-conformity which were inimical to Anglican polity. Nevertheless, Methodism was also the father to the first phase of the Evangelical revival *within* the Church of England.

Bishops and the Apostolicity of the Church
During the eighteenth century the intellectual climate of the Enlighten-ment permeated much of the Church, giving birth to a new 'broad church' party. This 'Latitudinarianism' became dominant until the birth of the Oxford Movement, usually thought to have begun with John Keble's Oxford Assize sermon in 1833. Keble's immediate protest was against the parliamentary suppression of ten Irish bishoprics. In the second and third decades of the nineteenth century Parliament took the

lead in a number of important administrative reforms of the Church, most notably the compulsory pooling of the English cathedral revenues to provide for a more equitable distribution of clergy stipends. Necessary as such reforms were, they were prosecuted by the state on the assumption that the Church of England was simply the spiritual aspect of the nation.

The Oxford Movement reminded the Church of its spiritual credentials. In the fourth of the *Tracts for the Times* Keble emphasized the apostolic descent of the ordained ministry and an emphasis on 'apostolic succession' became characteristic of the 'Tractarian' Movement. In origin this emphasis was against state interference in the proper spiritual affairs of the Church, rather than against churches without the historic episcopal succession. Its effect was, nevertheless, to stress the importance of episcopacy as a sign and instrument of the apostolicity of the Church. Although sharp controversy and John Henry Newman's eventual secession to Rome (1845) shook the early Tractarians, the movement continued to grow in influence. It transformed both the Church of England and other Anglican churches. Its later nineteenth century 'Anglo-Catholic' phase arose more as a response to pastoral need in the parishes than out of theoretical ecclesiology, especially the slum parishes of the new industrial cities. There was a strong emphasis on sacramental worship, music, ritual and the architectural setting of the liturgy.

The impetus of the Evangelical and Catholic revivals, together with the resources released by ecclesiastical reform, including the restoration of the Convocations, caused a substantial revival of church life during the nineteenth century. Hundreds of new parishes were established and eight new dioceses were formed. The office of suffragan bishop was also revived, as episcopacy was again seen in primarily pastoral terms. The Religious life of monks and nuns was restored to the Church. An order of deaconesses was created, though not as part of 'holy orders'. A national system of parochial church schools was established, and a number of new boarding schools were founded on Anglican principles.

By the middle of the nineteenth century there arose a more developed consciousness of there being a world-wide Anglican Communion. From 1867 the Lambeth Conference of bishops has met approximately every ten years and a strong sense of world-wide episcopal collegiality has developed, as has also the special role of the Archbishop of Canterbury in the fostering of collegiality and communion. The Lambeth Conferences have been particularly concerned with questions of evangelization and culture, discipline, the growth towards autonomy, and ecumenical relations, not least with the Nordic and Baltic churches.[1]

Ecumenical relations in England during the nineteenth century are best characterized by the word 'competition'. Rivalry between the Church of England and the Free Churches enhanced the Anglican emphasis on episcopacy. The denunciation of Anglican orders by Pope Leo XIII in 1896 equally distorted Anglican ecumenical emphasis by encouraging counter-apologetics which stressed Anglican episcopal continuity.

Theological controversy over ritual and ceremonial matters, including prosecutions in the civil courts, marred the close of the century. Biblical criticism and reaction produced fierce debate of another kind as the Church began to respond to the new knowledge of the secular sciences.

Church, State, Episcopacy and Synod

The first quarter of the twentieth century saw a continuation of church reform and development. Twelve more dioceses were created. Liturgical revision was begun. In 1919 there was a major readjustment in relations between Church and state in the passing of the Enabling Act and the creation of a national Church Assembly. By this parliamentary legislation a new House of Laity was added to the ancient houses of bishops and clergy of the Convocations of Canterbury and York. The new Assembly had power to prepare legislation on ecclesiatical matters for the consideration of Parliament. Parliament could not amend such legislation, only accept it or reject it. The modification worked well until the House of Commons twice rejected a draft revised Prayer Book accepted by the bishops, clergy and laity of the Church (1927-28). Between the wars the debate between criticism and tradition continued and developed, the Archbishops' Commission on Doctrine in the Church of England (1938) attempting to set new parameters of doctrinal interpretation.

---

[1] See Existing Agreements Between our Churches, above.

After 1945 a second period of organizational reform was inaugurated. The endowments of the Church were restructured by the establishment of the Church Commissioners (1948). Considerable time was spent by the Church Assembly and the Convocations on the revision of the canon law, no substantial changes having been made since 1604. The new code was promulged from 1964 and 1969. It is now revised regularly, revisions being made and new canons added from time to time as required. In 1970 the Church Assembly was replaced by a new General Synod, to which most of the powers of the Convocations were transferred. This gave the laity an increased share in decision-making; a special responsibility for worship and doctrine remains, however, with the House of Bishops. By the Worship and Doctrine Measure of 1974 the Church eventually had restored to it the power to revise its own liturgy, or rather, to authorize new and alternative services alongside the Book of Common Prayer. In a protocol agreed by the Prime Minister in 1977 the Church also achieved a decisive role in the appointment of its bishops for the first time for many centuries. Under the new arrangements a Crown Appointments Commission, composed of representatives of the wider Church and the diocese concerned, puts forward two names to the Prime Minister. They are usually in order of preference, though this may be disregarded. The Prime Minister nominates one of the two names to the Sovereign for appointment.

Much recent legislative attention has been focused upon pastoral and liturgical reform. The Alternative Service Book (1980) is widely accepted. On the other hand the ordination of women to the priesthood has caused considerable controversy both within and outside the Church. Women deacons were accepted in 1986-7 . In November 1992 the General Synod also accepted the ordination of women priests as an authentic development of the ordained ministry, but the bishops have found it necessary to make pastoral provision for the minority who do not accept this as legitimate. In the last few years there has been an increasing debate within the Church as to the appropriate relation between episcopacy and synodical government. The House of Bishops has increasingly been encouraged to take a more prominent responsibility for leadership when the 'parliamentary' procedures of the General Synod fail to unite the Church. As this debate about constitutional episcopacy is in its infancy, it cannot but be enhanced by closer relations with the Nordic and Baltic churches, many of which are experiencing similar tensions and asking similar questions.

Bishops and Unity

Although the Church of England has been engaged in two major ecumenical discussions with the English Free Churches since World War II, the stumbling block of the reconciliation of ministries between 'episcopal' and 'non-episcopal' churches has so far prevented their successful conclusion. Equally, Rome has not been able fully to endorse the Anglican - Roman Catholic Agreed Statement on Ministry and Ordination. Nevertheless these conversations, and the wider ecumenical discussion on ordained ministry in the Faith and Order Commission of the World Council of Churches (the Lima Statement: *Baptism, Eucharist and Ministry*), have enabled Anglicans to view other ministries more positively without denying the apostolicity of episcopacy. New Ecumenical Canons were thus promulged in 1989 which for the first time gave some official recognition to Free Church ministers. By extension, the same principles were applied to the Evangelical Church in Germany in the Meissen Agreement, accepted by the Church of England in 1990-1. As the Anglican churches in Britain and Ireland compare their history with that of the episcopal churches in the Nordic and Baltic region, the similarity of our stories will become more obvious. When coupled to our newer ecumenical understanding of episcopacy this recognition should give us well-founded confidence to take the further steps towards fuller communion recommended in *The Porvoo Common Statement*.

CHRISTOPHER HILL

WALES

Who were the first bishops in Wales is not recorded; British bishops were present at the Council of Arles in 314. They are identified as being the Bishops of York and London, and a third, possibly from Lincoln. Whether there were bishops in the western part of Britain that we now call Wales in unknown.

A sixth-century source (Gildas' *De Excidio*) refers to the presence of bishops and a seventh-century Life of St Samson describes Dyfrig as a *'papa'* or *'episcopus'*. The earliest unit of organization would seem to have been the *'clas'* church, similar to the minster in England. This was a mother church with a number of subsidiary churches under its control. This arrangement may have been the origin of a diocesan structure. The head of these community churches was an abbot. In some cases he would also be a bishop. We can identify fairly confidently that there were bishops in St David's, Llandeilo Fawr (both in West Wales), Bangor in North Wales and Llandaff in the south-east, but there may well have been at least six more. These bishops seem to have been independent of Canterbury. When Pope Leo III addressed all the people dwelling in the island of Britain in 789, he carefully defined the jurisdiction of the Archbishop of Canterbury as limited to England and the English.

With the coming of the Normans (1070) the Welsh dioceses were rapidly brought under the control of Canterbury, and bishops were appointed by the Crown, except in the case of Bangor, where the Welsh Prince of Gwynedd jealously guarded his right of appointment until the princedom was conquered by the English Crown in 1282. Urban of Llandaff (present-day Cardiff) was the first to make a promise of obedience to the Archbishop of Canterbury, in 1107. In 1188 Archbishop Baldwin of Canterbury travelled round Wales preaching the Crusade and asserted his rights as metropolitan; at the end of the thirteenth century Archbishop Peckham issued a series of instructions for the improvement of church life and clerical discipline in the Welsh dioceses. The Welsh Church had become part of the province of Canterbury, and was to remain so until 1920.

In the sixteenth century the Welsh Church became part of the reformed, established Church of England. Bishops were appointed by the Crown. The Welsh dioceses were poor, and bishops frequently combined their offices with more lucrative offices in England (e.g. a number of eighteenth century Bishops of Llandaff were Deans of St Paul's in London). Sadly, for a period of 150 years until 1870 no Welsh-speaking bishops were appointed, which inevitably meant that the bishops were alienated from a large part of their clergy and their flocks. This was one factor amongst others which led to the majority of the population becoming nonconformist, which in turn led to demands that the Welsh Church should lose its privileged position as the established Church.

Eventually acts of Parliament were passed in 1914 and 1919 and the Church was disestablished in 1920. The four ancient dioceses ceased to be a part of the province of Canterbury, and the Church in Wales came into being as a separate province of the Anglican Communion, with its own archbishop, bishops and synodical structure. Two more dioceses were founded in 1921 and 1923.

The Church in Wales elects its bishops by means of an electoral college which consists of the other bishops, three clerics and three laymen from each diocese, with a double representation from the vacant see. The college thus consists of 47 members. The bishops are the leaders of the Church, working within a written constitution which can only by changed by the Governing Body (synod) of the Church, voting in the three separate Houses of Bishops, Clergy and Laity. The bishops are especially responsible for matters of faith and order.

HUW JONES

SCOTLAND

In what ways was the Scottish Reformation distinctive? Whereas the Church of England might be described as 'nationalized Catholicism', the Scottish Reformation was opposed, not promoted, by the government. Yet it was not really a popular movement. The work of the late Professor Ian Cowan on the progress of the Reformation in the different localities in Scotland led him to conclude that

> On religious issues alone it is clear that the greatest strength of protestant support, with the exception of Kyle, was confined to a closely demarcated area on the east coast. Beyond these areas the reformers were clearly numerically weak. Yet political considerations were to favour this militant minority and enable them to achieve their religious goal.[1]

Furthermore, anti-French Scottish patriotism played a major role in the revolution of 1559 which deposed Mary of Guise from the Regency.

John Hamilton, Archbishop of St Andrews, had himself spearheaded a movement to remedy abuses in the Scottish Church, convening provincial councils for that purpose in 1549, 1552 and 1559; however, Cardinal Beaton's response to criticisms of the Church was severe repression.

A second distinctive feature of the Scottish Reformation was that, because it came later than on the Continent, different models of reform were being advocated in Scotland, one party favouring the English model and the other the more radical model of Geneva. John Knox, whose experience under Calvin helped to shape the Reformed Church in Scotland, was not opposed to that Reformed ideal 'the godly Bishop', and Professor Gordon Donaldson demonstrated conclusively that Knox's superintendents were a rationalized form of episcopacy.[2] The novelty of the Scottish situation was that the partisans of both models stayed together in one church for the first century of the Reformation, whichever party was in effective control from time to time. Professor T.C.Smout summarizes the position thus:

---

[1] I.B.Cowan, *The Scottish Reformation* (London, 1982), p.114.

[2] G.Donaldson, *The Scottish Reformation* (Cambridge, 1960), ch.V and the maps on pp.112f.

The reformed Church of Scotland broke to the surface in 1560, but it did not at that point assume all the characters which we now associate with it. For the next 130 years it went on changing and developing, twisting in its ecclesiastical polity first to one side and then to another to accommodate differing shades of religious opinion until finally, in 1690, it emerged as the classic presbyterian church of the eighteenth and nineteenth centuries, with its elders, deacons and ministers, its kirk-sessions, presbyteries, synods and General Assembly, its frequent but not invariable association with sabbatarianism and puritanism, and its convictions of ecclesiastical parity. Too often the whole scheme is imagined to have existed in the head of John Knox from the start, and only to have been prevented from seeing the light of day by the worldliness of kings and bishops. In fact Knox would have found presbyterianism unfamiliar and perhaps in some ways absurd: the development of the Reformation from 1560 to 1690 was a slow and organic process in which first one feature and then another was introduced and fought over, and in which the ideas and aspirations of Andrew Melville and seventeenth-century divines were at least as important as those of Knox.[3]

What then of the place of the historical episcopate as a strand of the Apostolic Succession of the Church? The Scots Confession of 1560 specifies three 'Notes' (marks, characteristics) 'by which the true Kirk is discerned from the false': the true preaching of the Word of God, the right administration of the sacraments and ecclesiastical discipline uprightly administered — 'without the same,' said the first *Book of Discipline* (church order), 'there is no face of a visible Kirk'. The aim of the reformers was the faithful re-creation (*reformatio*) of a Holy Catholic and Apostolic Church that had ceased to exist in visible form. The gospel called into being a Church markedly different, in several vital aspects, from the papal institution as it had come to be in sixteenth-century Scotland. As in England and in Scandinavia, therefore, the intention was demonstrable moral *discontinuity*. The Scots Confession saw a parallel between recent events in Scotland and the rebuilding of Jerusalem and its Temple after a seventy-year exile when the city remained razed and desolate. Where the objective is the restoration of the true Church of Christ, replacing the institution regarded as not the true Church, relatively little importance is attached to affirming signs of historical continuity. Professor Gordon Donaldson cited in support of this view Hooper and Cranmer in England, as well as in Scotland, Sir

---

[3] T.C.Smout, *A History of the Scottish People, 1560-1830* (London, 1969), p.62.

David Lindsay of the Mount and two reformers who adhered to the papal cause, Ninian Winzet and Abell.

Deprived of Bishops or Repudiating Episcopacy?

It was in the seventeenth century that Anglican writers began to distinguish between the necessity for the sake of reformation of doing without episcopal continuity, and the voluntary and unnecessary repudiation of it. The Scottish bishops (bishops having been re-introduced in Scotland by Charles I) had isolated themselves by their refusal to transfer their personal oath of allegiance from James VII (i.e. James II of England) to William III in 1689, forcing the new king to opt for presbyterianism in the Church of Scotland. The Scottish Episcopal Church thus came into distinct existence as a separate minority from the now-presbyterian established Church of Scotland. The Scottish Episcopal Church had the distinctive experience of being repressed, as a pro-French fifth column, by a British Government which used English troops for the purpose, and introduced Church of England worship (according to the English Book of Common Prayer, and conducted by English clergy) into Scotland. The underground Episcopal Church learned to value and to advocate 'a free, pure, ecclesiastical episcopacy,' appointed not by the Crown but by the Church, not supported by the state with either finance or temporal power (e.g. membership of the House of Lords), and not answerable to the state for the exercise of their ministry to the Church.

When 'The Thirteen United States of America' were recognized as independent by the Treaty of 1783, it became a matter of urgency for American Anglicans to have bishops of their own, rather than continue to be under the jurisdiction of the Bishop of London. They chose Dr Samuel Seabury and sent him to England for consecration, but the English bishops spent months discussing the form in which the act could legally be done. The Americans turned, therefore, to the Scottish Episcopal Church, whose understanding of episcopacy was more akin to their own, and whose liturgy they were willing to adopt as preferable to the English rite. The consecration of Seabury in Aberdeen on 14 November 1784 is an event the significance of which has increased, not only for the Scottish Episcopal Church, but for the whole Anglican Communion.

Toleration for the Scottish Episcopal Church came only when it was regarded as in no sense a threat to the political establishment. The Episcopal Church was suspected by the British government of being sympathetic to the Jacobite movement — that is to the successors of James II (James VII of Scotland) in opposition to the Protestant Succession of the Houses of Orange and Hanover. It was only with the death of Bonnie Prince Charlie in Rome (1788) leaving no successors, and only a brother, the celibate Henry, Cardinal, Duke of York, that the Jacobite movement left the realm of practical politics and entered that of romantic nostalgia. An Act of Toleration in 1792 offered relief to the Scottish Episcopalians, who in 1804, by the Declaration of Laurence-kirk, affirmed their agreement in doctrine with the Church of England, and reconciliation with the Qualified Chapels (that is, the legally imposed Church of England chaplaincies) proceeded apace.

Ordination

At the Reformation, the Scottish Church, in its anxiety to eschew all practices that were infected by superstition, spoke not of ordination, but of the 'inauguration' of ministers, and at first avoided using the imposition of hands. The imposition of hands was reintroduced in the second *Book of Discipline*, but may have taken many years to become general. It is now the valued and invariable practice of both the Episcopal Church (Anglican) and the Church of Scotland (Reformed).

What Ordinal was used in Scotland after the Reformation? The outlines were given in chapter IV (3) of the first *Book of Discipline* and, for a superintendent, V (3), and the details are carefully worked out by the Reverend Dr Duncan Shaw.[4] The initial provisions were replaced by the second *Book of Discipline*, passed by the General Assemblies of 1581, 1590 and 1591 and approved by Parliament in 1592. In 1610 the General Assembly laid down the rule of ordination by the Bishop. Although 1620 saw the publication of the 'Forme and Manner of Ordaining Ministers and Consecrating of Archbishops and Bishops, used in the Church of Scotland', that rite was not uniformly adhered to, being rivalled by both the 1560 *Book of Common Order* and the English Ordinal.

---

[4] D.Shaw, 'The Inauguration of Ministers in Scotland, 1560 to 1620', *Records of the Scottish Church History Society*, xvi (1966), 35-52.

One who was troubled in conscience about the lack of provision for ordination to a distinct diaconate was James Gordon, who became a Roman Catholic and a bishop in that church, succeeding Thomas Nicolson as (Roman Catholic) vicar apostolic in Scotland in 1718.

Nevertheless, the Scottish Episcopal Church has continued to witness to the historic episcopate as a gift of God for his whole Church, a gift we cannot renounce for the sake of unity, but must continue for the sake of unity. It has therefore been a development warmly welcomed by the Episcopal Church that a working party of the Multilateral Church Conversation in Scotland (which includes the Church of Scotland, the United Free Church of Scotland, the United Reformed Church, the Methodist Synod in Scotland, Congregational Union of Scotland and the Scottish Episcopal Church) has made a study of the subject and has recommended the adoption of the historic episcopate for a united Scottish Church. A technical problem for uniting episcopal and non-episcopal Churches is how the existing ordained ministries are related to the ordained ministry of the united Church in this connection. The Episcopal Church has drawn attention to the significantly different procedure adopted on the two occasions in the seventeenth century when the historic episcopacy was restored in Scotland.

> The three Scottish Bishops who went to Westminster for consecration on 21 October, 1610, were not required to accept Anglican ordination as Deacons and Priests as a preliminary step, and no English Archbishop took part in the rite, to make it clear that all was conferred was spiritual status, in no sense involving subordination to England.[5]

In 1662

> as only one of the pre-Covenant (i.e. pre-Civil War and Commonwealth) bishops survived, recourse was again had to England for consecration, and this time two of the four candidates, who had not been episcopally ordained, were required to accept ordination as Deacons and Priests before their consecration, but within Scotland ordination to the Diaconate was rare, and there was no general or compulsory re-ordination of men in presbyterian orders...[6]

The arguments presented in *The Porvoo Common Statement* help to put Anglican scruples into perspective, to take seriously the reformers'

---

[5] G.Donaldson, *Scotland: James V to James VII* (Edinburgh, 1965), p.206.

[6] *Ibid.*, p.364.

intention to 'restore the face of the Kirk among us', and to show how desirable it is that the Church of Christ should exhibit clearly the signs of continuing in the Apostles' doctrine and fellowship the breaking of bread and the prayers (Acts 2. 42).

ROBERT HALLIDAY

IRELAND

Little is known concerning the small and fragmented Christian Church which existed in Ireland prior to the major evangelistic movement associated with St Patrick in the fifth century. Patrick himself was both a bishop and a product of the (albeit declining) Romano-British civilization. The church he envisaged for Ireland was clearly to be a church organized on a diocesan basis with a monarchical-style episcopate rather similar to that which had emerged in the cities of Western Europe.

The very nature of Irish society, however, confounded Patrick's dream within a generation. Ireland had never been part of the Empire and was a society totally devoid of town life. The Irish Church developed as a distinctive monastic church rather in the Eastern tradition, with the abbot — although not necessarily in episcopal orders — as the primary source of ecclesiastical jurisdiction and the monasteries as the sole sources of pastoral care for those who lived around them. This monastic church of the Irish 'golden age' was famous for its manuscripts, its biblical scholarship and its contribution to the re-evangelization of Europe following the collapse of the Empire. Famous Irish monks in their travels in Europe frequently fell foul of diocesan bishops with whose jurisdiction they were not used to reckoning. At home the Church remained virtually isolated in its distinctiveness. Bishops were part of the personnel of most monasteries and were given their proper place within the liturgy. They perhaps had a special role too in relation to the preservation of good order and sound doctrine. The only time a question was officially posed by the Irish Church to Rome — in the mid-seventh century, concerning the dating of Easter — it seems to have been bishops who took the initiative.

The Viking invasions, which began in 795, were followed by a period when the invaders from Scandinavia settled down and founded urban trading centres on the coast. It was the descendants of the Vikings who were the founders of cities such as Dublin and Waterford in the tenth century. These city 'states' also became the first Irish dioceses and, cut off as they were from the rest of Irish society, their bishops looked for consecration to their trading partners across the sea and in particular to Canterbury. Doubts were expressed as to the regularity of consecrations in the monastic Irish Church, which, it was alleged, were carried out by one bishop only, rather than by the customary three or more.

In the late eleventh and twelfth centuries, Continental influences began to have their impact on the Irish Church as a whole. The papacy of Gregory VII (Hildebrand, 1073-85) began to take an active interest in this remote corner of the Celtic world, and through his correspondence with influential figures in Ireland Gregory broke a papal silence *vis-à-vis* the country, which had continued since the Easter controversy. Developing trading contacts with Europe were meanwhile making the Irish Church seem strangely idiosyncratic. Several of the Irish petty kings were anxious to enhance their kingship by being perceived as enthusiastic church reformers and reorganizers. It was such kings who were largely responsible for the arrival of continental religious orders, in particular the Cistercians, in Ireland around this time.

It was in this atmosphere that a number of synods were held, most notably that convened at Rathbreasail in 1111. Present at this synod was a papal legate, Gilbert, the author of a tract, *De Statu Ecclesie*, concerning methods of church organization. A diocesan system was adopted, with two metropolitan sees, Cashel, seat of the dominant O'Brien kings, in the South and Armagh in the North. The supposed claims of the latter to associations with St Patrick had been well publicized over the years by the secular overlords of the area, who sought thereby to strengthen their political position. The Norse sees were ignored in this scheme but at a further synod in Kells in 1152 they too were absorbed into the Irish system, with Dublin becoming a metropolitan see and Tuam in the west, in the area controlled by the now dominant O'Connor kings, becoming a fourth such see at the same time. Controversy was to rage throughout the middle ages, especially between the Archbishops of Armagh and Dublin, as to who was the overall primate. Eventually, following the precedent of Canterbury and York, the Archbishop of Armagh became accepted as 'Primate of All Ireland' and the Archbishop of Dublin as 'Primate of Ireland'.

It is hard to know just how effective the reforms of these synods were prior to the arrival of the Normans in Ireland in the 1160s and 1170s. Certainly the new cathedral chapters found it difficult to displace the monastic centres and there is no evidence at all of parochial development before the new wave of invaders arrived. The reasons which brought Henry II and the Normans to Ireland were complex in the extreme and related more to the expansionist ambitions of the Cambro-Norman barons than to any ecclesiastical considerations, although Henry chose to interpret his motives to the pope as a pious effort to reform effectively the Church in Ireland in reparation for the murder of Archbishop Thomas Becket. At a synod in Cashel soon after the invasion, it was decreed that the Church in Ireland should be organized in every way — liturgically, administratively and otherwise — on the lines of the English Church.

For a time the conquest seemed almost completely effective, with bishops approved by the royal administration being elected by the diocesan chapters, but the so-called Gaelic revival of the fourteenth century was to reduce English influence for the rest of the middle ages largely to the east of the island. The inevitable divisions within the Church should, however, not be overemphasized on a pastoral level. The usually English Archbishops of Armagh, for example, had no difficulty in being recognized as the successors to Patrick in the Gaelic areas of their province, or in holding visitations in the Gaelic suffragan sees. By the end of the middle ages, with the growth of direct papal influence in ecclesiastical appointments, the bishops of the area controlled by the Dublin government (called the Pale) were usually appointed by the papacy taking heed of royal influence at Rome, whereas the bishops of the Gaelic sees tended to come from local grandee families who had the resources to make their voices heard at the curia. The chaotic nature of the post-schism fifteenth-century papal bureaucracy, combined with the large number of obscure bishoprics in Ireland (the country as a whole contained no less than 36 bishoprics), meant that it was quite common for the papacy to appoint members of two rival families to the same see, apparently quite unaware of the inconsistency of its actions. Furthermore, the titles of small, virtually unworkable, Irish sees were used by ambitious English clergy, who had no intention at all of going to Ireland, as the means of obtaining coveted episcopal appointments. For example, between 1431 and 1433 no less than four 'Bishops of Dromore' were operating as suffragans in England, each having convinced the curia that their diocese was '*in partibus infidelium*'! Efforts to reduce the number of Irish dioceses, particularly by the royal government during the reign of Edward II (1307-27), had all come to naught. The result was a proliferation of sees in the area *inter Hibernicos*, where a form of hereditary episcopal succession within the ruling lineages tended to emerge and where celibacy was almost never observed. The bishops of the Pale, on the other hand, were often officials in the civil administration, attending Parliament and acting as royal advisers on Irish affairs.

One must not, however, take too negative a view of the late medieval Irish Church. The Gaelic bishops did not act in a manner that caused offence in their particular cultural context, and their support of the observant movement in the fifteenth-century mendicant orders caused a real spiritual revival in many areas. In the towns, chantries and collegiate churches offered much evidence of lay piety. Surviving evidence of fifteenth-century provincial synods shows a church by no means unconscious of its continuing duty to reform itself. Upon this church in the sixteenth century came two entirely unanticipated crises — the beginning of the Reformation under Henry VIII and the beginning of the efforts by the Tudor monarchs and their successors to reconquer the whole island and in due course to plant many areas of it with English settlers. Some of these plantations were conspicuously unsuccessful, but the plantation of Ulster in the seventeenth century by English and Scottish settlers was to give that part of Ireland the substantially protestant population which it still has.

As in England, the Tudor Reformation was an act of state, implemented by parliamentary legislation. It took many years before, for example, the last of the monasteries in remote areas were dissolved, but amongst the bishops, opposition to the various changes was minimized by a combination of pragmatism and personal convenience. Nearly all of the existing bishops in 1536 quietly accepted such limited changes as were inevitable and stayed in their sees. The episcopal succession continued uninterrupted — independently, it is worth noting, of the succession in England. Although a few enthusiastic protestants were imported into the Irish episcopate in subsequent years and the Book of Common Prayer was introduced into the Church in 1551, acquiescence seemed to be the attitude of the bulk of the Irish bishops as far as the political-cum-ecclesiastical pendulum-swings of the period were concerned. This applied both to Queen Mary's attempt to restore the authority of the papacy and to Elizabeth's eventual ecclesiastical settlement, which was accepted by all but two bishops.

The reasons why the bulk of the Irish population did not, however, adopt protestantism, but rather came to look to Rome for alternative structures of pastoral care, remain hotly contested. By the seventeenth century it was, however, becoming clear that Roman Catholicism was in some way identifiable with an anti-English embryonic nationalism. The reformers had failed to make effective use of the Irish language in their efforts — the Prayer Book had not appeared in Irish until 1608 and it was only through the labours of William Bedell (Bishop of Kilmore from 1629) that the first complete translation of the Bible in Irish was produced. The forces of the Counter-Reformation, particularly as expressed through the religious orders with which the Irish had an apparently natural affinity, were strong. The blood of the Roman Catholic martyrs accused by the government of treason also had its impact. But, perhaps above all, the early seventeenth-century reformed Church of Ireland became satisfied, except it seems in heavily-planted areas of Ulster, to regard itself as a church strengthening the position of a minority colonial elite, a church of civilized people as opposed to the almost barbarian masses who were thought to be scarcely worthy to be offered the civilities of protestantism. Even very much later on, the small farmers and the working classes, although never entirely absent, were sadly few in number within Church of Ireland life in the south.

Episcopacy itself had never been a theological issue at the Reformation or indeed during the early decades of the seventeenth century just portrayed, any more than had been the case in England. However, the temporary persecution of the Church of Ireland in the Cromwellian period was to lead apologists such as Bishop Jeremy Taylor to ponder the virtue of episcopacy as an essential to the Church's wellbeing and as a component of a comprehensive and peaceable church polity very different from that of the Puritans. After the turbulence of previous centuries, the restoration of episcopacy in the 1660s seemed to mark the beginning of a period of stability and confidence for the Church of Ireland. The Puritans, and indeed the narrowly Calvinistic strain within the Church itself, had both been overcome. On the other hand, the previously highly erratic efforts of the Papacy to re-establish the Roman Catholic hierarchy were beginning to achieve success. Hitherto, persecuted bishops had left their charges in the care of vicars-general, and during much of the Cromwellian period only one Roman Catholic bishop had remained in Ireland. However, a brave — indeed unique— attempt was gradually made to put in place a full hierarchy whose members were entirely without temporalities.

The eighteenth century was the period of the so-called 'protestant nation' in Ireland. The bishops, appointed of course by the Crown, sat in a Parliament in Dublin which was coming to see a substantial measure of political separation from England as being expedient for Ireland. The Penal Laws kept the majority religious community very much in its place, with restrictions on education, worship, ministry, land inheritance and participation in local government. Some of these laws seemed to exist more to be, as it were, officially broken than to be upheld, but nevertheless they represented a constant source of friction. For the Anglo-Irish, this was a period of confident cultural achievement — the age of Berkeley and Burke. All was shattered with the Act of Union in 1800, when the English government, exploiting the corruption of the Irish Parliament itself, acted to put an end to any drift towards separatism. The Irish Parliament was abolished and Irish bishops became members of the Westminster House of Lords. The Church of Ireland and the Church of England became, for the ensuing seventy years, one united church.

During the nineteenth century the rise of liberalism in particular made the position of the established Irish Church seem untenable. Already in 1833 Parliament had acted to downgrade the metropolitan sees of Tuam and Cashel to ordinary bishoprics and to reduce the total number of bishops to twelve, which remains the present figure. Previously, the number of Irish bishops and the idleness of some of them had been a cause of scandal, and Irish sees had been used as sources of income for friends of the government who continued to live in England. The 1833 act of perceived Erastianism, of the Church's spiritual mission being legislated for by parliamentary decision, actually provoked Keble's Assize Sermon at Oxford which is generally held to have begun the

Oxford Movement. Demands for disestablishment grew louder, particularly in the aftermath of Roman Catholic Emancipation in 1829, and the wealth of the Irish bishops, the pastors of a small minority of the population, became a favoured target. W. E. Gladstone, himself a loyal Anglican churchman, favoured complete disestablishment and disendowment at a stroke rather than the endless legal erosion of the position of a church that still remained in theory shackled to the state. Disestablishment, for him, would not only end a great public wrong, it would liberate the Irish clergy from a false position and open a freer path for the exercise of their real ministry.

Disestablishment came into effect on 1 January 1871, despite the vehement opposition of the Irish bishops in the House of Lords to the principle involved. Lay members of the Church rallied bravely to the cause of financial reconstruction, but theologically the blow fell at a most inopportune time. The evangelical movement had been strong in Ireland — in Ulster in particular — and in the early synods of the disestablished Church there was a considerable determination among the lay members to ensure that all possible steps were taken to ensure that the Irish Church did not go the Romeward way of several of the leading Tractarians. Hence a regime of canons, only moderated in recent years, was imposed upon the worship of the Church to stress its emphatically protestant character. The bishops of the *Ancien Régime* faced an almost vulgar hostility in the early synods, for the sympathy of some of them with the Tractarians was well known. For a while the threefold ministry and the Ordinal seemed in danger. In the end, however, moderate counsels prevailed, a minimalist approach was taken to Prayer Book revision and the Church resolved to maintain communion with the sister Church of England and therefore with the rest of what was emerging as the Anglican Communion throughout the world.

The bishops, under the new system, became a separate House in the new General Synod. (They rarely, however, sit alone when the whole Synod is in session.) Changes touching the formularies or doctrines of the Church would in future require the consent of two-thirds majorities of laity and clergy voting seperately. If a particular measure was passed by laity and clergy in one Synod but was rejected by a majority of the bishops, that measure could be introduced again at the next General

Synod, and if passed again by laity and clergy, it could only be vetoed by the bishops if two-thirds of them opposed the measure and gave their reasons in writing. This thorny question of the episcopal veto, and therefore of the relationship of the bishops to the new synodical structure in matters of doctrine, was extremely contentious in the 1870s, but in fact the veto has never been exercised and the House of Bishops rarely even actually votes as a separate House in the General Synod. The Church of Ireland, despite early tensions and subsequent political divisions in Ireland, has shown a remarkable tendency to obey its own rules and to display consensus. This is seen, not just in the widely-accepted continuing work of liturgical revision in recent years, but most notably in the remarkably pacific acceptance, by substantial majorities, of the opening of the priesthood and the episcopate itself to women in 1990.

In the immediate aftermath of Disestablishment, bishops, including the Archbishop of Dublin, were elected by diocesan synods comprising the clergy and representatives of the people of the vacant see. (Only the Archbishop of Armagh was to be elected by the bishops from amongst their own number.) This system became perceived as unsatisfactory, as it failed to represent the interests of the wider Church in the selection of its bishops and tended to favour a cautiously predictable pattern of clerical advancement within individual dioceses. At present, bishops are selected by an electoral college system that has evolved through various forms. Lay and clerical representatives of the vacant diocese are joined by representatives of the other dioceses within the province (Armagh or Dublin). The election is presided over by the metropolitan, and representatives of the House of Bishops also participate. If the college is unable to agree on a candidate who has the support of two-thirds of both clerical and lay electors, the election lapses to the House of Bishops — an eventuality that occurs from time to time. The Archbishop of Armagh remains the choice of the bishops.

Political changes since Disestablishment have had little or no impact on the organization of the Irish Church. Dioceses, even individual parishes, straddle the political border. The independence from Britain of all but six north-eastern countries in 1922 resulted in the partition of the country, and the majority of members of the Church of Ireland now live in Northern Ireland. On the other hand, church administration remains centred on Dublin, and seven of the twelve bishops live in the Republic, seeing to the needs of dioceses that tend, especially in the south and west, to be geographically large because sparsely populated.

For various reasons, the Church of Ireland population in the South dropped significantly after Partition, partly because of the departure of British troops and civil servants and their dependents. Decline seems at present to have levelled off, and in a more favourable ecumenical climate the contribution of the small Anglican community and its episcopal leaders to the national life and to Christian witness is highly appreciated, notwithstanding the fact — often remarked upon by visitors to Ireland — that this tiny minority still remains virtually the exclusive user of all the ancient cathedrals and Christian sites. Severance from Britain, which in the 1920s was a difficult step for many southern protestants to take, has been entirely accepted, and the Church of Ireland, which in fact nurtured many of the early patriots as well as the authors of the attempted revival of the Irish language in the late nineteenth century, has been encouraged to stress its Irishness anew. In Northern Ireland most members of the Church would tend to adopt a Unionist position and the role of the bishops in fostering reconciliation and hope in a society still torn by sectarian and terrorist violence is inevitably a difficult one. It is notable that the House of Bishops, despite its essential unity, reflects in its own personnel the differences of political outlook which some would say enrich the contemporary Church.

What then is distinctive about the practice of episcopacy in Ireland as a result of our particular history? First of all, given the size of the Church, there are still quite a lot of bishops. It is possible for bishops to visit the parishes of their diocese frequently, and to be accessible Fathers-in-God to their clergy. The Church has never found it necessary to resort to suffragan/assistant bishops and all bishops in active service are diocesans.

Secondly, when compared, for example, with their colleagues in the Church of England, the Irish bishops have had considerable experience of being 'bishops in synod'. They have at times been rebuffed by the Synod when their guidance on a moral issue was not accepted, and they have learned what it means to be politely criticized. Nevertheless, the fact remains that the bishops have learned to behave constitutionally almost by instinct and that the General Synod is a place where the mind of the Church is fairly readily discerned rather than the divisions of the Church exposed. So it is that the power of the bishops to defend, as it were, the faith over against the Synod, although thought necessary in the 1870s, has never needed to be used. Perhaps the greatest tribute one could pay in this context to the influence and leadership style of the Irish bishops is that they have tended to demonstrate the truth of the assertion that a leader is at his best when people barely know that he exists.

MICHAEL BURROWS

ORDERS AND ORDINATION

Denmark, Norway and Iceland: A Historical Study

It was once widely believed by those concerned about episcopal fellowship and the historic episcopate that at the Reformation in the sixteenth century the Church in Sweden retained the historic episcopate in bishop and see, whereas the Church in Denmark lost it. This opinion is still encountered today. Put rather baldly, it is claimed that Sweden, like the Church of England, has retained the historic episcopate, but in Denmark the succession was clearly interrupted in the Reformation of the sixteenth century; therefore Danish bishops stand neither in the same succession nor in the same episcopal fellowship as those of Sweden and the Anglican Communion. This judgement, of course, has had understandable consequences. Can a Danish pastor be invited to celebrate at an Anglican altar? Should Anglicans communicate at Danish or Norwegian or even Icelandic Lutheran altars (since both Iceland and Norway depended historically on Denmark for the derivation of their post-Reformation church order)? For some Anglicans the answer is decidedly No, since the lack of succession in the Lutheran churches of Denmark, Norway and Iceland puts the churches of those countries outside the fellowship of those churches linked by the communion of their bishops with one another and casts doubt on the validity and regularity of their ordained ministry.

Since 1951, this particular piece of historical judgement has been subjected to closer scrutiny.[1] According to these further researches, at the beginning of the sixteenth century there were seven sees (dioceses) on Danish territory, including the archiepiscopal see of Lund (now Swedish). Like other medieval prelates, the Danish bishops were wealthy landowners, and powerful both locally and in the government of the country. They were also unpopular. Already, in the reign of Christian II, the king (suitably advised) had proposed a reform of a much disliked episcopal college. In the Law Books of 1522 he urged that all ecclesiastical cases should be tried in Roskilde and not sent to Rome, and that

---

[1] Cf. especially 'Anglo-Scandinavian Conversations, Oslo, March 1951: notes submitted by the Danish Delegation concerning the Danish Church', compiled by F.R.Stevenson (unpublished typescript).

the bishops' courts should deal only with matrimony and adultery. He recommended further that the clergy should no longer be able to inherit land (unless they chose to marry); that the bishops themselves should not be absent on great feasts, should preach and instruct their people, and should not parade around the streets accompanied by a band of pipes and drums. They should arrange for the people of town and village to be taught the Lord's Prayer, the Creed and the *Ave Maria* in Danish. The spirit of reform was clearly biting, and the butt of much criticism was the episcopate.

It is not clear how influential Christian II's proposals were. Some say that they scarcely moved anyone. One recommendation, however, did endure, and that was an ever growing determination to avoid all appeals to Rome. This was the beginning of a break with the papacy, and the final separation from Rome was not far away. It did not need a divorce or a crisis. The pope (Leo X) had met his Waterloo when Church and state unanimously refused to allow a North Italian Cardinal to be enthroned as Archbishop of Lund. As A.J.Mason writes, 'This daring act of Leo's, more than anything else, caused the eventual loss of Denmark to the Papacy'.[2] Christian II having fled from the country, his successor Frederick I abolished the episcopal court of Roskilde altogether, together with the whole of Christian II's legislation, and simply ordained that Rome would no longer be involved in episcopal appointments in Denmark.

But in severing from Rome, other problems emerged. The first concerned the archiepiscopal see of Lund. Disagreements between king, canons and pope led to the appointment (after a six-year interregnum) of a presbyter who was never consecrated bishop. This was to recur elsewhere. In 1530

> presbyters took office as bishops of Fyn and Roskilde, thus leaving only five consecrated bishops occupying their sees... By 1535 only three remained... Of these, Bille and Munk were heavily involved in the 'Counts' Feud' of 1534-36 and in 1536 lost their liberty as civil rebels and were deprived of office. Only Ahlefeldt remained, and his see was not properly part of the Danish kingdom but lay in the duchy of Slesvig-Holsten. *Thus for some years before the Bugenhagen ceremony the Danish presbyterate had been virtually the only active ministry within the kingdom.*[3]

---

[2] A.J.Mason, 'The Loss of the Succession in Denmark', *Church Quarterly Review*, xxxii (1891), 149-187, p.156.

[3] 'Anglo-Scandinavian Conversations...' (see n.1 above), pp.1-2 (italics added).

This did not augur well for the future of the episcopate. Still more uncomfortable was the situation created in 1526 when Frederick allowed Lutheran preachers to ply their trade freely in the country. Four years later, they had established a considerable presence. In 1530, inspired by the popularity of the Lutheran advance, a leading Lutheran preacher, Peder Laurensen, drew up what became known as the Copenhagen Confession (similar in style to the Augsburg Confession), a statement of Reformation principles. The bishops returned a broadside. It was to be their last stand.

Frederick died in 1533. It fell to the government to elect a successor, as the royal family did not have a right of succession. The nobles and the bishops dithered, and Christian II marshalled his mercenaries in an attempt to return. Civil war broke out. Frederick's son, also called Christian, commanded considerable support in Jutland and eventually succeeded in putting down the uprising. He was named king and took office as Christian III. At a meeting of the *Rigsdag* in 1536, the bishops were again in the dock. It was complained that they had failed to elect a king quickly enough, that they had dithered when the rebellion was at its height, that they had divided the estates of the Crown among themselves and their friends, that no one knew who was the Archbishop of Lund, as so many had claimed the see for themselves, and that if anyone criticized them (the bishops), it was always the complainer who came off worst. But the main accusation, as E.H.Dunkley writes, was that 'when the throne was vacant they had postponed the election of a King and thereby plunged the country into civil war'. This, Dunkley believes, was substantially true.[4]

Denmark, then, looked set to lose its bishops, at least that particular group. On his election, Christian III lost no time in bringing about a change. All seven bishops were deposed and imprisoned. A new order was drawn up (the *Kirkeordinans* of 1537, finally ratified in 1539), which in many respects was very conservative. The orders of bishop and presbyter were retained, with a prescribed form for the consecration of bishops. The order also preserved cathedral chapters and religious houses, on condition that the canons, monks and nuns submitted to Lutheran theological education. Communion in both kinds was introduced, but vestments were retained as in the past.

---

[4] E.H.Dunkley, *The Reformation in Denmark* (London, 1948), p.74.

But the order had to be implemented, and it was with this intent that Christian III invited Dr Bugenhagen, a man in priest's orders but exercising a superintendent ministry in the reformed church in Wittenberg, to 'apply' the (as yet incomplete) *Kirkeordinans*.[5] Bugenhagen accordingly crowned the king and his consort and then 'ordained' seven superintendents to fill the seven vacant sees in Denmark and one to fill a vacancy in Norway. On the one hand, this marked a new beginning for the Danish Church, a break with the miseries and corruptions of the past; but, as A.J.Mason observes, this was not 'a case of deliberate preference for presbyterian ordination, as in some countries'. 'The men now set apart or almost all of them were already presbyters, and they were to be made *something more*, and for the future to have sole authority to ordain.'[6] Bearing in mind, then, that it was intended that these should be superintendents or bishops and that the order of bishop was foundational to the 1539 church order, we have to look once more at the charge that Bugenhagen, in priest's orders, had no authority to consecrate.

We have to remember first that Bugenhagen himself was exercising a superintendent style of ministry in the German Lutheran Church. H.Hering, in his study of Bugenhagen, relates that Electoral Saxony at the time needed two superintendents, one at Wittenberg, which was the seat of the University and the fountain of the new reforms, and the other in the town of Kemberg.[7] Bugenhagen was appointed to the first of these, an appointment which he held *in parallel* with that of being chief pastor of the church in Wittenberg. Hence there can be no doubt about the fact that Bugenhagen was much more than an ordinary pastor or parish priest, and the visitation which he carried out very shortly after his appointment shows him exercising a distinctly episcopal style of ministry.

---

[5] On the appointment of Bugenhagen as superintentendent, see H.Hering, *Doktor Pomeranus Bugenhagen* (Schriften des Vereins für Reformationsgeschichte, vol. vi, 1888, no. 22), p.94.

[6] A.J.Mason, *op.cit.*, p.186 (italics added).

[7] *Loc.cit.*: 'Die Ordnung suchte ferner einer Bedürfnis einer kirchlichen Aufsicht noch durch ein höheres Amt zu dienen. Zwei Ober-Superattendenzen wurden für die chursächsischen Lande eingerichtet, die eine in Wittenberg als dem Sitz der Universität..., die andere in Kemberg... Die erstere wurde Bugenhagen übertragen, und sollte überhaupt mit der Pfarre in Wittenberg als einer Metropolis der sächsischen Lande verbunden bleiben'.

The trouble with the term 'superintendent' is that in English it sounds like a civilian officer in a blue uniform, an official of the state, a bureaucrat, a man whose main task is to inspect and to control. In German, however, 'Superintendent' is simply a term for the man with a ministry of *episcope* an overseer, a *superintendens*. Bugenhagen himself considered the two terms as entirely interchangeable. On 21 November 1537 he wrote to Christian III, 'To comfort Your Majesty, I won't conceal from you the fact that God achieves much good by the instrument of his poor bishops or superintendents'.[8] It is also instructive to discover what a sixteenth-century Lutheran superintendent was supposed to be and do. In a number of church orders this office is carefully described. For example, in Albertine Saxony the superintendent is appointed with the approval of the local prince; he must be both learned and godly; and his prime ministry is to the clergy, whom he must visit, instruct, warn and admonish, correct when necessary, and help in any way he can. He must not be so young that they cannot respect him, but be a man of experience who will be ready to be called out when needed, will listen to sermons, and advise and contribute wherever he can. He has a special care for those preparing to be ordained; he must also be particularly solicitous for the widows of the clergy, seeing them into proper care before the appointment of a new pastor.

Such a ministry is essentially episcopal. It is certainly not that of a parish priest or pastor. Nor is the theology behind this that every minister is bishop in his own parish. Very early on in the German Reformation it was discovered that a ministry of unity and pastoral care of the clergy was essential if the Church was to survive. Hence the appointment of superintendents. One major theological difference from the medieval understanding of the historic episcopate was that Lutherans seem to have believed the superintendent ministry of *episcope* to have emerged from the presbyteral order, instead of seeing the presbyterate as a development from the episcopate. So, for example, in the church order of Joachim II, Margrave of Brandenburg, in 1540, it is expressly declared (quoting St Jerome) that in the primitive Church, bishop and presbyter

---

[8] 'Ich wil E.M. zu troste nicht verbergen das Got durch seine arme Bischofe oder Superintendenten viel guts ausrichtet' (Letter to Christian III, 21 Nov 1537 in *Dr Johannes Bugenhagens Briefwechsel*, ed. O.Vogt (reprint Hildesheim, 1966), p.156.

were alternative titles for the same office; that presbyters ordained their successors (*vide* the Pastoral Epistles — the laying on of hands of the presbytery), and that for the sake of unity and good order certain presbyters had to be raised to superintendent status. It remains true, however, that whatever the appeal to history, in practice the Church of Denmark remained very traditional. The consecrations by Bugenhagen were considered *extraordinary but valid*; and ever thereafter only bishops consecrated, only bishops ordained.

Let us then stand back for a moment and look at what happened in Denmark. Political and social upheavals trapped the existing episcopate in the death rattle of an expiring world. They could not survive, either as individuals or as a credible spiritual leadership. They were voted out, discredited, badly treated. But martyrdom was a title that would not stick; there was no John Fisher among them. Three were not bishops at all; the remaining four had lost all credibility. The choice before the newly elected king was either to restore the episcopate, choosing new men in collaboration with the rest of the European Church, or to go for the new presbyterian order which flourished at Geneva and in Zurich. As it happened, there was a third choice, namely to look to Germany rather than to Switzerland. Christian III had been formerly prince of Schleswig and closely associated with Wittenberg. Hence he was in a position both to understand and to adopt a reformed and essentially pastoral style of oversight, free from the trammels of property and state office, free also from the interference of non-Danish-speaking delegates from Rome. Such was the Lutheran pattern of superintendent minister — a bishop 'by any other name', a bishop in task and in calling, a bishop in the understanding of those who appointed him. Appointed he certainly was, solemnly with the laying on of hands. Questionings there may have been about the *successio personalis*. But the appointment of men with the task of the care of all the churches to the ancient historic sees, the concern that they should teach and guard the faith once delivered to the saints and keep a close eye on the way in which the Christian faith was presented by pastor and people, makes them in a very real sense the inheritors, guardians and transmitters of the one apostolic faith. They actually visited the parishes (as is evidenced by the *Visitatsbog* of the first post-Reformation Bishop of Sealand), and saw to it that preaching was better done and that the people read the

Scriptures in Danish. They are today, when they meet together, the representatives and uniters of the clergy and people from the most far-flung islands to the civilization of the metropolis. Denmark has, therefore, a ministry which is genuinely episcopal, true to the apostolic faith, true to the whole concept of apostolic order. Further, it has to be remembered that the Danish succession has been continued unbroken since 1537, which in itself is a sure indication of intent to continue what always had been. It is on the basis of this continuity that Anglicans should now be able to move forward beyond the hesitations about episcopacy in the Danish, Norwegian and Icelandic Churches which characterized our earlier agreements.

Rites of Ordination
A study of the rites of ordination to the episcopate of the British and Irish Anglican churches and the Nordic and Baltic Lutheran churches shows the extent to which we have a common understanding of ministry and an intention to ordain to the same offices of ministry in the Church of God.[9] All our churches ordain to the episcopate and presbyterate and have a form of diaconate.[10] In Denmark and Sweden the second order is called 'priest'; in Norway, Estonia and Latvia the order is that of 'pastor'. In Finland church law and the rite of ordination use the word 'priest'; the more common usage is 'pastor'. The consecration (ordination) of bishops is, however, what most fundamentally concerns the dialogue between our churches. The following essential features emerge from a study of our churches' rites of ordination to the episcopate.

(i) *Context*
The consecration of bishops takes place

(a) within the eucharist— or usual Sunday service (Norway);

(b) in the cathedral of the diocese in which the new bishop is to serve (Finland, Norway, Denmark, Iceland, Wales, Ireland and Scotland) — or at Uppsala (Sweden) — or in the province to which the diocese belongs (England), and

---

9 I am more than grateful to the Nordic Ecumenical Institute at Uppsala for their diligence in supplying the Nordic and Baltic texts.

10 Cf. S.Platten and J.Halliburton, 'Deacons', below.

(c) is conducted by the archbishop of the province, presiding bishop, Bishop of Copenhagen as *primus inter pares* (Denmark); Primus of the Scottish Episcopal Church. The chief consecrating bishop is assisted by other bishops (England Wales, Ireland and Scotland and Sweden), by bishops and priests (Denmark); by assistants appointed by the presiding bishop (Norway, Finland, Estonia, Latvia).

(ii) *Service of the Word*
The liturgy of the word which precedes the liturgy of the sacrament varies from country to country.

(iii) *Presentation of the candidate and declaration that he has been elected*

Note the presence of a notary (lawyer) in the rites of England, Wales, Ireland, Finland, Sweden and Latvia. In England and in Ireland the candidate is presented by two bishops; in Denmark, the candidate is presented by the dean of the cathedral; in Norway by the chairman or vice-chairman of the diocesan council; in Scotland, by the dean of the diocese, a representative of the laity of the diocese and a member of the college of bishops.

(iv) *Sermon(s)*
In Sweden, Denmark, Finland and Norway, England, Wales, Ireland and Scotland the sermon (by the consecrating bishop or another) comes after the Scripture readings; in Estonia, the sermon comes at the very beginning. In Norway, Denmark and Estonia the new bishop also preaches after his consecration.

(v) *Scripture readings*
These are lessons dealing with commissioning, service, bishops, shepherding, priesthood, preaching and guiding, etc.

(vi) *Questioning of the candidate and declaration of his duties*
(a) The new bishop is called upon to confess his faith, saying the Nicene Creed (Finland and Norway) and the Apostles' Creed (Latvia) — as in the Eastern rites of ordination.

(b) The bishop is called upon to see to the preaching of the word and the administration of the sacraments, to preserve himself and his own household as an example, to build up the Church of God (all churches).

To preserve the apostolic faith (Norway); 'hold to sound doctrine' (Denmark); 'teaching the Christian faith and upholding catholic doctrine' (Scotland); to declare his 'belief in the faith which is revealed in the holy Scriptures and set forth in the catholic creeds' (England). To have oversight over the diocese (Sweden); to 'ordain and inspect, visit, take and give counsel, listen and make decisions' (Sweden). 'He shall... serve the oneness in Christ' (Sweden), 'you are to be the centre of unity' (Wales); 'be a supporter of priests and congregations in your diocese' (Denmark); 'banish error and keep good order in the Church' (Latvia). He is to be chief pastor and head of the Church... to preside over synods and consistories... to preside over choice and ordination of candidates (Estonia); to 'further the unity of the Church' (England); 'to ordain and send out new ministers' (Scotland and Ireland); 'You are to be the guardian of discipline in the Church' (Wales).

There is in fact a remarkable consistency in the portrait of a bishop's duties as set out in the rites of consecration.

(vii) *Veni Creator* — Denmark and Finland, England, Ireland, and Scotland: before consecration; Sweden afterwards. Others have space for hymns.

(viii) *Consecration*

(a) Vesting in cope and giving of episcopal insignia — (staff and ring) before the consecration in Denmark, Latvia and Finland, after the consecration in Sweden (where the mitre is also worn); in Scotland (vesting according to custom), in Ireland (vested with the episcopal habit) and in Wales (ring and pastoral staff). In Ireland, the new bishop is also given the Bible.

(b) Laying on of hands by presiding bishop or archbishop with other bishops, clergy and assistants.

(c) A prayer of consecration — a prayer to ask the grace of God for the candidate to do the work of a bishop, preaching, teaching, guiding, looking after the people and parishes in his diocese.

Note the belief expressed in some of these prayers that the pastoral office was given to the Church from the beginning (Finland), a ministry associated with the apostles (Norway and Denmark).

(ix) *Conclusion*

The Eucharist or main Sunday service continues.

4. Some Conclusions

(a) It is quite clear that the intention of these rites is to continue and ordain to the ministry of pastoral and spiritual oversight which from apostolic times has been the task of the bishop.

(b) The ordaining minister is a bishop; the candidate to be ordained is called bishop after his consecration.

(c) All the essential and traditional elements of a rite of ordination in the Western Church are present — Presentation of the Candidate, Examination of the Candidate, Prayer for the Holy Spirit, Laying on of Hands with Prayer by all bishops present and the Vesting of the new bishop in cope and with other insignia (pastoral staff, ring and mitre (in Sweden only)).

(d) The readings that may be chosen express what any episcopal church would want to say about the life and work of its bishops.

(e) The prayer of consecration also describes what any episcopal church would understand about the life and work of a bishop as chief pastor and guardian of the faith.

There seems therefore so much in common between Anglican and Lutheran understandings of episcopacy that we ought to be sharing more fully in one another's ecclesial and ministerial life.

JOHN HALLIBURTON

THE RITES OF ORDINATION
TO THE EPISCOPATE IN THE BRITISH, IRISH, NORDIC AND BALTIC CHURCHES

The 'job description' and the prayer accompanying the laying on of hands are reprinted below.

1. **Church of England (Alternative Service Book 1980)**

   A bishop is called to lead in serving and caring for the people of God and to work with them in the oversight of the Church. As a chief pastor he shares with his fellow bishops a special responsibility to maintain and further the unity of the Church, to uphold its discipline, and to guard its faith. He is to promote its mission throughout the world. It is his duty to watch over and pray for all those committed to his charge, and to teach and govern them after the example of the Apostles, speaking in the name of God and interpreting the gospel of Christ. He is to know his people and be known by them. He is to ordain and to send new ministers, guiding those who serve with him and enabling them to fulfil their ministry.

   He is to baptize and confirm, to preside at the Holy Communion and to lead the offering of prayer and praise. He is to be merciful, but with firmness, and to minister discipline, but with mercy. He is to have a special care for the outcast and needy; and to those who turn to God he is to declare the forgiveness of sins.

   The Prayer

   Send down the Holy Spirit upon your servant N for the office and work of a bishop in your Church.

   Almighty Father, fill this your servant with the grace and power which you gave to your apostles, that he may lead those committed to his charge in proclaiming the gospel of salvation. Through him increase your Church, renew its ministry, and unite its members in a holy fellowship of truth and love. Enable him as a true shepherd to feed and govern your flock; make him wise as a teacher, and steadfast as guardian of its faith and sacraments. Guide and direct him in presiding at the worship of your people. Give him humility, that he may use his authority to heal, not to hurt; to build up, not to destroy. Defend him from all evil, that as a ruler over your household and an ambassador for

Christ, he may stand before you blameless, and finally, with all your servants, enter your eternal joy.

Accept our prayers, most merciful Father, through your Son Jesus Christ our Lord, to whom, with you and your Holy Spirit, belong glory and honour, worship and praise, now and for ever. **Amen.**

2. Church of Ireland

Bishops are called to lead in serving and caring for the people of God and to work with them in the oversight of the Church. As chief pastors they share with their fellow bishops a special responsibility to maintain and further the unity of the Church, to uphold its discipline, to guard its faith and to promote its mission throughout the world. It is their duty to watch over and pray for all those committed to their charge, and to teach and govern them after the example of the Apostles, speaking in the name of God and interpreting the gospel of Christ. They are to know their people and be known by them. They are to ordain and to send new ministers, guiding those who serve with them and enabling them to fulfil their ministry.

They are to baptize and confirm, to preside at the Holy Communion and to lead the offering of prayer and praise. They are to be merciful, but with firmness, and to minister discipline, but with mercy. They are to have special care for the sick and for the outcast and needy; and to those who turn to God they are to declare the forgiveness of sins.

The Prayer

We praise and glorify you, almighty Father, because you have formed throughout the world a holy people for your own possession, a royal priesthood, a universal Church. We praise and glorify you because you have given us your only Son Jesus Christ to be the Apostle and High Priest of our faith, and the Shepherd of our souls. We praise and glorify you that by his death he has overcome death; and that, having ascended into heaven, he has given his gifts abundantly to your people, making some, apostles; some, prophets; some, evangelists; some, pastors and teachers; to equip them for the work of ministry and to build up his body. And now we give you thanks that you have called this your servant, to share this ministry entrusted to your Church.

Send down the Holy Spirit upon your servant... whom we consecrate in your name for the office and work of a bishop in your Church.

Almighty Father, fill this your servant with the grace and power which you gave to your apostles, to lead those committed to *his* charge in proclaiming the gospel of salvation. Through *him* increase your Church, renew its ministry and unite its members in a holy fellowship of truth and love.

Enable *him* as a true shepherd to feed and govern your flock, to be wise as a teacher and steadfast as a guardian of the faith and sacraments of your Church. Guide and direct *him* in presiding at the worship of your people. Give *him* humility, to use *his* authority to heal, not to hurt; to build up, not to destroy. Defend *him* from all evil, that as a ruler over your household and an ambassador for Christ *he* may stand before you blameless, and finally with all your servants enter your eternal joy.

Accept our prayers, most merciful Father through your Son Jesus Christ our Lord, to whom, with you and your Holy Spirit, belong glory and honour, worship and praise, now and for ever. **Amen.**

The newly-ordained bishop is vested with the episcopal habit. The Archbishop gives the Bible to the newly-ordained Bishop, and says

Receive this Book: here are words of eternal life. Take them for your guide, and declare them to the world.

Keep watch over the flock of which the Holy Spirit has appointed you shepherd.

Encourage the faithful, restore the lost, build up the body of Christ; that when the Chief Shepherd shall appear, you may receive the unfading crown of glory.

3. **Scottish Episcopal Church**

A bishop follows in the succession of the apostles whom Christ sent to proclaim the Gospel to the world and to bear authority in the community of faith. With his fellow bishops he oversees and cares for the universal Church. As one under authority he must be attentive to the Holy Spirit who leads us into all the truth; called into the fellowship of Christ's disciples, he must seek the Father's will.

Within his diocese, he ordains and sends out new ministers. He guides and serves the priests and deacons who share his responsibility to nurture the community of the baptised.

There is one Lord and Master, by whose authority a bishop must teach and enable others to bear their witness, so that God's Word may have free course to enlighten his people and heal the nations.

There is one Shepherd, at whose command a bishop must seek to know his flock and be known by them.

There is one great High Priest of the new covenant, in whose name a bishop presides over the church's offering and calls all to be of one mind and purpose, that in unity they may present to the Father a single, holy, living sacrifice.

The Prayer

God and Father of our Lord Jesus Christ, you call us in your mercy; you sustain us by your power. Through every generation, your Wisdom supplies our need. From the beginning you chose the people of Abraham, raised up rulers and priests, and never left the sanctuary of your covenant without its servants. In the fulness of time, you founded your Church by the word of your grace, choosing in Christ, before the world was made, those whose lives would proclaim your glory. You have chosen N. your servant to be a bishop in the Church.

The Primus and the other Bishops lay hands upon the Bishop-Elect.

Pour now upon him your power, the Spirit who leads and guides, the Spirit you gave through your beloved Son to the apostles to build the living sanctuary of the new covenant.

Grant N. authority to shepherd your flock; in the name of Christ the one High Priest to offer the gifts of your holy church; to forgive sins as you command, to order ministries as you direct, and by that power which you gave to your apostles, to loose the bonds of wickedness and to let the oppressed go free. Through Jesus Christ your Son our Lord with whom and in whom in the unity of the Holy Spirit, glory, honour and power are yours, now and for ever. **Amen.**

4. Church in Wales

A bishop is called to be a chief minister and pastor. You are to be the centre of unity, a teacher of the Faith and a guardian of discipline in the Church. You are to watch over the people committed to your charge, and, after the example of the chief Shepherd, to know the flock and to be known by them. You are to lead and guide the priests and deacons in your care, and to be faithful in ordaining and sending out new ministers. You are to proclaim the gospel of our Lord Jesus Christ, and to be the chief minister of the sacraments of the New Covenant. You are to confirm the baptised, and guide the people of God in the way of eternal life.

The Prayer

SEND DOWN THY HOLY SPIRIT UPON THY SERVANT N. FOR THE OFFICE AND
WORK OF A BISHOP IN THY CHURCH;

may he glorify thee in the midst of thy people, and offer spiritual
sacrifices acceptable unto thee. Give him grace to proclaim at all
times the good news of reconciliation; and to use the authority given
him, not to hurt and destroy, but to serve and to heal. Defend him
against the assaults of the devil, that as a ruler over thy household
and as an ambassador for Christ, he may stand before thee blameless,
and finally, with all thy servants, enter thy eternal joy; through Jesus
Christ our Lord, the chief Shepherd and great High Priest, who lives
and reigns with thee and the Holy Spirit, one God, world without
end. **Amen.**

The Archbishop gives the Bible to the new Bishop, saying:

Be a faithful steward of the Word of God and of his holy sacraments.
Guard the Faith, and exercise without reproach the high office and
ministry to which you have been called.

*The Archbishop then places the ring on his finger and presents the
pastoral staff, saying*:

Care for the flock of Christ; maintain the unity of the Faith; support
the weak; heal the sick; bind up the broken; encourage the faithful;
seek and restore the lost. Be merciful, but with firmness; minister
discipline, but with mercy; that when the chief Shepherd shall appear,
you may receive the unfading crown of glory.

5. **Church of Denmark**

You have now heard, how the Lord has instituted the ministry of the
word and through his apostles has witnessed to its necessity for his
Church on earth. As the Lord now entrusts you with this holy
ministry and furthermore charges you with the task of exercising
oversight in his church, it is his will that you shall be vigilant in your
calling and keep watch over yourself and the congregations which
are entrusted to you, that you walk faithfully in his sight as a dutiful
servant of the Lord, that you hold to the sound doctrine as found in
the prophetic and apostolic Scriptures and witnessed to in the
Confessional Writings of our Church, and in all respects take care to
exercise your ministry without deference to any person, but with
integrity to the glory of God's name and the edification of the
congregation. Be a supporter of the priests and congregations in your

diocese. Strengthen the weak, seek out the erring, be merciful without tolerating evil, rebuke without forgetting mercy. And when the world despise the Gospel, let it be your comfort that it is God's work you are doing and not your own, and that our Lord Jesus has promised to be with his Church always, even to the end of time, that his servants may cheerfully carry out their calling and finish the race set before them with joy.

The Prayer

Let us with all our hearts pray that God Himself may form you and make you fit for your ministry:

Lord our God, heavenly Father, we pray that you will acknowledge this your servant N. who is now entrusted with the ministry of a bishop in the diocese of N. Give him/her your Holy Spirit, that he/she may undertake his/her office to the glory of your name and may hold to your Holy Gospel preaching your Son, Jesus Christ, crucified and risen, as our only salvation. Strengthen him/her that he/she may faithfully exercise oversight over the congregations, guide the perplexed, comfort those who fear, teach and rebuke, and with the truth of the word of God resist all error, and let your Holy Gospel remain with us pure and untainted that we thereby may receive the blessed fruit of eternal life, through your Son, Jesus Christ our Lord.

6. Evangelical-Lutheran Church of Finland

Tend the flock of God that is your charge, not by constraint but willingly, not for shameful gain but eagerly, not as domineering over those in your charge, but being examples to the flock.

In the Finnish rite there is no 'job description' as such. First, the bishop-elect recites the Nicene Creed. Then he promises that he will see to it that 'the Gospel is truly preached, the sacraments administered according to Christ's institution and the congregations, cared for according to the order of our church'.

The actual consecration prayer is as follows:

By the authority vested in me by the Church of Christ, according to the will of God, I hereby consecrate you to the office of Bishop of the diocese of X, in the Name of the Father and of the Son and of the Holy Spirit. Amen.

Then follows the *Veni Creator*, during which the bishop is vested in cope, pectoral cross and crosier. Then a prayer as follows:

Holy Father, eternal God. We thank you and praise you for sending your Son, Jesus Christ, to be our Saviour, for founding your Church and instituting the pastoral office. We pray: Grant the gift of the Holy Spirit to your servant, X, who has now been consecrated to the office of Bishop. Stir up the gifts of grace which you have given to him. Grant that he may preach the Gospel clearly, and in everything edify your Church. Help him to be rooted in your Word and show himself to be your true servant in his teaching and life. Grant him the skill rightly to direct this diocese. Help him to support church workers and others in positions of responsibility. Grant him wisdom, patience, friendliness and humility. Bless this diocese. Grant us all eternal joy through Jesus Christ our Lord, who with you and the Holy Spirit lives and reigns eternally. Amen.

7. Evangelical-Lutheran Church of Iceland

Brother, you have heard the word of the Lord and his apostles. God wants everybody to be saved and to come to the knowledge of the truth. He has therefore instituted the service of his word and sent his Church to preach it. By his grace he has called you to this service and entrusts you now with a wider role in his Church as a shepherd. What he demands of you is faithfulness and vigilance in your calling and that you will build on the only foundation which is laid, the Lord Jesus Christ, that you take heed to yourself and all the flock with which you are being entrusted, that you abide in God's word as revealed in Holy Scripture and according to the witness of our Church in its confessions.

You are to lead your Church by meekness and firmness, defend it against heresy and strengthen it in the faith which it has been given once and for all. Be a good advising father to your fellow servants, support the weak and correct those who stray. Be merciful without tolerating evil, reprimand but do not forget clemency. And when you suffer because the world scorns the sound teaching, you shall remember with thanks that it is God's mission you have undertaken, not your own, and that our Lord Jesus Christ says: Fear not, I have overcome the world.

His is the work, his grace is sufficient for those who follow him and trust in him.

The Prayer

Almighty everlasting Father, accept in grace your servant N. Give him your Holy Spirit so he may fulfil his calling truthfully, to the glory of your holy name. Let him be true to your word and preach your Son crucified and risen as the only Saviour and Lord. Strengthen him to tend your congregations with care and watchfulness, teach, reprimand and guide with meekness, firmness and wisdom and seek only honour in being truthful to you and your holy will, for the blessing of your Church and for the salvation of your children.

For the sake of your son, Jesus Christ our Lord. Amen.

8. Church of Norway

You have heard the word of God concerning the duties of a bishop, the requirements and the promises of this office and how important it is for the church of God on earth. As the Lord (continues to)* entrust(s) you with the ministry of Word and Sacrament, and now gives you the duties of a bishop, he requires that you be self-disciplined and vigilant in your calling.

— You shall feed the Church of the Lord with the Bread of Life and take heed to yourself and to all the flock entrusted to your care.

— You shall preserve the apostolic teaching according to the confession of our Church, and guide and encourage the servants of the Lord in the congregation.

— You shall fulfil your duties faithfully, and with your fellow servants seek to promote and preserve the unity in God's church, to the praise and honour of his holy name.

_____, do you promise before God that you will do this with faithfulness according to the grace, God himself will give you.

* *The words 'continues to' shall be omitted when the one being consecrated has not previously been ordained.*

The Prayer

Almighty God, the Father of our Lord Jesus Christ, look in favour upon this your servant and consecrate him to his task. Grant him your Holy Spirit, so that he performs his duties to the upbuilding of your church and to the glory of your holy name. Strengthen him that he remain steadfast in your Word and rightly preach the Gospel of Jesus Christ. Grant him, in word and in deed, to be an example for those who believe in you.

Fill him with vigilant love, so that in faithfulness to you he looks after the congregations and those who serve them. Help him to show wisdom when he gives comfort and advice, when he teaches, gives encouragement and admonishes, so the holy gospel may be preserved in its purity and the unity of your church be promoted among us, through your Son, Jesus Christ, our Lord. Amen.

9. Church of Sweden

The church is God's people, Christ's body, a temple of living stones, Christ being the corner stone. In this people of God, where we are all called through baptism to bring the gospel to the whole world, the bishop has a special calling. A bishop shall have oversight over the diocese and its congregations. *He* is responsible for God's Word being preached in purity and clarity, for the sacraments being rightly administered, and for the works of charity being practised according to God's will. A bishop shall ordain and inspect, visit, take and give counsel, listen, make decisions and in all *his* work strengthen God's people in the task of discerning the signs of the time and of bearing witness to God's mighty acts for the whole creation. Holding the office of bishop, *he* shall live as a servant of Christ and shall be a shepherd for God's flock. With vigilance and wisdom, *he* shall serve the oneness in Christ toward the church's edification and renewal in the Spirit, so that the love of God becomes visible in the world. The calling of a bishop will now be entrusted to you. Meet people tenderly and with respect. Together with them, seek the way God wills and let it be your endeavour to let faith, doctrine and life become one.

The Prayer

... You choose among us servants for your gospel, that people may come to faith, the church be renewed and the creation restored. From you we receive *him* who now is being ordained a bishop.

The Archbishop and the assistants lay their hands on the head of the bishops elect:

O Lord, come to NN with your Holy Spirit, and take *him* into your service as bishop in your church.

O God we now beseech you

(The congregation joins in with the rest of the prayer)

Give this your bishop steadfastness in serving the gospel, faithfulness in wisdom and caring for your people. Give *him* the courage, strength and patience *he* will need, and keep *him*, O God, always close to you. May *he* live evermore deeply in faith, hope and love. Through Jesus

173

Christ our Lord, who lives and reigns with you and the Holy Spirit, one God, now and for ever. Amen.

(After the giving of the pectoral cross, cope and mitre and crosier, the Archbishop says:)

In apostolic manner by prayer and the laying on of hands in God's name, NN has been ordained a bishop. Receive *him* as an ambassador for Christ.

10. Estonian Evangelical-Lutheran Church
(Summary)

A special authority and responsibility has been passed down from the apostles upon the bishop to teach and lead the church, to administer discipline and to ensure that the gospel is purely preached and that proper order is maintained in the church.

The bishop is the chief pastor and head of the church. He regulates the ministry of the pastors and ensures that they are fulfilling their responsibilities and leading a life worthy of the gospel. He also serves as their pastor.

The bishop calls together the General Synod and presides over it. He also calls and presides over all meetings of the Consistory.

It is the bishop's responsibility to appoint, call together and preside over all commissions for examining ordination candidates, commissions for examining prospective church workers, and all other commissions of the church. He ordains pastors. He suggests candidates for dean and installs them. He calls and presides over all meetings of the deans.

The bishop executes or appoints someone to approve all budgets of the church and church organizations.

The Prayer

Holy Father, Everlasting God, we praise and glorify you that you have sent your Son, Jesus Christ, to free us, and have built your church and placed shepherds over it. We ask you, give the gift of your Holy Spirit to your servant N, who has been blessed into the office of archbishop. Kindle the gifts of grace that you have placed within him that he might purely preach the gospel and in all things build up your church. Help him to grow ever more deeply in your Word, that he may in teaching and life be an example of true faith. Give him discernment, that he might rightly lead the EELC. Help him to support all pastors and others in positions of leadership. Give him wisdom, patience, warmth and humility. Bless the EELC. Give us all everlasting joy through our Lord and Saviour Jesus Christ, who lives with you and the Holy Spirit, now and forever. Amen.

11. Evangelical Lutheran Church of Latvia

There is no 'job description' as such in the rite supplied. The archbishop-elect is led into the church and commanded to listen to the Scriptures which describe the work of a bishop. After which the ordaining archbishop says:

> May God grant you grace to keep these words firmly in your heart that they may be to you a guide to your life and at all times may remind you of the high responsibility of your office and may increase your zeal to serve our great Master Shepherd. The congregations which are entrusted to you expect that you will fulfil the important office of Archbishop, which we transmit to you today, as a true servant of Jesus Christ.

In the promises, the archbishop-elect is asked to hold fast the word of God, to banish all error, to see that Christ is preached and the sacraments duly administered. He is also charged with keeping a good order in the congregations of the Church.

Then the ordaining archbishop says:

> By the authority given to me in my office, I hereby transmit to you the office of Archbishop in the Evangelical Lutheran Church of Latvia, in the name of the Father and of the Son and of the Holy Ghost.

The new archbishop receives pectoral cross, cope and crosier. Then the ordaining archbishop says:

> We thank thee, almighty God, eternal Father, that thou hast in thine eternal love given us thine only begotten Son, Jesus Christ to be our Saviour; who through his death has redeemed us, has ascended into heaven, sent the Holy Ghost and has bestowed on his church many diverse spiritual gifts. We ask thee to grant to thy servant, to whom now the office of oversight in thy church has been entrusted, the gift of the Holy Ghost; may he lead him into all truth and keep him in the clear light of the Gospel. Help him to carry out his office faithfully, and to secure the increase of thy Church. Whether he is honoured or despised, praised or blamed, may he always show himself to be thy Servant: great in patience, trustworthy in work,

earnest in prayer, clear and competent in teaching, solid in forbearance, firm in steadfast love and in the truth of thy Word, armed with the spiritual weapons of thy power, in order that he may also be a true and skilled householder, who himself at the end of his time may enter eternal heavenly joy, through Jesus Christ, our Lord, who with thee and the Holy Ghost liveth and reigneth in divine glory, world without end. Amen.

12. Evangelical-Lutheran Church of Lithuania

See the statement and prayer quoted in Aldonis Putce, 'Episcopacy in our Churches: Lithuania', above.

DEACONS

At the time of the Reformation in the sixteenth century, the Church of England (including Wales at that time) and the Church of Ireland continued to ordain to the threefold ministry of bishop, priest and deacon. Like the minor orders (which the Church of England rejected), the diaconate was seen as a step towards the priesthood; and for four hundred and more years following (the practice continues today) candidates for the priesthood served a probationary year as a deacon in their first parish. In Scotland, deacons in the Reformed Church followed the Continental model. The ordination of deacons in a distinct order was rare until the nineteenth century saw conformity with the practice of the Church of England in the Scottish Episcopal Church.

More recently in some provinces within the Anglican Communion, the diaconate has been understood in a broader context. In the Episcopal Church of the United States, for example, men and women have been ordained to a distinctive diaconal ministry, serving as pastoral assistants or readers and in other areas of pastoral and teaching work. In the Roman Catholic Church, some men (usually married and therefore ineligible for the priesthood) have been called and ordained to the 'permanent diaconate'. In the Anglican churches also (more recently) many women ordained to the diaconate have explored what this distinctive ministry actually entails and have contributed much to its proper understanding. This is also true in Wales, which was the first of the British and Irish Anglican churches to ordain women to the diaconate (1980). In some dioceses women deacons have been appointed 'clerics in charge' with full responsibility for a parish or a group of parishes. Some men too have been ordained deacon and have asked specifically not to proceed to the priesthood. The order of deacon is seen to be historic, to emphasize the caring and serving role of all ministry, and its distinctive form to be a revival of an emphasis nearly lost to the Church. Hence in the Church of England today this distinctive form of the diaconate runs parallel with the traditional use of the diaconate as a year's preparation for the priesthood. The Scottish Episcopal Church, after thirty years' study, is now promoting a distinctive diaconate, often to men and women, which is not understood as a probationary step to the priesthood. The question of a permanent diaconate in Ireland has surfaced only on a few occasions, most notably during the brief period between the ordination of women to the diaconate and the priesthood. This was so brief that questions relating to a permanent diaconate had insufficient time to take root or gain momentum.

The Churches of Sweden, Norway, Finland and Denmark and the Baltic churches have a long tradition of those trained in caring and teaching skills who work alongside the pastor. The Church of Iceland has recently revived this tradition, which was broken in the eighteenth century. They are called deacons, but are not considered an order in the same sense as bishops and pastors (priests, presbyters). In Denmark, for example, they are known as pastoral co-workers. They are professionally trained in social work, nursing and catechetics, and in the parish their duties range from health care and pastoral counselling to social work and instructing the young in the Christian faith. The deacon in the Norwegian, Icelandic and Swedish Churches fulfils a similar role (though in Norway there is a special office of catechist). Social and health care with special church training is also central to the work of a deacon in Finland. In Estonia, the deacon is charged to assist the pastor and to serve the congregation.

In all seven countries, the deacon is solemnly appointed — by the laying on of hands with prayer by the bishop in Norway, Sweden, and Finland, and by a special commissioning, not necessarily by the bishop, in Denmark. The deacon is similarly commissioned in Latvia and Estonia. Except in Sweden, the deacon is seen as a member of the laity rather than of the clergy (though in Norway the deacon sits with church workers in the Synod and not on the bench of the laity). Deacons also assist with the distribution of Holy Communion in parishes and for the sick in hospitals. In Norway and Sweden they take a special part in the liturgy.

The Nordic and Baltic churches have the diaconate under review and are exploring its role. Unlike the traditional Anglican way, which has set the deacon alongside the priest in the liturgy and in the parish in preparation for ordination to the priesthood, the Nordic churches have preserved a strong tradition of a special ministry whose first task is to respond to social need but which is also closely associated with the parish, an association symbolized by the deacon's taking part in the liturgy. Such a ministry is diaconal in a very distinctive sense; it has much to say to other churches which are looking to discover the true role of the diaconate in the Church today.

STEPHEN PLATTEN
JOHN HALLIBURTON

INITIATION AND CONFIRMATION

All our churches are asking radical questions about initiation rites and procedures: baptism, admission to communion, catechesis and confirmation.

The Current Situation

(i) *The Nordic Lutheran Churches*

Although there has been a reduction in the number of those coming forward to confirmation, particularly in Denmark and Sweden, nevertheless the number of those confirmed in the Nordic churches remains very much higher than in the Church of England. In Finland it is still over 90 per cent of young people aged about 15 years.

(ii) *The Baltic Lutheran Churches*

After the establishment of atheistic Communism in the Baltic States in 1940 the numbers of those coming forward for baptism and confirmation were reduced dramatically. However, the government's attitude began to change towards the end of the 1980s, and since then numbers have rapidly increased. For example, in 1987 in Estonia 1,532 people were baptized and 1,179 confirmed. In 1990 comparable figures were 18,608 and 11,691.

(iii) *The British and Irish Anglican Churches*

Some 33,000 young people under the age of 16 were confirmed in the Church of England in 1990. In a total population of some 10 million young people the proportion who have been confirmed in the Church of England up to that age will therefore be very small, and however estimated will not be likely to be much more than one per cent. In the Church in Wales 12,233 infants and children under 11 were baptized in 1991, of which only 4,356 were confirmed. A quarter of this number were adults. In Scotland and Ireland there are no central statistics available.

Catechesis

In the Nordic countries confirmation follows a six- to eight-month period of careful and intensive catechesis, and is administered by a priest. In the Church of England the period and style of catechesis varies considerably, and some parishes are experimenting with or have developed an educational programme of young people which continues beyond confirmation, though many parishes still have a brief period of preparation. Both in England and in the Nordic countries the churches find that many young people cease to come to church after confirmation.

Admission to Communion

Partly for this reason, in all our churches experiments have begun to admit children to communion before confirmation. In Denmark and Sweden the practice is widespread. In Norway it is less widespread, but permitted. In England it is permitted as an experiment in some dioceses and parishes, but not in others. The Church in Wales is soon to initiate a similar experiment. However, in the Church of England the general rule remains in force that only those who have been confirmed by a bishop (or 'are ready and desirous to be confirmed') may be admitted to communion. In Ireland there is an on-going pastoral debate about the Church's approach to and preparation for confirmation. In particular the link between confirmation and admission to the eucharist is being questioned by many. A select committee of the General Synod is examining the issues surrounding the communion of the baptized but unconfirmed.

It is important that children who have been accustomed to receive communion before confirmation in one of our churches should not be forbidden communion when visiting or residing in the area of another church. No canonical changes are needed to ensure that this happens, but an appropriate procedure needs to be established.

History of Confirmation

In all our churches the meaning of confirmation has been debated in recent years. Historically, confirmation appears to have been a development of the prayer for the gift of the Spirit (traditionally associated with the anointing of the candidate after the rite of baptism). In the East this prayer has remained within the baptismal rite as 'chrismation'. In the West, in the case of infants it was separated from baptism and came to be performed later, normally by a bishop in some parts of Europe, but not always and not everywhere.

At the Reformation both Lutheran and Anglican reformers emphasized the importance of catechesis, and indeed this emphasis had already been prominent in some parts of the Church, especially under Franciscan influence before the Reformation. In the Church of England, however, when a bishop was not available to confirm, anyone 'ready' (i.e. duly catechized) for confirmation could be admitted to communion, even though the Church of England retained the rite of confirmation by a bishop. In the Nordic countries catechesis became very important, but the rite of confirmation ceased for two hundred years. Only under pietistic influence was confirmation restored in the Nordic countries. The argument for the restoration was that persons who had been baptized as infants should have the opportunity to confirm that they had come to a personal faith by taking 'a formal oath before the Lord' (confirmation order for Denmark and Norway).

This interpretation of confirmation has been held by many church people, although many theologians for several decades have tried to persuade confirmands and their parents that the word confirmation first of all should be understood to mean an act whereby God confirms the promise given to the Christian in baptism and received by the gift of faith.

Confirmation Rites

In the Anglican churches the rite of confirmation includes an examination of the candidates, and a personal profession of faith in which they re-affirm the promises made on their behalf at baptism. It contains a prayer for the gift of the Spirit and the laying on of hands by the bishop on each candidate. It has been suggested that the new confirmation rite in the recent English Alternative Service Book (1980) might have lost some of the proper eschatological emphasis. *Confirmation 1987* is widely used in the Church of Ireland.

The episcopal role in confirmation has for over a hundred years been deeply embedded in the pastoral practice of the Anglican churches. In most Nordic countries episcopal visitations in the past have focused on the whole range of parochial life, and since the Reformation bishops have never confirmed, therefore Lutherans have difficulty in understanding the importance of the role of the bishop in connection with confirmation in the Anglican tradition. In the Anglican churches bishops tended in the past to focus their visits on confirmation services (though this is beginning to change). Parish education programmes in the past also focused largely on confirmation preparation. This in part accounts for the difficulty many Anglicans have in considering any alternative to episcopal confirmation.

In the Nordic and Baltic churches the rites vary, but all contain an opportunity for a personal profession of faith (in the form of questions on the Apostles' Creed) and a prayer that the candidate may be strengthened to live in the grace of baptism and so obtain eternal life. In all the rites the reference to baptism as the sacrament which bestows the gift of the Holy Spirit is clear. In some churches there is a blessing with the laying on of hands by the priest. In the Swedish liturgy there is a prayer for the descent of the Holy Spirit ('May the Good Spirit of God lead you in all your ways'). We believe that the Nordic and Baltic churches might re-examine their confirmation rites to see if the invocation of the Holy Spirit was sufficiently emphasized.

Church Membership

All our churches agree that we become members through baptism. However this was so much taken for granted in earlier centuries that Swedish canon law omitted to mention it, assuming that every citizen of Sweden would have been baptized. The result has been that legally and canonically everyone with a Swedish parent is assumed to be a member of the Church of Sweden unless he or she specifically asks not to be. Today therefore some half a million Swedes are counted as members of the Church of Sweden without having been baptised. The bishops of the Church of Sweden wish to amend canon law to make baptism a requisite for church membership, but this has not yet been enacted. There is some opposition to this step, since many people do not wish to sever a remaining link, however tenuous, with half a million people who wish to be associated with the Church but are not willing to be baptized.

Other churches are not required to recognize unbaptized Swedes as church members, since the Porvoo Declaration always refers to 'baptized members' in this context. It is to be noted, however, that unbaptized parishioners also have rites in the Church of England; for example, marriage.

In the Church of England, baptized members in good standing of other Trinitarian churches are admitted to communion, even if they are not confirmed by a bishop (Canon B 15A). This is also true of the Church in Wales, which has recently permitted members of other churches in certain circumstances to be entered on electoral rolls of parishes and to serve as officers in the local parish. In Ireland eucharistic hospitality also pertains, though as good practice rather than as formal legislation. However, we suggest that the Church of England change its canons so as to recognize confirmation by a priest in the Nordic and Baltic churches. Presbyteral confirmation is already widely practised in other episcopal churches.

In the Porvoo Declaration, the participating churches would commit themselves 'to regard baptized members of all our churches as members of our own'.[1] We believe that in addition, members of one of our churches resident in the area of another should be enabled to exercise rights, for example, of electing to or being elected to serve on representative bodies of that church.

General Recommendations

It has become clear to us that our churches are facing a similar period of questioning about the integration and nurture of young people in our churches in a secular age. We approach this challenge with very different catechetical experience, differing liturgies and differing pastoral practice. We recognize that we all practise a rite of confirmation in episcopally ordered churches.

We therefore recommend, if possible even before any agreement is formally ratified between our churches, that our churches take every opportunity to consult with one another on the theological, educational, pastoral and liturgical aspects of Christian initiation.

GERHARD PEDERSEN
MARTIN REARDON

---

[1] *The Porvoo Common Statement*, para. 58.b(iii).

DOCTRINAL STATEMENTS AND DECLARATIONS OF ASSENT

1. Church of England

a. CANON A5: OF THE DOCTRINE OF THE CHURCH OF ENGLAND

The doctrine of the Church of England is grounded in the Holy Scriptures, and in such teachings of the ancient Fathers and Councils of the Church as are agreeable to the said Scriptures. In particular such doctrine is to be found in the Thirty-nine Articles of Religion, the Book of Common Prayer, and the Ordinal.

[The documents to which this Canon refers are:

(i) The *Thirty-nine Articles of Religion* (1571)

(ii) The *Book of Common Prayer* (1662)

(iii) The Form and Manner of Making, Ordaining and Consecrating of Bishops, Priests and Deacons, annexed to the Book of Common Prayer and commonly known as the *Ordinal* (1662)]

b. CANON C 15: OF THE DECLARATION OF ASSENT

1(1) The Declaration of Assent to be made under this Canon shall be in the form set out below:

Preface
The Church of England is part of the One, Holy, Catholic and Apostolic Church worshipping the one true God, Father, Son and Holy Spirit. It professes the faith uniquely revealed in the Holy Scriptures and set forth in the catholic creeds, which faith the Church is called upon to proclaim afresh in each generation. Led by the Holy Spirit, it has borne witness to Christian truth in its historic formularies, the Thirty-nine Articles of Religion, the Book of Common Prayer and the Ordering of Bishops, Priests and Deacons. In the declaration you are about to make will you affirm your loyalty to this inheritance of faith as your inspiration and guidance under God in bringing the grace and truth of Christ to this generation and making Him known to those in your care?

Declaration of Assent
I, A B, do so affirm, and accordingly declare my belief in the faith which is revealed in the Holy Scriptures and set forth in the catholic

creeds and to which the historic formularies of the Church of England bear witness; and in public prayer and administration of the sacraments, I will use only the forms of service which are authorised or allowed by Canon.

2. Church of Ireland

a. THE CONSTITUTION OF THE CHURCH OF IRELAND, ADOPTED BY THE GENERAL CONVENTION IN THE YEAR 1870: PREAMBLE AND DECLARATION

In the Name of the Father, and of the Son, and of the Holy Ghost. Amen: Whereas it hath been determined by the Legislature that on and after the 1st day of January, 1871, the Church of Ireland shall cease to be established by law; and that the ecclesiastical law of Ireland shall cease to exist as law save as provided in the 'Irish Church Act, 1869', and it hath thus become necessary that the Church of Ireland should provide for its own regulation:

We, the archbishops and bishops of this the Ancient Catholic and Apostolic Church of Ireland, together with the representatives of the clergy and laity of the same, in General Convention assembled in Dublin in the year of our Lord God one thousand eight hundred and seventy, before entering on this work, do solemnly declare as follows:-

I

1. The Church of Ireland doth, as heretofore, accept and unfeignedly believe all the Canonical Scriptures of the Old and New Testament, as given by inspiration of God, and containing all things necessary to salvation; and doth continue to profess the faith of Christ as professed by the Primitive Church.

2. The Church of Ireland will continue to minister the doctrine, and sacraments, and the discipline of Christ, as the Lord hath commanded; and will maintain inviolate the three orders of bishops, priests or presbyters, and deacons in the sacred ministry.

3. The Church of Ireland, as a reformed and Protestant Church, doth hereby reaffirm its constant witness against all those innovations in doctrine and worship, whereby the primitive Faith hath been from time to time defaced or overlaid, and which at the Reformation this Church did disown and reject.

II

The Church of Ireland doth receive and approve *The Book of the Articles of Religion,* commonly called the Thirty-nine Articles, received and approved by the archbishops and bishops and the rest of the clergy of Ireland in the synod holden in Dublin, A.D. 1634; also, *The Book of Common Prayer and Administration of the Sacraments, and other Rites and Ceremonies of the Church, according to the use of the Church of Ireland; and the Form and Manner of Making, Ordaining and Consecrating of Bishops, Priests and Deacons,* as approved and adopted by the synod holden in Dublin, A.D. 1662, and hitherto in use in this Church. And this Church will continue to use the same, subject to such alterations only as may be made therein from time to time by the lawful authority of the Church.

III

The Church of Ireland will maintain communion with the sister Church of England, and with all other Christian Churches agreeing in the principles of this Declaration; and will set forward, so far as in it lieth, quietness, peace, and love, among all Christian people.

IV

The Church of Ireland, deriving its authority from Christ, Who is the Head over all things to the Church, doth declare that a General Synod of the Church of Ireland, consisting of the archbishops and bishops, and of representatives of the clergy and laity, shall have chief legislative power therein, and such administrative power as may be necessary for the Church, and consistent with its episcopal constitution.

b. DECLARATION FOR SUBSCRIPTION

I, A.B., do hereby solemnly declare that —

(1) I approve and agree to the Declaration prefixed to the statutes of the Church of Ireland, passed at the General Convention in the year of our Lord one thousand eight hundred and seventy.

(2) I assent to the Thirty-nine Articles of Religion, and to the Book of Common Prayer, and of the ordering of Bishops, Priests, and Deacons. I believe the doctrine of the Church of Ireland, as therein set forth, to be agreeable to the Word of God; and in public prayer

and administration of the sacraments I will use the form in the said Book prescribed, and none other, except so far as shall be allowed by the lawful authority of the Church.

(3) [against simony]

(4) [against pluralism]

(5) [canonical obedience]

(6) I promise to submit myself to the authority of the Church of Ireland, and to the laws and tribunals thereof.

3. Scottish Episcopal Church

a. [no equivalent]

b. DECLARATION OF ASSENT

I,... do solemnly make the following Declaration. I assent to the Book of Common Prayer and to the Ordering of Bishops, Priests and Deacons. I believe the doctrine of the Church as therein set forth to be agreeable to the Word of God, and in public prayer and administration of the Sacraments I will use the form in the said Book prescribed and none other except so far as shall be allowed by lawful authority in this Church.

4. Church in Wales

a. [no equivalent]

b. DECLARATION AND UNDERTAKING

I, J... S... do solemnly declare my belief in the Faith which is revealed in the Holy Scriptures and set forth in the Catholic Creeds and to which the historic formularies, namely: the Thirty-nine Articles of Religion, the Book of Common Prayer and the Ordering of Bishops, Priests and Deacons, as published in 1662, bear witness; and in public prayer and administration of the sacraments, I will use only the forms of service which are allowed by lawful authority, and none other.

And I hereby undertake to be bound by the Constitution of the Church in Wales, and to accept, submit to, and carry out any sentence of judgment which may at any time be passed upon me by the Archbishop, a Diocesan Bishop or any Court of the Church in Wales.

5. Church of Denmark

a. CONFESSIONAL BASIS

The Apostles' Creed

The Niceno-Constantinopolitan Creed

The Athanasian Creed

The Augsburg Confession of 1530

Luther's Small Catechism

b. EXTRACT FROM THE RITE FOR CONSECRATING A BISHOP: ADMONITION OF THE OFFICIATING BISHOP

You have now heard, how the Lord has instituted the ministry of the Word and through his apostles has witnessed to its necessity for his Church on earth. As the Lord now entrusts you with this holy ministry and furthermore charges you with the task of exercising oversight in his Church, it is his will that you shall be vigilant in your calling and keep watch over yourself and the congregations which are entrusted to you, that you walk faithfully in his sight as a dutiful servant of the Lord, that you hold to the sound doctrine as found in the prophetic and apostolic Scriptures and witnessed to in the Confessional Writings of our Church, and in all respects take care to exercise your ministry without deference to any person, but with integrity to the glory of God's name and the edification of the congregation.

6. Evangelical-Lutheran Church of Finland

THE CONFESSION OF THE CHURCH IS STATED IN THE CHURCH LAW AS FOLLOWS:

The Evangelical-Lutheran Church of Finland confesses that Christian faith which, having its basis in the Holy Word of God, the Prophetic and Apostolic books of the Old and the New Testament, is articulated in the three main creeds of the ancient Church and in the unchanged Confession of Augsburg and in the other confessional books of the Lutheran Church which are included in the *Book of Concord*, and holds as the highest law of the confession that unshakeable truth, clearly declared in these confessional books, that the Holy Word of God is the only rule by which all doctrine must be examined and judged in the Church.

b. At the ordination of pastors the ordinands confess their faith in the words of the Apostles' Creed, then the bishop asks the following three questions:

— Do you want in the name of the Triune God to enter into the office of a pastor and to administer it rightly and faithfully to the glory of God and to the nurture of the congregation?

— Do you want to remain faithful to the pure Word of God, to avoid false doctrine, to preach fearlessly and to administer the holy sacraments according to His ordinance?

— Do you as well want to strive so to live, that your life will be a pattern for your congregation?

After the ordinands have given affirmative answers to these questions, the vows are attested in an oath which includes the contents of the doctrinal basis of the Evangelical-Lutheran Church of Finland quoted above.

At the ordination of a bishop the ordinand confesses his faith in the words of the Niceno-Constantinopolitan Creed and then the ordaining bishop asks the following three questions:

— You have accepted the vocation to the bishop's office in the Diocese of N.N. Do you want to administer this office rightly and faithfully according to the Holy Word of God and the order of our church?

— Do you want to oversee that the Gospel is rightly preached, the sacraments are administered according to the ordinance of Christ and the congregations are taken care of according to the order of our church?

— Do you want to further all that nurtures the Church of Christ and strive so to live, that your life will be a pattern for the congregation?

After the ordinand has given affirmative answers to these questions he has to attest the vows in an oath which includes the doctrinal basis of the church and a promise to remain faithful to the Bible's teaching concerning the office of oversight and its obligations.

7. Evangelical-Lutheran Church of Iceland

Since Iceland was a part of the Danish state at the time of the Reformation, the Icelandic national church was established on the same confessional basis as the Danish. For this reason the Icelandic church accepts the following five confessional documents: The Apostles' Creed, the Nicene Creed, the Athanasian Creed, Luther's Small Catechism and the Augsburg Confession of 1530 (see especially Einar Sigurbjörnsson, *Kirkjan játar* (Reykjavik, 1980), pp. 10, 27).

At the ordination of priests, the bishop reads the following admonition, which the ordinand vows to observe:

> ...I now solemnly urge you: to preach God's Word pure and undefiled, as revealed in the prophetic and apostolic writings, according to the witness of our Evangelical Lutheran Church in its confessions; to administer the Holy Sacrament as Christ commanded with reverence... (*Icelandic Church Handbook* (Reykjavik, 1981), pp. 187-88).

The same emphasis is found in the Letter or Certificate of Ordination presented by the bishop to the ordinand:

> Whereby... according to the vow which he has taken before me, he is bound to perform his office faithfully and diligently and to walk before God with prudence in his way of life and daily conduct, in a manner befitting God's servant. He is bound to adhere in every article to the prevailing laws and customs of the church, to preach God's Word truly and purely to his congregation according to Holy Scripture and in the spirit of our Evangelical Lutheran Church, to administer the Lord's Holy Sacrament with reverence... (Letter of Ordination for priests of the Icelandic National Church).

8. Church of Norway

a. CONFESSIONAL BASIS

A law of 1687 established as the confessional for the Church of Norway:

The Apostles' Creed

The Nicene Creed

The Athanasian Creed

Luther's Small Catechism

The Augsburg Confession of 1530

b. At the ordination of pastors, the Bishop says:

You have heard the Word of God concerning the ministry, its requirements and its promises, how rich it is in glory, and how essential it is for God's Church on earth. As the Lord is now entrusting you with the ministry as a pastor in our church, I hereby direct and exort you:

— that you preach the Word of God with clarity and in purity as it is given to us in the Holy Scriptures and as our church testifies to it in its confessional writings, and that you administer the holy sacraments as instituted by Christ and in accordance with the ordinances of our church....

9. Church of Sweden

a. DECLARATION ON THE FOUNDATION DOCUMENTS OF THE CHURCH OF SWEDEN CONCERNING FAITH, CONFESSION AND DOCTRINE, ISSUED ON 30TH SEPTEMBER 1992

By decision of the General Synod of the Church of Sweden the following Declaration is made under Section 7 paragraphs 1 and 3 of the Church of Sweden Act 1982

1 The faith, confession and doctrine of the Church of Sweden, which is manifested in its worship and life, is founded upon God's holy Word, as given in the prophetic and apostolic scriptures of the Old and New Testaments; is summarised in the Apostolic, Nicene and Athanasian creeds and in the original text of the Augsburg Confession of 1530; is affirmed and acknowledged in the Resolution of the Uppsala Assembly of 1593; and is explicated and elucidated in *The Book of Concord* and in other documents approved by the Church of Sweden.

2 The books authorised for use in divine worship in the Church of Sweden are, in addition to the authorised Swedish translation of the Bible, *The Church of Sweden Service Book, The Swedish Hymn Book, The Swedish Lectionary* and *A Little Prayer Book,* which have been accepted by the General Synod of the Church of Sweden as expressions of the faith, confession and doctrine of the Church of Sweden.

3 The foundation documents of the Church of Sweden are the Bible, the creeds, the documents and the Books of Worship which, in accordance with paragraphs 1 & 2, set forth her faith, confession and doctrine.

This declaration is effective from 1st January 1993.

On behalf of the Central Board of the Church of Sweden

Bertil Werkström

Gösta Wrede

b EXTRACT FROM THE ORDINATION MASS FOR BISHOPS: QUESTIONS

Will you hold fast to the faith of the Church, defend it, and see to it that God's word be preached in purity and clarity as it is given in the Holy Scripture and as the Confessions of our church bear witness thereto, and that the sacraments be rightly administered?

Yes.

Will you in your work follow, keep and protect the orders of our church and foster the oneness in Christ?

Yes.

10. Estonian Evangelical-Lutheran Church

a. The Doctrine of the EELC is found in the Old Testament, the New Testament, the Apostles' Creed, the Nicene Creed, the Athanasian Creed and the Lutheran Confessions collected in the *Book of Concord,* namely:

1. The Augsburg Confession of 1530

2. Its Apology

3. The Smalcald Articles

4. Luther's Small and Large Catechism

5. The Formula of Concord

b. Oath of Ordination for priests of the EELC:

...With diligence and loyalty will I enlighten both young and old in the Word of God and administer the Holy Sacraments as Jesus Christ has instituted them, and I will maintain fully the secrecy of the confessional. . .

11. Latvia

a. CONFESSIONAL BASIS

The Apostles' Creed

The Nicene Creed

The Augsburg Confession

Luther's Small Catechism

b. ORDINATION PROMISE

I shall hold fast to the teachings of Luther and to the main Creeds of the Christian faith.

12. Evangelical-Lutheran Church of Lithuania

a. STATUTE OF THE EVANGELICAL-LUTHERAN CHURCH OF LITHUANIA (1990)

In the name of God, the Father, the Son and the Holy Spirit. Amen. The Evangelical Lutheran Church of Lithuania, as a community organized of Christ and His Gospel, confesses as the only basis of her teaching and life the canonical books of the Old and the New Testament, and in explaining the Holy Scripture keeps to the Apostolic, Nicene and Athanasian Creeds, the unchanged Augsburg Confession, the Catechisms of Martin Luther and other writings gathered in the *Book of Concord*, as they came into being in the flow of the history of Christianity.

Since 18th June 1968 the Evangelical-Lutheran Church of Lithuania is a member of the Lutheran World Federation (LWF), which unites Lutheran churches in all continents, and is seeking among them spiritual communion (*koinonia*).

THE MOST SIGNIFICANT
ANGLICAN-LUTHERAN ECUMENICAL TEXTS

1. At the World level

a. *Anglican-Lutheran International Conversations: The Report of the Conversations 1970-1972 authorized by the Lambeth Conference and the Lutheran World Federation* (London: SPCK, 1973). Reprinted as *The Pullach Report 1970-72* in Harding Meyer and Lukas Vischer (eds), *Growth in Agreement: Reports and Agreed Statements of Ecumenical Conversations on a World level* (New York: Paulist Press; Geneva: World Council of Churches, 1984), pp. 13-34.

b. Anglican-Lutheran Joint Working Group: Anglican-Lutheran Relations: *The Cold Ash Report* (London: Anglican Consultative Council; Geneva; Lutheran World Federation, 1983).

c. Anglican-Lutheran International Continuation Committee: *The Niagara Report*. Report of the Anglican-Lutheran Consultation on Episcope, Niagara Falls, September 1987 (Cincinnati: Forward Movement Publications, 1988).

2. At the European level

a. Anglican-Lutheran European Commission; *Anglican-Lutheran Dialogue: Helsinki Report 1982* (London: SPCK, 1983).

3. Nordic and Baltic

a. *The Church of England and the Church of Sweden*. Report of the Commission appointed by the Archbishop of Canterbury..., with Three Appendices (London: A. R. Mowbray, 1911).

b *The Church of England and the Church of Finland*. A Summary of the Proceedings at the Conferences held at Lambeth Palace, London, on October 5th and 6th, 1933, and at Brandö, Helsingfors, on July 17th and 18th, 1934. In *Lambeth Occasional Reports 1931-8*, pp. 115-187.

c. Report of the Joint Commission appointed by the Archbishop of Canterbury and the Archbishop of Turku, July 1934. In Vilmos Vajta (ed.) *Church in Fellowship: Pulpit and Altar Fellowship Among Lutherans* (Minneapolis: Augsburg, 1963), pp. 199-200. [Oddly, the

'Summary of Proceedings' (para 7), does not include the Commission's actual report and recommendations.] Reprinted in G. K. A. Bell (ed.), *Documents on Christian Unity: Third Series 1930-1948* (London: Oxford Press, 1948), pp. 146-147.

d. *Conferences between representatives appointed by the Archbishop of Canterbury on behalf of the Church of England and Representatives of the Evangelical Lutheran Churches of Latvia and Estonia* (1936-38). In *Lambeth Occasional Reports 1931-8 (London: SPCK, 1948), pp. 205-261.*

e. *The Church of England and The Churches of Norway, Denmark and Iceland.* Report of the Committee appointed by the Archbishop of Canterbury in 1951..., with Three Appendices (London: SPCK, 1952).

4. **Germany** [Anglican - Lutheran/Reformed/United]

The Meissen Agreement: Texts (Council for Christian Unity Occasional paper No.2, 1992).

5. **USA: Lutheran-Episcopal Dialogue**

a. *Lutheran-Episcopal Dialogue: A Progress Report* (Cincinnati: Forward Movement Publications, [1973]).

b. W.G. Weinhauer & L. Wietelmann (eds), *The Report of the Lutheran-Episcopal Dialogue: Second Series 1976-1980* (Cincinnati: Forward Movement Publications, 1981).

c. *The Lutheran-Episcopal Agreement: Commentary and Guidelines* (New York: Lutheran Church in Ameria, 1983): see also *Handbook for Ecumenism* (New York: Episcopal Church Ecumenical Office, 1989).

d. Lutheran-Episcopal Dialogue, Series III: W.A. Norgren & W.G. Rusch (eds), *Implications of the Gospel.* (Minneapolis: Augsburg; Cincinnati: Forward Movement Publications, 1988).

e Lutheran-Episcopal Dialogue, Series III: W.A. Norgren and W.G. Rusch (eds), *Toward Full Communion and Concordat of Agreement* (Minneapolis: Augsburg; Cincinnati: Forward Movement Publications, 1991).

FULL TEXT OF PARAGRAPHS CITED IN FOOTNOTES TO THE COMMON STATEMENT

3. W.A. Norgren and W.G. Rusch (eds), *Implications of the Gospel. Lutheran-Episcopal Dialogue, Series III* (Minneapolis and Cincinnati, 1988) (*LED III*), ch. III, paras 33-7, 51-7.

The Church as Necessary Implication of the Gospel

33.   It is to be expected that the issues of greatest sensitivity related to full communion between Episcopalians and Lutherans would occur in ecclesiology. On the basis of Article 7 (VII) of the Augsburg Confession Lutherans have traditionally emphasized that the preaching of the gospel 'in its purity' and the administration of the sacraments 'according to the gospel' are 'sufficient for the true unity of the Christian church.' Lutherans have asked whether doctrine, proclamation, and administration of the sacraments reflect an authentic understanding of the gospel before entertaining the prospect of full communion with non-Lutheran churches. Anglicans have traditionally stressed the importance of order to assure the authentic administration of the sacraments. Episcopalians have asked, among other things, whether churches have the historic episcopate before entertaining the prospect of full communion with them.

34.   In 1982, when the predecessor bodies of the Evangelical Lutheran Church in America and the Episcopal Church recognized each other as churches 'in which the Gospel is preached and taught,' this was done on the basis of official conversations both in Europe and the United States of America which revealed a significant shared understanding of the gospel of justification by grace for Christ's sake through faith (Anglican-Lutheran European Regional Commission, 1983, pp. 8-10; Lutheran-Episcopal Dialogue II, 1981, pp. 22-25). The agreement on the sacraments (ALERC, pp. 10-14; LED II, pp. 25-29) and on apostolicity (ALERC, pp. 14-20; LED II, pp. 31-43 was sufficient to permit both churches to take the historic step of establishing 'Interim Sharing of the Eucharist' as they continued to work toward full communion. These agreements encourage us to affirm together what we understand about the church. It is our conviction that the gospel of the reign of God means that the church is called to be an eschatological community. This does not mean that the church is identical with the reign of God. Understanding the church as eschatological community, however, confirms the fresh approach to apostolicity begun by LED II and opens new possibilities for understanding questions of order envisioned when LED III was mandated.

35.   To begin, we confess and affirm the necessary relationship between the gospel and the church. While God calls each of us by name and gives each of us personal faith, this confession and affirmation requires special attention in the American context because of the pervasive presence of religious individualism in that context. Because many of the European immigrants who came to the North American continent were seeking to escape the oppressive qualities of established churches, and because post-Enlightenment culture often identified Christianity with morality, it became relatively easy for persons to identify themselves as Christians without becoming part of the church. The revival practice of asking hearers simply to 'accept Jesus as personal savior' coupled with the scarcity of clergy on the frontier contributed to the separation of gospel from church. Currently, much religious television encourages and reinforces the individualism endemic to our religious history.

36.   We must describe the necessary relationship between gospel and church with some care. The common history of our churches in the 16th century continues to remind us of the dangers of religious oppression, especially the insistence that church controls gospel or that the church believes something other than the gospel which calls it into being. We confess and affirm that church and gospel are necessarily related because both have to do with the reign of God. The gospel is grounded in the history of Jesus as the breaking in of the end-time reign of God. The goal and consequence of the mission of Jesus is nothing less than the renewed people of God now open to and called to include all peoples. Hence the church is the principal implication of the gospel in human history. The end-time reign of God implies and calls into being the end-time messianic community.

37.   The mission of Jesus not only implies community. It requires community for its continuance. The church is called to be the explicit bearer of the gospel in history. There is no faith in Jesus, the Christ, as the grounding of the reign of God without the visible and audible proclamation of the gospel in word and sacraments. And there is no proclamation of the gospel in word and sacraments without a community and its ministry (Rom. 10.14-20). Word and sacraments are embedded and embodied in the end-time community and its life. The call of the gospel is not to individualized and isolated faith. It is the call that persons be translated from communities dominated by the reign of death to the community created and liberated by the Christ's reign of life. The authentic alternative to oppressive religious institutionalism is not religious individualism but rather a community shaped by the gospel of the Christ as the crucified one.

The Church's Polity Is Life Together for Witness to the Gospel

51.   This topic confronts our churches with the most obvious, although not the only, obstacle to full communion not only because there are actual differences in governance and ordination between our churches but also because there are differences in understanding the function of bishops and in the significance attached to the historic episcopate. When polity is understood in terms of specific forms, such understanding determines the way our respective churches raise questions about it. To Lutherans it seems that Episcopalian emphasis on the historic episcopate and its authority to ordain could be an unwarranted addition to the gospel. To Episcopalians the Lutheran view that, when there is agreement on the gospel, polity can become an adiaphoron seems an unwarranted indifference with regard to something that is at least an implication of the gospel. In this document we will not deal with all the issues related to polity. Another document of this dialogue will be devoted to the group of topics mandated by the 1982 resolutions authorizing Interim Sharing of the Eucharist, namely, 'historic episcopate, and ordering of ministry (bishops, priests, and deacons) in the total context of apostolicity'. If we understand polity as disciplined life together, then we can here give an account of how the gospel defines and shapes the polity of the church; how, in fact, the polity of the church is an implication of the gospel.

52.   Polity is normally defined as a 'politically organized community.' But if the gospel is that the reign of God has begun and will triumph, then this cannot mean politics as usual. 'You know that those who are supposed to rule over the Gentiles lord it over them, and their great men exercise authority over them. *But it shall not be so among you*' (Mark 10.42-43, italics added). Hence, polity in the church must

mean the visible life together of the community which believes that Jesus is the Christ, that the messianic age has begun, that the reign of God will finally triumph. Polity includes governance, but it is more than governance. It includes the ordering of ministries, but it is more than the ordering of ministries. It is the way the church as the body of Christ under historical conditions is freed by the gospel so to live together so that the patterns and powers of its life reflect and witness to the reign of God rather than to the patterns and powers of the 'old age.' Polity in the church thus testifies to the fact that the gospel gives life to a visible, historical community. Further, polity reflects to the church and the world at large the church's utter dependence on the one gospel. We therefore confess and affirm that the church witnesses to the gospel by the way its members live together, that the way its members live together should reflect both the resurrection victory of Jesus and his way of ministry up to and including the cross. Hence polity is fundamentally the gift of discipleship in its essential corporate dimension. The Messiah serves the people of God, calls that people to be the seed bed of the new reconciled and reconciling humanity, and shapes that people's life and mission by the power and character of his own ministry.

53.   Two characteristics of Jesus' teaching about the ministry of the messianic community are represented by the terms 'to send' (*apostellein*) and 'to serve' (*diakonein*).* Because Jesus is sent as the Christ by the Father, he sends the community which confesses him as the Christ with his same mission (Mark 9:37 and parallels; Matt. 10.5-15 and parallels; John 3.17; 4.38; 17.3,8,18,21,23,25; 20.21). In a certain sense the church's 'apostolicity' *is* its mission, the subject of Section 5 of this document. Equally important is the way the church engages in its mission. *Diakonia* 'is the service performed for the unifying and preservation of the church, the service which establishes and maintains the faith.'** In contrast to secular rule the church was not to be constituted by coercive power. Nor was it to be constituted by learned power (1 Cor. 1.18-25), by magical power (Acts 8.18-24; Acts 16.16-24), or religious power (Heb. 13.10-16). Rather, Jesus brings in the reign of God as the one who serves (Luke 22.27 and parallels; John 13.1-20). The reign of God did not come through visible power. It came through one who was a slave for slaves, one who was poor for the poor, one who was a servant for servants.*** Even those who have been given the charism of leadership exercise their leadership 'in the Lord' (1 Thess. 5.12-13), as those whose worship is to present themselves as living sacrifices (Rom. 12.1-8, esp. 7 and 8).

* Massey H. Shepherd Jr., 'Ministry, Christian,' *The Interpreter's Dictionary of the Bible*, Vol. III (Nashville: Abingdon, 1962), p. 386.

** Leonhard Goppelt, *Apostolic and Post-apostolic Times* (London: Adam and Charles Black, 1970), p. 177.

*** 'To serve means to demonstrate love to mankind out of a faith which forgoes the use of right and power and seeks God's help in Jesus. This love is to be demonstrated for the same purpose as it was by Jesus, to inspire a faith in God and compassion for others.' Goppelt, *ibid.*, p. 178.

54.   Both mission and servanthood are characterized by diversity of concrete expression in the New Testament and other writings which take us well into the 2nd Century C.E. The Twelve, resident in Jerusalem, represent a corporate apostolate which witnessed to the messiahship of Jesus within Judaism and kept the emerging

Gentile mission in contact with its Jewish matrix. Side by side was the ministry of the Seven (Acts 6-8), often regarded as the origin of the diaconate but more accurately described as a missionary ministry similar to an apostolate like that of Paul. Many of the Pauline churches were apparently led by a presbyter-bishop, while the corporate leadership of elders, derived from synagogue administration, seems to have functioned in the churches described by Luke and the Pastoral Epistles. The leadership of presbyters persisted even at Rome until well into the second century, long after the monarchical episcopate had established itself in Syria and Asia Minor. These offices did not exhaust the forms ministry took in earliest Christianity, for there is abundant evidence of the importance of 'charismatic' leaders in both the Pauline (1 Corinthians 12-14; Romans 12; Ephesians 4) and Johannine traditions (1 John 2.20-27; 4.1; 3 John 9-10; Rev. 1.9-11).

55.   The unity and reconciliation effected by the inbreaking reign of God embraces a fruitful, but sometimes turbulent, diversity among us. The church, from the beginning, knew a rich variety of activities in its life together, some of which served particularly to undergird its unity. We list a few of these.

   a.   *The sharing of goods* with those in need is held up in the New Testament writings as a characteristic of church life. Luke describes the earliest community in Jerusalem as exceptionally generous (Acts 4.32 - 5.11); Paul, later on, collected an offering from churches of his founding to help that church in a time of need (e.g., 2 Corinthians 8-9); and the letters of John (1 John 3.16-18) and James (1.26-27) insist on such sharing as a fundamental Christian duty.

   b.   *Intercessory prayer* focused the Christians' concern for one another. Paul, for example, asked for such prayers for himself from the church at Rome (Rom. 15.30).

   c.   *Admonition and correction* were devoted to preserving community among those in disagreement. To accuse is to expose an enemy and break community. To admonish is to love a friend and preserve community in the midst of conflicts. Thus Paul could rebuke Peter (Gal.2.11-15) without, it seems, breaking their partnership in the gospel.

   d.   *Suffering* for the sake of the gospel, for the sake of the community, also served to further the word of proclamation (Acts 5.41; 2 Cor. 6.4-5; 11. 23-29; Col. 1.24-29).

   e.   *Love and humility* were prominent themes of moral exhortation, for, by putting others first, we promote the unity of the church (1 Corinthians 13; Phil. 2.1-11; 1 John 4.20; Mark 10.42-45).

In these and other ways, the church sought to practice the unity which is one of its cardinal characteristics (John 17.20-21) without obliterating the diversity which made its life vital.

56.   In addition to mission, servanthood, diversity, and unity as dimensions of the church's life together, there is still another dimension that we believe can also be found in the life of the early church. A contemporary description of it is found in the agreed statement of Lutherans and Catholics in Dialogue V, *Papal Primacy and the Universal Church*, p. 20, which identifies collegiality and subsidiarity as norms for the renewal of the church's polity in general and the office of universal pastor in particular.

Collegial responsibility for the unity of the church... is of utmost importance in protecting those values which excessive centralization of authority would tend to stifle... The collegial principle calls all levels of the church to share in the concern and responsibilities of leadership for the total life of the church.

The *principle of subsidiarity* is no less important. Every section of the church, each mindful of its special heritage, should nurture the gifts it has received from the Spirit by exercising its legitimate freedom. What can properly be decided and done in smaller units of ecclesial life ought not to be referred to church leaders who have wider responsibilities. Decisions should be made and activities carried out with a participation as broad as possible from the people of God. Initiatives should be encouraged in order to promote a wholesome diversity in theology, worship, witness, and service. All should be concerned that, as the community is built up and its unity strengthened, the rights of minorities and minority viewpoints are protected within the unity of faith.

57. · It should be evident from the preceding paragraphs that the earliest centuries of the church's history hold before us a rich vision of the church's polity as life together in response to the gospel. Measuring its current life in terms of these examples, the church confesses by the power of the gospel that it exists in a broken and anticipatory form. It confesses its brokenness in its relation to Judaism; its own disunity; its too frequent identification with oppressing establishments; its failures of compassion, peacemaking, justice, inclusivity, stewardship, and pastoral discipline. The power of the gospel is seen not only in the church's freedom to confess its brokenness and sin but also in its freedom for reform. Indeed, the refusal to undertake evident and necessary reform is a possible indication that a community has hardened itself against the gospel. The ordination of women by our churches is a specific example of a recently undertaken reform. The importance of this action as an example of how our polity is a witness to the gospel of the reign of God calls for lengthier treatment.

4. *Baptism, Eucharist and Ministry* (WCC Faith and Order Paper No. 111, 1982) (*BEM*), *Ministry*, para. 5.

5. The Holy Spirit bestows on the community diverse and complementary gifts. These are for the common good of the whole people and are manifested in acts of service within the community and to the world. They may be gifts of communicating the Gospel in word and deed, gifts of healing, gifts of praying, gifts of teaching and learning, gifts of serving, gifts of guiding and following, gifts of inspiration and vision. All members are called to discover, with the help of the community, the gifts they have received and to use them for the building up of the Church and for the service of the world to which the Church is sent.

5. Roman Catholic / Lutheran Joint Commission, *Ways to Community* (Geneva, 1981), para. 9.

9. Like every good gift, unity also comes from the Father through the Son in the Holy Spirit.

The will and work of the Father is 'in Christ as a plan for the fullness of time, to unite all things in him' (Eph. 1.10). In the Father is the origin of all the Son does for unity. 'And he has put all things under his feet and has made him the head over all things for the church, which is his body, the fullness of him who fills all in all' (Eph. 1.22-23).

6. *Ibid.*, para. 34.

34. Unity in Christ does not exist despite and in opposition to diversity, but is given with and in diversity. The work of the one unifying Spirit of God does not begin with the uniting of the already separated, but rather creates and maintains diverse realities precisely in order to lead them into the unity of love.

14. *The Truth Shall Make You Free: The Lambeth Conference 1988* (London, 1988), p. 204: resolution 4, para. 4.

This Conference:

1. Receives with gratitude the *Cold Ash Report* (1983) of the Anglican-Lutheran Joint Working Group and approves its recommendations (see *Emmaus Report*, pp. 82-84).

2. Welcomes the *Niagara Report* of the Anglican-Lutheran Consultation on *Episcope* (1987), recognises in it a substantial convergence of views, and commends it to the member Churches of the Anglican Communion for study and synodical reception.

3. Recommends that the permanent body already established by the Anglican Consultative Council and the Lutheran World Federation to co-ordinate and assess developing Anglican-Lutheran relationships (the Anglican/Lutheran International Continuation Committee) be renamed as the Anglican-Lutheran International Commission; and asked to undertake the following tasks in addition to its existing terms of reference:

(a) to integrate in a broader document the theological work already accomplished in international, regional and local dialogues;

(b) to explore more thoroughly the theological and canonical requirements that are necessary in both Churches to acknowledge and recognise the full authenticity of existing ministries (see *Niagara Report*, para. 94);

(c) to advise with sensitivity on the actual pastoral practices of our Churches in regard to the celebration of God's Word and Sacraments, especially the Holy Eucharist;

(d) to produce a report which will indicate the degree of convergence of views on the ordained ministry of bishops, presbyters and deacons.

4. Recognises, on the basis of the high degree of consensus reached in international, regional and national dialogues between Anglicans and Lutherans and in the light of the communion centred around Word and Sacrament that has been experienced in each other's traditions, the presence of the Church of Jesus Christ in the Lutheran Communion as in our own.

5. Urges that this recognition and the most recent convergence on apostolic ministry achieved in the *Niagara Report* of the Anglican-Lutheran Consultation on Episcopacy (1987) prompt us to move towards the fullest possible ecclesial recognition and the goal of full communion.

6. Recommends to member Churches, subject to the concurrence of the Lutheran World Federation, that:

(a) Anglican and Lutheran Churches should officially establish and encourage the practice of mutual eucharistic hospitality if this is not already authorised where pastoral need exists and when ecumenical occasions make this appropriate;

(b)   The Provinces of our Communion should make provision for appropriate forms of 'interim eucharistic sharing' along the following lines:

(i)   They should by synodical action recognise now the member Churches of the Lutheran World Federation as Churches in which the Gospel is preached and taught;

(ii)   They should encourage the development of common Christian life throughout their respective Churches by such means as the following proposals of the *Niagara Report:*

(a) Eucharistic Sharing and Joint Common Celebration of the Eucharist;

(b) meetings of Church leaders for prayer, reflection and consultation, thus beginning joint *episcope*;

(c)   mutual invitation of Church leaders, clergy and laity, to synods, with a right to speak;

(d) common agencies wherever possible;

(e) exploring the possibility of adjusting boundaries to assist local and regional co-operation;

(f) Covenants among Church leaders to collaborate in *episcope.*

(g) joint pastoral appointments for special projects;

(h) joint theological education and training courses;

(i)   sharing of information and documents;

(j)   joint mission programmes;

(k) agreed syllabuses for Christian education in schools, joint materials for catechesis and adult study;

(l)   co-operation over liturgical forms, cycles of intercession, lectionaries and homiletic materials;

(m) welcoming isolated clergy or diaspora congregations into the life of a larger group (see ALERC *Helsinki Report*, 5);

(n) interchange of ministers to the extent permitted by canon law;

(o) twinning (partnership) between congregations and communities;

(p) joint programmes of diaconal ministry and reflection on issues of social responsibility;

(q) joint retreats and devotional materials.

(iii)   they should affirm by synodical action now on the basis of the consensus documents of Anglican-Lutheran International Conversations that the basic teaching of each respective Church is consonant with Scripture and that Lutheran teaching is sufficiently compatible with the teachings of the Churches of the Anglican Communion so that a relationship of *Interim Sharing of the Eucharist* may be established between these Churches under the guidelines appended.

APPENDIX

Guidelines for Interim Sharing of the Eucharist

(a)　The Churches of the Anglican Communion extend a special welcome to members of the Lutheran Churches to receive Holy Communion on the understanding that the Lutheran Churches will do likewise. This welcome constitutes a recognition of eucharistic teaching sufficient for Interim Sharing of the Eucharist.

(b)　Bishops of dioceses of the Anglican Communion and bishops/presidents of Lutheran districts and synods may by mutual agreement extend their regulations of church discipline to permit common, joint celebration of the Eucharist within their jurisdictions according to guidelines established by respective synods.

In this case:

When a joint Eucharist is held in an Anglican church an Anglican bishop or priest should preside, using an Anglican liturgy, with the Lutheran preaching; when a joint eucharist is held in a Lutheran church a Lutheran should preside using a Lutheran liturgy, with the Anglican preaching. This is not concelebration, nor does it imply rejection or final recognition of either Church's eucharist or ministry. The liturgical arrangements, including the position of the ministers in relation to the altar, should take into account local circumstances and sensitivities.

15. *I Have Heard the Cry of My People: Proceedings of the 8th Assembly of the Lutheran World Federation, Curitiba, Brazil, 29 January - 8 February 1990*, p. 107.

On the basis of concrete steps toward full communion between Lutherans and Anglicans in several parts of the world and in the light of the resolution passed in 1988 by the Lambeth Conference (the bishops of the Anglican Communion),

This Assembly

1.　wishes to take up the concern of the Seventh LWF Assembly that closer relationships be furthered through the world between LWF member churches and churches of the Anglican Communion (cf. Budapest Resolutions 4.4, 4.5, 4.7);

2.　is pleased to note that relations between Anglicans and Lutherans have taken decisive official steps forward, notably between

• The Episcopal Church/USA and the Evangelical Lutheran Church in America,

• The Church of England and the Evangelical Church in Germany and the Federation of Evangelical Churches in the GDR,

• The Anglican Church/Canada and the Evangelical Lutheran Church in Canada;

3.　is informed that formal conversations are underway between the Church of England and the Nordic and Baltic Lutheran churches;

4.　is aware of relationships between Anglican and Lutheran churches in other parts of the world which in practice manifest a high degree of church fellowship;

5.　notes that the 'Niagara Report' of the 1987 Anglican-Lutheran Consultation on Episcopé, based on previous A-L conversations, projects a way to resolve the issue of the historic episcopate which has been an obstacle to A-L church fellowship;

6.　expresses its joy that the 1988 Lambeth Conference of the bishops of the Anglican Communion officially

- recognized in the Niagara Report 'a substantial convergence of views',
- recommended it to its member churches 'for study and synodical reception',
- urged that 'the most recent convergence on apostolic ministry achieved in the "Niagara Report"... prompt us to move towards the fullest possible ecclesial recognition and the goal of full communion', and
- 'subject to the concurrence of the Lutheran World Federation', recommended a series of joint steps toward that goal;

7. resolves

7.1 that the LWF renew its commitment to the goal of full communion with the churches of the Anglican Communion, and that it urge LWF member churches to take appropriate steps toward its realization;

7.2 that LWF acknowledge with gratitude the 1988 Resolution on A-L relations of the Lambeth Conference and that it concur with that Conference's recommendations to Anglican and Lutheran churches;

7.3 that the LWF note with thanksgiving the steps toward church fellowship with national/regional Anglican counterparts which LWF member churches have been able to take already and that it encourage them to proceed;

7.4 that the Anglican-Lutheran International Commission both arrange for further global studies and reports which may be needed, and the ALIC be prepared to assist Anglican and Lutheran churches in taking steps toward full communion.

16. *Pullach*, para. 17.

17.The Anglican and the Lutheran Churches hold that it is Jesus Christ, God and Man, born, crucified, risen, and ascended for the salvation of mankind, in whom all Scriptures find their focus and fulfilment. They are at one in accepting the Holy Scriptures of the Old and New Testaments as the sufficient, inspired, and authoritative record and witness, prophetic and apostolic, to God's revelation in Jesus Christ.

17. *Helsinki*, para. 20

20.We therefore share a common understanding of God's justifying grace, i.e. that we are accounted righteous and are made righteous before God only by grace through faith because of the merits of our Lord and Saviour Jesus Christ, and not on account of our works or merits (cf. LED 1980, pp. 22-3). Both our traditions affirm that justification leads and must lead to 'good works'; authentic faith issues in love. We understand sanctification in relation to justification not only as an expression of the continuity of justification, the daily forgiveness of sins and acceptance by God, but also as growth in faith and love both as individuals and as members of the Christian community.

and *Meissen*, para. 15 (vi).

(vi)   We believe and proclaim the gospel that in Jesus Christ God loves and redeems the world. We 'share a common understanding of God's justifying grace, i.e. that we are accounted righteous and are made righteous before God only by grace through faith because of the merits of our Lord and Saviour Jesus Christ, and not on account of our works or merits... Both our traditions affirm that justification leads and must lead to "good works"; authentic faith issues in love'.*

* Helsinki, para. 20; cf. paras 17-21.

18. *All Under One Christ. Statement on the Augsburg Confession by the Roman Catholic / Lutheran Joint Commission.* Augsburg, 23 February 1980 (published with *Ways to Community* (Geneva, 1981)), para. 14.

14. A broad consensus emerges in the doctrine of justification, which was decisively important for the Reformation (CA IV): it is solely by grace and by faith in Christ's saving work and not because of any merit in us that we are accepted by God and receive the Holy Spirit who renews our hearts and equips us for and calls us to good works.*

* cf. CA IV, VI and XX, The Book of Concord, pp. 30ff, 41ff: Malta, Nos. 27 and 48.

19. *Salvation and the Church. An Agreed Statement by the Anglican - Roman Catholic International Commission — ARCIC II* (London, 1987), para. 19.

19. As justification and sanctification are aspects of the same divine act, so also living faith and love are inseparable in the believer. Faith is no merely private and interior disposition, but by its very nature is acted out: good works necessarily spring from a living faith (Jas. 2.17ff). They are truly good because, as the fruit of the Spirit, they are done in God, in dependence on God's grace.

The person and work of Christ are central to any understanding of the relation between salvation and good works. God has brought into being in the person of his Son a renewed humanity, the humanity of Jesus Christ himself, the 'last Adam' or 'second man' (cf. 1 Cor. 15.45, 47). He is the firstborn of all creation, the prototype and source of our new humanity. Salvation involves participating in that humanity, so as to live the human life now as God has refashioned it in Christ (cf. Col. 3.10). This understanding of our humanity as made new in Christ by God's transforming power throws light on the New Testament affirmation that, while we are not saved *because of* works, we are created in Christ *for* good works (Eph. 2.8ff). 'Not because of works': nothing even of our best achievement or good will can give us any claim to God's gift of renewed humanity. God's recreating deed originates in himself and nowhere else. 'For good works': good works are the fruit of the freedom God has given us in his Son. In restoring us to his likeness, God confers freedom on fallen humanity. This is not the natural freedom to choose between alternatives, but the freedom to do his will: 'the law of the Spirit of life in Christ Jesus has set me free from the law of sin and death... in order that the just requirement of the law might be fulfilled in us' (Rom. 8.2, 4). We are freed and enabled to keep the commandments of God by the power of the Holy Spirit, to live faithfully as God's people and to grow in love within the discipline of the community, bringing forth the fruit of the Spirit.*

* cf. Article 10 of the Thirty-nine Articles: 'we have no power to do good works pleasant and acceptable to God, without the grace of God by Christ preventing us, that we may have a good will, and working with us *(cooperante)*, when we have that good will.' This echoes Augustine's language about 'prevenient' and 'co-operating' grace (*De Gratia et libero arbitrio* 17.33).

Inasmuch as we are recreated in his 'own image and likeness', God involves us in what he freely does to realise our salvation (Phil. 2.12ff). In the words of Augustine: 'The God who made you without you, without you does not make you just' (*Sermons* 169.13). Thus from the divine work follows the human work: it is we who live and act in a fully human way, yet never on our own or in a self-sufficient independence. This fully human life is possible if we live in the freedom and activity of Christ who, in the words of St Paul, 'lives in me' (Gal. 2.20).

20. *Meissen*, para. 15 (ii);

(ii)   We accept the Niceno-Constantinopolitan and Apostles' Creeds and confess the basic trinitarian and christological dogmas to which these creeds testify. That is, we believe that Jesus of Nazareth is true God and true Man, and that God is one God in three persons, Father, Son and Holy Spirit.*

* cf. *Pullach*, paras. 23-25.

23.   The Anglican and the Lutheran Churches are at one in accepting officially the Apostles' and Nicene Creeds. These Creeds are used regularly in their worship and in their teaching. They recognize the Athanasian Creed as giving a true exposition of the trinitarian faith.

24.   They believe that these Creeds are authoritative summaries and safeguards of the Christian faith. Their authority is established in the first place by their faithful witness and interpretation of the biblical message, and in the second place by their acceptance and use in the Early Church. They, therefore, hold a unique place among all confessional documents.

25.   The acceptance of these Creeds implies agreement between both Communions on the fundamental trinitarian and christological dogmas.

21. Thirty-Nine Articles of Religion.

VIII.   *Of the Three Creeds*

The Three Creeds, *Nicene* Creed, *Athanasius's* Creed, and that which is commonly called the *Apostles'* Creed, ought thoroughly to be received and believed: for they may be proved by most certain warrants of holy Scripture.

22. Augsburg Confession.

I [God]

We unanimously hold and teach, in accordance with the decree of the Council of Nicaea, that there is one divine essence, which is called and which is truly God, and that there are three persons in this one divine essence, equal in power and alike eternal: God the Father, God the Son, God the Holy Spirit. All three are one divine essence, eternal, without division, without end, of infinite power, wisdom, and goodness, one creator and preserver of all things visible and invisible. The word 'person' is to be understood as the Fathers employed the term in this connection, not as a part or property of another but as that which exists of itself.

Therefore all the heresies which are contrary to this article are rejected. Among these are the heresy of the Manichaeans, who assert that there are two gods, one good and one evil; also that of the Valentinians, Arians, Eunomians, Mohammedans, and others like them; also that of the Samosatenes, old and new, who hold that there is only one person and sophistically assert that the other two, the Word and the Holy Spirit, are not necessarily distinct persons but that the Word signifies a physical word or voice and that the Holy Spirit is a movement induced in creatures.

III [The Son of God]

It is also taught among us that God the Son became man, born of the virgin Mary, and that the two natures, divine and human, are so inseparably united in one person that there is one Christ, true God and true man, who was truly born, suffered, was crucified, died, and was buried in order to be a sacrifice not only for original sin but also for all other sins and to propitiate God's wrath. The same Christ also descended into hell, truly rose from the dead on the third day, ascended into heaven, and sits on the right hand of God, that he may eternally rule and have dominion over all creatures, that through the Holy Spirit he may sanctify, purify, strengthen, and comfort all who believe in him, that he may bestow on them life and every grace and blessing, and that he may protect and defend them against the devil and against sin. The same Lord Christ will return openly to judge the living and the dead, as stated in the Apostles' Creed.

23. *Meissen*, para. 15 (iii).

(iii)   We celebrate the apostolic faith in liturgical worship. We acknowledge in the liturgy both a celebration of salvation through Christ and a significant factor in forming the *consensus fidelium*. We rejoice at the extent of 'our common tradition of spirituality, liturgy and sacramental life' which has given us similar forms of worship, common texts, hymns, canticles and prayers. We are influenced by a common liturgical renewal. We also rejoice at the variety of expression shown in different cultural settings.*

* *Helsinki*, para. 31; *God's Reign and our Unity (GROU)*, para. 62; *BEM, Baptism*, paras 17-23, *Eucharist*, paras 27-33, *Ministry*, paras 41-44.

24. *Meissen*, para. 15 (vii);

(vii)   We believe that the Church is constituted and sustained by the Triune God through God's saving action in word and sacraments, and is not the creation of individual believers. We believe that the Church is sent into the world as sign, instrument and foretaste of the Kingdom of God. But we also recognise that the Church stands in constant need of reform and renewal.*

* *Helsinki*, paras 44-51; GROU, paras 29-34.

Helsinki, paras 44-51;

44.   The Anglicans and Lutherans agree in their basic approach concerning the understanding of the Church. For them the Church of Jesus Christ is not constituted by individual believers who choose to come together to form the Church. We believe the Church to be a given reality both divine and human. The Church, the communion of the living and departed believers of all times and places, has been, is, and will remain until the final fulfilment of all things in Jesus Christ.

45.   The Triune God constitutes and sustains the Church through his saving action in Word and Sacrament. He keeps the people of God the Body of Christ, the Temple of the Holy Spirit in the truth. He calls and gathers people into communion with him and with one another and sends them as messengers and co-workers into the

world. Thus, the Church is called to be the new humanity in Jesus Christ and, consequently, to be a sign and instrument of God's will for all humanity.

46.   Anglicans and Lutherans confess the Church as one, holy, catholic, and apostolic. We reaffirm the short exposition of these four 'marks' in the Pullach Report (ALIC, paras. 51, 53-6).

47.   The Church, as a divine reality and the first-fruits of the Kingdom of God, transcends our present finite reality. At the same time, being a human institution and organization, it participates in all the ambiguities and frailties of the human condition. It is always in need of reform and renewal.

48.   Anglicans and Lutherans, together with other Christians, have rediscovered the communal character of the Church at a time of loneliness and estrangement. The Church lives in *koinonia* and is a community in which all members, lay or ordained, contribute their gifts to the life of the whole.

49.   In this perspective of *koinonia*, we are able to agree with the description of the Church offered by the Anglican - Roman Catholic International Commission: 'In the New Testament it is clear that the community is established by a baptism inseparable from faith and conversion, that its mission is to proclaim the Gospel of God, and that its common life is sustained by the eucharist. This remains the pattern for the Christian Church. The Church is the community of those reconciled with God and with each other because it is the community of those who believe in Jesus Christ and are justified through God's grace. It is also the reconciling community, because it has been called to bring to all mankind, through the preaching of the Gospel, God's gracious offer of redemption' (ARCIC, Introduction, para. 8).

50.   Living in *koinonia* the Church does not exist by itself and for itself. It is not a self-sufficient island. Rather, it is called to worship and praise God and to bring before him all the joys, sufferings and hopes of humankind. It is sent into the world to continue Christ's loving service and to witness to his active presence among all people. It is an instrument for proclaiming and manifesting God's sovereign rule and saving grace (cf. ALIC, para. 59).

51.   Anglicans and Lutherans therefore agree that the mission of the Church arises necessarily from its nature. They confess together that their Churches have often failed to be obedient to their God-given mission. In Europe, the fact that some of the Anglican and Lutheran Churches were, or are still, established and have the character of 'folk churches' has sometimes endangered their mission. These Churches have often identified themselves with prevailing political structures and ideologies. But such abuses should not obscure the importance of the necessary relation between the Gospel and the culture of the society to which the Church is sent.

25. *Meissen*, para. 15. (iv);

(iv)   We believe that baptism with water in the name of the Triune God unites the one baptised with the death and resurrection of Jesus Christ, initiates into the One Holy, Catholic and Apostolic Church, and confers the gracious gift of new life in the Spirit.*

* *Helsinki*, paras 22-25; *GROU*, paras 47-61.

Helsinki, paras 22-25.

22.   We reaffirm the statement on baptism in the Pullach Report (ALIC, paras. 64-6) and recognize in the Faith and Order text on baptism (BEM, pp. 2-7) the faith which our two communion share. It is therefore sufficient for our purpose to underline some basic convictions.

23.   In both our traditions the sacrament of baptism has always been seen as intimately related to God's gift of forgiveness and justification (cf. para. 21). Baptism is the effective means by which God brings persons into the community of the church and whereby he adopts them into a new relationship as his sons or daughters. The gift of baptism, rightly understood, is inseparable from faith and conversion, that is the continuous return to the new relationship with God established in baptism.

24.   A feature of Anglican and Lutheran liturgical revision has been an increasing stress on baptism as the sacrament of incorporation into Christ and his Church. When seen in this perspective, infant baptism still the predominant practice in Europe is to be understood as entry into the communion of those whose sins are forgiven, which is itself a forgiving community. Whether infant or adult, the gift of baptism is freely given, not earned. God takes the decisive initiative through the sacramental action of the Church. But God's gifts are not mechanical and they have to be appropriated personally, for the whole of Christian life is a gracious relationship of faith, repentance, forgiveness and sanctification.

25.   As a consequence of our common understanding of baptism and our similar pastoral and liturgical practice, Anglicans and Lutherans have both experienced similar tensions in the face of the gradual secularization of modern Europe. In both Churches there is a lively debate on the appropriate baptismal policy to be pursued in largely 'post-Christian' urbanized cultures. In our attempts to involve the whole Christian community in the responsibility for the Christian upbringing of baptized children we can learn much from one another.

Neither tradition today would simply identify the Church with society. Nevertheless Anglicans and Lutherans also resist the temptation to regard the Church as a gathered sect having no relation to the culture or society within which it finds itself. At this point our common understanding of baptism and of our pastoral task reflects an agreement on the nature of the Church.

26. *Pullach*, para. 67.

67.   In the Lord's Supper the Church obediently performs the acts commanded by Christ in the New Testament, who took bread and wine, gave thanks, broke the bread, and distributed the bread and wine. The Church receives in this way the body and blood of Christ, crucified and risen, and in him the forgiveness of sins and all other benefits of his passion.

27. *Anglican - Roman Catholic International Commission. The Final Report.* Windsor, September 1981 (London, 1982) (ARCIC I), *Eucharistic Doctrine*, para. 5.

5.   Christ's redeeming death and resurrection took place once and for all in history. Christ's death on the cross, the culmination of his whole life of obedience, was the one, perfect and sufficient sacrifice for the sins of the world. There can be no repetition of or addition to what was then accomplished once for all by Christ. Any attempt to express a nexus between the sacrifice of Christ and the eucharist must not obscure this fundamental fact of the Christian faith.* Yet God has given the

harist to his Church as a means through which the atoning work of Christ on cross is proclaimed and made effective in the life of the Church. The notion of emorial as understood in the passover celebration at the time of Christ i.e. the making effective in the present of an event in the past has opened the way to a clearer understanding of the relationship between Christ's sacrifice and the eucharist. The eucharistic memorial is no mere calling to mind of a past event or of its significance, but the Church's effectual proclamation of God's mighty acts. Christ instituted the eucharist as a memorial (*anamnesis*) of the totality of God's reconciling action in him. In the eucharistic prayer the church continues to make a perpetual memorial of Christ's death, and his members, united with God and one another, give thanks for all his mercies, entreat the benefits of his passion on behalf of the whole Church, participate in these benefits and enter into the movement of his self-offering.

* The early Church in expressing the meaning of Christ's death and resurrection often used the language of sacrifice. For the Hebrew *sacrifice* was a traditional means of communication with God. The passover, for example, was a communal meal; the day of atonement was essentially expiatory; and the covenant established communion between God and man.

28. *BEM, Eucharist,* para. 2.

2. The eucharist is essentially the sacrament of the gift which God makes to us in Christ through the power of the Holy Spirit. Every Christian receives this gift of salvation through communion in the body and blood of Christ. In the eucharistic meal, in the eating and drinking of the bread and wine, Christ grants communion with himself. God himself acts, giving life to the body of Christ and renewing each member. In accordance with Christ's promise, each baptized member of the body of Christ receives in the eucharist the assurance of the forgiveness of sins (Matt. 26.28) and the pledge of eternal life (John 6.51-58). Although the eucharist is essentially one complete act, it will be considered here under the following aspects: thanksgiving to the Father, memorial of Christ, invocation of the Spirit, communion of the faithful, meal of the Kingdom.

29. *Helsinki,* para. 28.

28. Although Christ is present and active in the entire eucharistic celebration, Anglicans and Lutherans have also affirmed a particular sacramental presence of Christ (cf. ALIC, para. 67). In virtue of the living Word of Christ and by the power of the Holy Spirit the bread and wine are the sacrament of Christ's body and blood. In the Lord's Supper, Jesus Christ, true God and true man, crucified, risen and ascended, is truly present in his body and blood under the elements of bread and wine (cf. ALIC, para. 68). Under these elements Christ comes to us in order to renew our entire being.

While both our Churches have traditionally understood the effects of the eucharist in terms of forgiveness, Anglicans and Lutherans today also wish to stress its fruits in the building up of the community of the Church and in the strengthening of faith and hope and of witness and service in daily life. In the eucharist we already have a foretaste of the eternal joy of God's kingdom.

30. *BEM, Ministry,* para. 17.

17.   Jesus Christ is the unique priest of the new covenant Christ's life was given as a sacrifice for all. Derivatively, the Church as a whole can be described as a

priesthood. All members are called to offer their being 'as a living sacrifice' intercede for the Church and the salvation of the world. Ordained minist related, as are all Christians, both to the priesthood of Christ, and to the priest of the Church. But they may appropriately be called priests because they ful particular priestly service by strengthening and building up the royal and proph priesthood of the faithful through word and sacraments, through their prayers intercession, and through their pastoral guidance of the community.

31. *Niagara*, para. 68.

68. We believe that all members of the Church are called to participate in its apostolic mission. They are therefore given various ministries by the Holy Spirit. Within the community of the Church the ordained ministry exists to serve the ministry of the whole people of God. We hold the ordained ministry of word and sacrament to be a gift of God to his Church and therefore an office of divine institution. (Helsinki Report, 32-42).

Meissen, para. 15 (viii)

(viii) We believe that all members of the Church are called to participate in its apostolic mission. They are therefore given various ministries by the Holy Spirit. Within the community of the Church the ordained ministry exists to serve the ministry of the whole people of God. We hold the ordained ministry of word and sacrament to be a gift of God to his Church and therefore an office of divine institution.*

* *Helsinki*, paras. 32-43, GROU, paras 91-97; *BEM, Ministry,* paras 4 and 12.

Helsinki, paras 32-42.

32. In the context of the broad ecumenical discussion on the ordained ministry, Anglicans and Lutherans increasingly note much agreement and similarity in their understanding and practice of the ministry. This wider ecumenical discussion, including multilateral dialogue in Faith and Order and the bilateral conversations of our two Communions both between themselves and with the Roman Catholic Church, has led Anglicans and Lutherans to rediscover considerable common ground in their understanding of the ordained ministry. This understanding was shaped by the Reformation tradition as well as by their common insistence on continuity with the biblical witness and the tradition of the early Church. This rediscovery has helped them to conclude that the obvious differences in the ordering of their ministries no longer imply a deeper ecclesiological difference. Such a difference was in fact never recognized officially by the two Communions.

33. This agreement and convergence on the level of doctrine is complemented and furthered by the common pastoral and liturgical experience of ministry in our Churches. We have learned that in the Anglican and Lutheran Churches pastors are called to fulfil very much the same functions and responsibilities. They face similar challenges, problems and opportunities. As for the office of bishop in our Churches, this similarity of practice is even more important in view of certain differences in the interpretation of the significance of the office of bishop.

34. Together with other Churches, Anglicans and Lutherans are rediscovering the importance of the ministry of the whole People of God, *the general priesthood of all baptized believers.* This priesthood has its foundation in the unique priesthood of